A
Century
of
American
Icons

A Century of American Icons

100 PRODUCTS AND SLOGANS FROM THE 20TH-CENTURY CONSUMER CULTURE

EDITED BY MARY CROSS

An Oryx Book

GREENWOOD PRESS
Westport, Connecticut • London

Library of Congress Cataloging-in-Publication Data

A century of American icons / 100 products and slogans from the 20th-century
consumer culture / edited by Mary Cross.
    p. cm.
  Includes bibliographical references and index.
  ISBN 0–313–31481–0 (alk. paper)
  1. Advertising—Brand name products—United States—History—20th century. 2.
Advertising—United States—History—20th century. 3. Imagery
(Psychology)—History—20th century. 4. Consumption (Economics)—United
States—History—20th century. I. Cross, Mary, 1934–
HF6161.B4 C46   2002
658.1'0973'0904—dc21   2002066114

British Library Cataloguing in Publication Data is available.

Library of Congress Catalog Card Number: 2002066114
ISBN: 0–313–31481–0

First published in 2002

Greenwood Press, 88 Post Road West, Westport, CT 06881
An imprint of Greenwood Publishing Group, Inc.
www.greenwood.com

Printed in the United States of America

The paper used in this book complies with the
Permanent Paper Standard issued by the National
Information Standards Organization (Z39.48–1984).

10 9 8 7 6 5 4 3 2 1

Copyright Acknowledgments

The author and publisher gratefully acknowledge permission for the use of the following
material:

"Where's the Beef?" slogan used by permission of Wendy's International.

To our students

Contents

Illustrations

Preface

This book is a result of the collaboration of faculty of the English and Communication Department at Fairleigh Dickinson University, Madison, New Jersey. I am grateful to them all for their scholarly commitment to this project and to Danielle Cruz, research assistant. We would like to thank our editor at Greenwood Press, Rob Kirkpatrick, for his thoughtful comments and editing, as well as Greenwood editor Debra Adams for initiating the project.

Introduction

The Product as Icon

Strictly speaking, this book is an iconology, that is, an interpretation of images and representations that have reached the status of icons. But this book is also about advertising, that quintessentially American salesmanship in print and pixels that gives us capitalism in its everyday buy-me form. Can there be icons in advertising? It is the premise of this book that there can be and that, throughout the past great century of American advertising, many products have attained monumental, iconic status by virtue of the cultural impact created for them by advertising. Products become iconic when advertising and its strategies of persuasion and repetition turn them into cultural artifacts, carving them as it were into the Mount Rushmore of consumer desire.

An icon, in the ancient world, was a physical image, a monumental figure, a sacred representation to be worshipped. The physical image itself was sacred; in the 8th and 9th centuries, iconoclasts were those who literally broke or destroyed such images. In the 21st century, the word "icon" has a much more secular meaning, though a secular icon can still attract its own throng of worshippers. Some say celebrities—dead or alive—have become iconic. There are iconic figures in history, in the movies, in music, in art—and in advertising. In the movies, some iconic American products, say a can of Coca-Cola or a package of Reese's Pieces, have become virtual shorthand for American culture: the little alien, E.T., eating his Reese's in the movie, is one of us. The path to iconicity is short—and sometimes short-lived—in ad time. One good marketing campaign and one good image or slogan can make an icon out of a Wendy's or a Volkswagen overnight. And an Andy Warhol can give the final imprimatur to the advertised product, turning Campbell's soup cans and Chanel perfume bottles into icons for museums.

Both pop art and pop culture look to advertising for inspiration because advertising is transformative not only of products but also of culture, and over the course of the last century it has, in its own way, transformed the way in which Americans live. The average citizen today is bombarded by thousands of advertising messages a day, from the Internet, television, newspapers, magazines, billboards, posters, signs, and mailings to the labels and brands appearing on clothing and the ads attached to supermarket carts. The same citizen a hundred years ago might have encountered advertising only in an occasional newspaper or magazine. Even then, in such a sparse media environment, the messages of advertising were powerful and hard to resist. From the beginning, they delivered visions of status and social success along with promises of clear skin (Ivory Soap), odor-free bodies (Odorono), and shiny kitchens (Bon Ami). Offering to cure everything from dyspepsia to melancholia in the case of patent medicine (Carter's Little Liver Pills), or suggesting the easy acquisition of luxury goods (Cadillac), they were and are even today almost the only public messages about what to do and how to live that most people encounter. Advertising set popular standards of behavior, and people tried to live up to the ads. They still do. Transformative, indeed, advertising speaks our cultural history and reveals to future generations our whole way of life in the products it celebrates.

That is another reason for putting together this volume. It has been compiled in view of a distinct knowledge gap that grows wider with each succeeding generation, as the names and purposes of some of America's most popular and influential products are lost to memory, along with their cultural moment. Spam, for instance, once a convenient—and during World War II, necessary—canned meat, has today become a name applied to junk e-mail. Spam in a can is still sold, but very few young people have ever heard of it. To an older generation, however, Spam represents part of the World War II experience in America when it was the only kind of meat any housewife could buy, with or without ration coupons. Other products, like Levi's jeans or Crackerjack, endure without any hint of their longevity—both over 100 years old—in American life. A reference book such as this provides to new generations of students and adults a convenient way of accessing this information and learning about the iconic, culture-defining products often mentioned in the fiction and history books they read.

The iconic products in this book were selected, first, because the advertising campaigns that made them known gave them images or words that were so memorable and, eventually, so familiar, that they became enormously significant, long-lasting elements of American culture, iconic in their power to capture the desire and imagination of the American consumer. Most of the icons discussed here became so because of a physical image: the product itself, or a character—human, animal, or cartoon—representing the product in an ad, like Mr. Peanut, or the design of a car, or an artist's rendering of the product that gave it meaning. Other icons were chosen because the words used to describe them—slogans, jingles, and taglines—gave the product a memorable, mythic stature that enshrined it in the 20th-century consumer mind and culture. A slogan like "Where's the Beef?" can leave its origins behind and enter the culture on its own.

The second reason these products, images, and slogans are included in this book is that they became part of America's history and enduringly tell its story, like an archeological dig. Advertising is, after all, the language of capitalism, speaking volumes about the ways in which Americans lived, behaved, and imagined themselves because of the products advertising made iconic. Most of the consumer goods presented here, some more than 100 years in existence, are being still sold, or are being revived, today. Even a World War I poster of Uncle Sam and a 1930s fitness program of Charles Atlas are enjoying a 21st-century revival, and products long forgotten, like a 1900s patent medicine or a 1920s Packard, speak eloquently of their time and place.

In a century of advertising greats, there were inevitably many other contenders for a place in this book of 100 icons. We have tried in every case to give them honorable mention in articles about similar products.

Organized by decade, this volume presents 100 products selected as prominent representatives of their time in American advertising and consumer culture. While many products that came to prominence in the 20th century had their origins in the 19th century, and while many overlap their decades significantly, entries were assigned to a particular decade based on the time in which they had the most impact, either because they were then brand new, daring, or best-sellers, or they had built momentum over years of advertising campaigns to have a significant cultural influence at that point, potent artifacts of their time. Thus, for example, we can show how the products of the 1940s, like the first television sets, reflected postwar life in America and gave impetus to one of the biggest boom times in our history. Or how the products of the 1990s, like Microsoft Windows, reflect some of the same adventurous optimism a new century can inspire. While a decade-by-decade structure is artificial in some ways, it has the advantage of giving manageable shape to the varied historical conditions in which these products flourished.

The title of each entry is either the name by which the product is commonly known, or the name of the iconic figure that was used to advertise the product (for example, the Marlboro man). Each entry discusses the product's history and the decade in which it began or flourished as an advertising icon. In addition, the entry discusses some of the methods and strategies used to advertise the product, its significant competitors, and its reception by consumers.

How Advertising Creates Icons

Icons are first of all visual, physical objects. They take up space in reality and in the mind, and they are full of meaning, whether religious, psychological, cultural, or personal. A picture is always worth a thousand words, but iconic presences, less tangible, can also be created verbally, embuing an idea or a brand name with symbolic power so that it too is full of meaning, taking on almost plastic form in the mind. An icon, whether word or picture, is, in addition, ideological in the sense that it reflects the values, needs, and aspirations of a culture. It becomes part of the story that a society tells itself, mythic in expressing cultural narratives important to that society.

As an icon maker, American advertising, assisted by powerful media, cannot be beat. Its persuasive methods, graphics, wit, and, above all, constant repetition create huge auras of need and desire around consumer products so compelling that they haunt the conscious—and the unconscious—lives of the target audience. Advertising in America *is* the story America tells itself, whether it wants to or not, co-opting the American Dream of abundance and serving it up in constant, delectable form. Advertising takes chopped meat—or toilet tissue or chewing gum or a soft drink—and makes a metaphor out of it, giving it meaning it never had before, creating its story, pumping it up, putting it out there, over and over again. These consumer goods acquire the meanings and stand for the lifestyles people aspire to, allowing them to participate in the story by buying something. The motivational strategies of advertising, which if nothing else is hyper-aware of its audience, make products the answer to every need, including needs people sometimes were not aware they had. Buying the product and owning it satisfy many psychic needs, if only for a little while, because of the mythic proportions advertising has given it.

Actually, it is necessary for advertising to make icons out of the things it promotes. The product is the hero of an ad, and the more substantial and real it is, the more desirable it is. Ever since the beginning of advertising in America, promoting the brand name itself has been a crucial goal of advertising. Companies want to establish their brand names as a signal to consumers that goods under that name are trustworthy and reliable. To brand the name on the consumer's mind requires heavy repetition and memorable logos, trademarks, and images. Today in advertising, branding is considered as important as promoting the actual products, and the effort makes virtual icons of company names and their graphic logos—for example, the Nike swoosh.

Television, perhaps the best thing ever invented to sell something, is an icon maker par excellence. In league with advertising, television catapults the image of a car or a beer into a nearly tangible form, an image larger than life. And images go directly to the brain, no reading required. Advertised products can be presented in their full sensory splendor: light, sound, color. Jump cuts à la MTV make fast connections among images of the product, juxtaposed with pictures of happy people using it, all washed in living color and swelling music, perhaps overlaid with a persistent product jingle. "Life Is Good," says Coca-Cola, proceeding in a rapid succession of images to connect iconic cans of Coke to the good part. Plagued by the zapping consumer in charge of the remote control, television commercials have become shorter, sharper, and more attention getting to arrest the viewer in mid-zap.

Advertising on the Internet has not been as successful, as agencies working to discover new ways to make it better will be the first to admit. Online, consumers have too many choices, too many links to hold still for a pitch. Yet every product and every manufacturer has its own Web site for consumers to "visit" these days, with special offers and light and sound shows to grab the attention. Icons of trademarks and logos populate the space, but advertising's conquest of cyberspace is merely a border skirmish at the moment. Stay tuned.

The print media have one advantage over television and the Internet as vehicles for advertising: they keep the message around longer, in hard copy as it were. A magazine can sit around a dentist's office for months hawking its wares in full color and with clever copy. Newspapers give ads the cachet of the right now and allow a message to be repeated day after day and sink in. Print media, like television shows and Web sites, are carefully aimed at target audiences. Advertising space is sold in the media on guarantees of audience size and composition. Thus an advertising media planner can buy up space that will reach just girls between the ages of 13 and 17, or target big-spending baby boomers, or capture the attention of pet owners. The prime category advertisers aim at today is the 18-to-34-year-old group of consumers whose brand loyalties are considered malleable.

The attention advertising pays to the consumer, the end-user of the product, is legendary and profitable. Demographic studies, psychological analyses, focus groups, surveys, polls, even grocery store scanners scrutinize American consumers closely and endlessly to discover the motivational triggers that will get them out of the house and into the store. Products like cars or sneakers are positioned to appeal to needs for status and belonging, health concerns can move food off the grocery shelves, and sex appeal can sell almost anything.

It is not so amazing after all that advertising can create icons out of the products it pitches. The visual, repeated presence of the physical product, the metaphoric meanings attached to it, its reflection of human need and aspiration, and the story it weaves into people's lives build cultural significance into consumer goods, sometimes giving products an iconic life beyond their own. Over the last century, advertising has learned many strategies for giving brands and consumer goods the status of icons. From the beginning when advertising was just about getting information out to the public, to today's sophisticated motivational approaches, advertising has made itself so much a part of daily life that its products are inextricably tied up with how we live and think about ourselves. The icons of 20th-century American advertising and consumer culture are here because, in the end, they have come to symbolize the experience of living as an American. As Marshall McLuhan, the communication guru and author of *Understanding Media*, said, ads are "the richest and most faithful daily reflections that any society ever made of its entire range of activities" (232).

REFERENCES

Fishwick, Marshall, and Ray B. Browne. *Icons of Popular Culture*. Bowling Green, OH: Bowling Green University Popular Press, 1970.

Goodrum, Charles, and Helen Dalrymple. *Advertising in America: The First 200 Years*. New York: Harry N. Abrams, 1990.

McLuhan, Marshall. *Understanding Media*. New York: New American Library, 1964.

Rothenberg, Randall. "The Advertising Century." *Advertising Age*, Special Issue (Spring 1999): 9–16, 130–33.

Icons of the 1900s

America began its second century full of optimism and promise. The economy was strong (on September 6, 1900, the Dow Jones index closed above 100 for the first time, at 100.28), the standard of living was rising, and there was peace abroad. There was no federal income tax. In 1900 a traveling salesman named L. Frank Baum published *The Wonderful Wizard of Oz*, a book depicting a dream land over the rainbow. America itself seemed to have over-the-rainbow possibilities at the beginning of what would come to be known as the "American Century."

The few years before and after the turn of the century were marked with an unprecedented number of inventions which revolutionized the way Americans lived in the years to come. The automobile and electric power changed everything. Thomas Edison had invented the phonograph (1877) and the lightbulb (1879); George Eastman had produced a camera for the masses (1888); the Wright brothers flew an airplane (1903); and Henry Ford came up with an American horseless carriage, the Model T car (1908). Countless others invented everything from the aspirin tablet (1853) to the X-ray (1895) and the zipper (1893), and Commander Robert Peary discovered there was a North Pole (1909).

Nonetheless, at the beginning of the century, people were still hitching horses to their carriages, women were still being laced into corsets and swathed in heavy long skirts, and indoor plumbing was not universal. In 1900 the population of the United States was still heavily agrarian; 40 percent of its 76 million people lived on farms. Bolstered by an immigration rate of about 400,000 a year until World War I, the population had nearly tripled since the Civil War. There were just forty-five states; three territories awaited statehood: Oklahoma, Arizona, and New Mexico. The Klondike gold rush was over, the oil and tobacco moguls of the Gilded Age were facing antitrust suits, and William McKinley was serving his second term as president. When McKinley was assassinated in 1901, Vice President Theodore Roosevelt, acclaimed for his "Rough Rider" leadership during the brief Spanish-American War of 1898, became president and stayed president as a kind of idol of the masses over a long period of domestic tranquility.

Encouraged by the happy times, a burgeoning population, and a strong economy, merchants and manufacturers saw their chance to capitalize on the increasing demand and consumerism that had begun to make themselves felt in American society. Such businessmen began to realize the value of advertising their products to inform the public and to create demand. Mail-order houses such as Sears' Roebuck and Montgomery Ward, had sprung up late in the 19th century to cater to isolated rural populations, and department stores such as John Wanamaker's in the cities launched advertising campaigns, which began to exert a broad cultural influence on how and why people spent their money and established an ethic of consumerism based on self-expression and status, which marked so much of the advertising to come. Thorstein Veblen's *The Theory of the Leisure Class*, published in 1899, had anticipated this process, and he coined the phrase "conspicuous consumption." The concept had been around at least since the ancient Egyptians, but advertising acted powerfully in shifting the preferences of the consuming public toward status purchasing and working in order to buy more luxuries, a trend which continues today.

Advertising had gotten a real foothold in America late in the 19th century, spurred on by the vivid posters and hyperbolic announcements of patent medicine. Print ads for patent medicines started to appear in little religious magazines and Sunday school weeklies. By 1900 3,500 magazines were being published in the United States. When publishers discovered that they could make more money by selling ads than by selling subscriptions, they created household names out of such products as Ivory Soap, Welch's Grape Juice, Hires Root Beer, and Kodak cameras. Even highbrow literary publications, including *Harper's*, *Atlantic*, and *Century* magazines, were not above selling advertising space, but they confined ads to a special section at the back. Women's magazines, such as the *Ladies' Home Journal*, learned how valuable their large female readership was to advertisers, and the emphasis on women as the primary household purchasers continues today. In 1905 an adman named Earnest Elmo Calkins had published a how-to book, *Modern Advertising*, to help advertisers learn the proper strategies to reach customers. Ad agents, operating on their own in large numbers at the end of the 19th century, monopolized the selling of space for publishers, but N. W. Ayer and Son of Philadelphia, one of the first two advertising agencies (and still in existence), changed all that by offering to serve the client, not just the media. Advertising agencies sprang up, primarily in New York City along Park Avenue, and the age of American advertising was well launched by the second decade of the century.

Many of the products advertised in the 19th century were ingredients in food—for example, Royal Baking Powder, Pillsbury's Flour, and Baker's Chocolate—which emphasized their purity. Soap and toilet articles, however, led the field in advertising dollars and continued to do so into the early days of the 20th century as national advertising took hold, competition increased, and brand names offered a simple way for consumers to make purchasing decisions. The story of how manufacturers and merchants began to etch their brands and trademarks into the American consciousness follows, as we trace the creation of Uneeda Biscuit from the cracker barrels of old, the rise of Ivory Soap from the depths of the lye tub, the promotion of wheat cereals as cures for whatever ails one, and the arrival of the first ready-to-eat, time-saving foods.

References

"The Century: 100 Years of News, Social Trends & Entertainment." *Contra Costa Times*. October 6, 1999. <http://www.contracostatimes.com/special_reports/century/stories/dcr06690.htm>.

Evans, Harold. *The American Century*. New York: Alfred A. Knopf, 1998.

Morgan, Hal. *Symbols of America*. New York: Viking Penguin, 1987.

Norris, James D. *Advertising and the Transformation of American Society, 1865–1920*. Westport, CT: Greenwood Press, 1990.

Veblen, Thorstein. *The Theory of the Leisure Class*. New York: Modern Library, 1931.

Mary Cross

Bon Ami Scouring Powder

The newly hatched chick on the red-and-yellow can of Bon Ami scouring powder is one of America's earliest trademarks. Introduced in 1886 by the J. T. Robertson Soap Company in Manchester, Connecticut, it is still the brand image of Bon Ami, which is French for "good friend." The slogan to go with the chick, "Hasn't scratched yet," was added in 1901 by a company promotion man who knew his chickens: newborn chicks do not scratch for food. The slogan was meant to assure consumers that the scouring powder contained few abrasives that would scratch surfaces. In an advertising campaign conducted in 1980 to revive the brand, another slogan was added: "Never underestimate the cleaning power of a 94-year-old chick with a French name."

John T. Robertson, who had been working for another soap company, decided to start his own company to make a nonabrasive soap that would not scratch surfaces like glass. He set up shop in an old Connecticut gristmill and concocted a cleanser from feldspar, tallow, and caustic soda which was popular with housewives who could now polish their mirrors as well as their sinks with it. In the early 1900s, the company, now run by the Childs family, owners of the gristmill, hired advertising agent A. W. Erickson to launch a campaign. He ran full-page ads in women's magazines featuring the chick in reproductions of oil paintings by artist Ben Austrian. The pictures were so popular they were made into prints. Free samples of the cleanser were handed out door-to-door, and a children's book, *The Chick That Never Grew Up*, with the character Princess Bon Ami was published.

Other cleansers on the market at the turn of the century, equally iconic, included Old Dutch Cleanser, picturing a sturdy woman in Dutch costume, and Gold Dust, featuring an image of black twins. Old Dutch, a scouring powder produced by the Cudahy Packing Company of Omaha, Nebraska, put the Dutch girl on its product in 1905 and, later, the slogan "Chases Dirt." She was appropriated during World War I to sell bonds and used in cartoons about Teddy Roosevelt's trust-busting campaign. The cleanser, now owned by Purex, is still sold with a modernized Dutch girl image. Gold Dust, made by N. B. Fairbank Company, was a popular cleanser from the 1880s to the 1950s. Its icon, a pair of black children as menial laborers, is representative of then-tolerated stereotypes. This cleanser is no longer on the market.

Bon Ami was the leading cleanser through the Great Depression until after World War II. Sold several times, it went into a decline until 1971 when it was purchased by the Faultless Starch Company of Kansas City, which added Bon Ami to its corporate name and managed to revive the brand in 1974 as environmental concerns in the 1970s gave it a new advantage. Bon Ami contained none of the dyes, phosphates, chlorine, or perfume then being targeted by environmentalists. Sales climbed 12 percent in the first six months of a national magazine advertising campaign in the early 1980s. Off the endangered species list, Bon Ami, still sporting its chick and slogan, is now sold in various forms as an aerosol and a glass cleaner as well as the traditional cleanser.

References

"Buying Bon Ami." Celebrating Greater Kansas City: Faultless/Bon Ami Company. <http://www.urbantapestry.com>.

Margolin, Victor, Ira Brichta, and Vivian Brichta. *The Promise and the Product: 200 Years of American Advertising Posters*. New York: Macmillan, 1979.

Saporito, Bill. "Has-Been Brands Go Back to Work." *Fortune*. April 28, 1986: 123.

Mary Cross

Campbell's Soup

In 1900 Campbell's Soup won the gold medallion that has been represented on its label for more than 100 years. The original medal was awarded for excellence at the Paris Exposition and graced the red-and-white Campbell cans until 2000 when the company reduced the medal to the size of a dime so that the label, made famous by artist Andy Warhol, could be given a more contemporary look, including pictures of the soup.

The company, first known as Joseph Campbell & Company, was founded in 1869 to can tomatoes in Camden in the Garden State of New Jersey where grew the giant beefsteak tomatoes Campbell claimed could fill a single can. In 1893, when the U.S. Supreme Court ruled that the tomato, long classified as a fruit, was to be designated a vegetable for trade purposes, the Campbell company formed an advertising committee and bought up space in New York City, Washington, D.C., and Saint Louis for 100 large signs to promote its new, ready-to-serve Beefsteak Tomato Soup.

Joseph Campbell bought out his first partner, Abraham Anderson, and expanded the company with his nephew, Arthur Dorrance, who introduced the condensed version of Campbell's Soups. By 1902 there were twenty-one varieties of Campbell's Soup, a number that did not change for the next thirty years. Since soup takes a long time to simmer, workers in the plant had nothing to do while they waited to can it. Joseph Campbell thought up a new product in 1904 to solve the productivity problem, Campbell's Pork & Beans, which workers could can while they waited for the soup to simmer.

During the same year, a pair of tomato-cheeked Campbell Kids, drawn by Philadelphia illustrator Grace Wiederseim, began to appear on streetcar advertisements. The Campbell Kids, an immediate hit, personalized the brand so well that the company used them on everything from postcards to lapel pins and, in 1910, as a pair of dolls.

The Campbell Soup Kids have had remakable longevity. They were used to sell Liberty Bonds during World War I, they danced the Charleston in the 1920s, and they slimmed down and lost their roly-poly look in the 1980s. In the 1990s, they were singing rap on television in a campaign designed by Backer Spielvogel Bates to promote Campbell's Teddy Bear Soup.

Campbell's used its first magazine advertisement, in 1905, in *Good Housekeeping*, to let the public know it had sold a phenomenal 16 million cans of soup in 1904 (by the company's 125th anniversary in 1994, it could claim that it was selling more than seventy cans per second).

Campbell's continued to advertise primarily in magazines, so much so that the "Campbell Soup position" became a standard: on a right-hand page facing a full page of editorial text. In 1907 the Joseph Campbell Company began to publish a series of cookbooks and meal planners, a clever move showing housewives how to hasten meal preparation by using canned soup. One of the prime ingredients, Campbell's Mushroom Soup, created in 1934, is still the basis of many recipes today.

The company's long-standing "M'm! M'm! Good!" slogan was created in 1931 for its radio ads, a campaign handled by Batten, Barton, Durstine and Osborne (BBDO). By the 1950s, Campbell's Soup was doing its first television commercials, sponsoring shows like *Lassie* and *Peter Pan*. The company hired a Hollywood actor named Ronald Reagan to be one of its spokesmen.

In the 1950s and 1960s, Campbell's Soup acquired several companies, including Pepperidge Farm, V-8 Juice, Swanson's, and Godiva Chocolates. The owner of Franco-American since 1915, Campbell's introduced SpaghettiOs in 1965. New, health-conscious versions of Campbell's soups have helped the company maintain its lead in the soup market.

The red-and-white Campbell's Soup can (the colors, chosen in the 19th century, were those of Cornell University) was immortalized by artist Andy Warhol in the 1960s. The painting has been hung in many museum exhibitions as an example of pop art.

References

Collins, Douglas, *America's Favorite Food: The Story of Campbell Soup Company*. New York: Harry N. Abrams, 1994.
"Company History." Campbell Soup Company. October 31, 2000. <www.campbellsoup.com/center/history>.
Watkins, Julian Lewis. *The 100 Greatest Advertisements: Who Wrote Them and What They Did*. New York: Dover Books, 1959.

Mary Cross

The Ford Model T

Although Henry Ford did not advertise it at first, his Model T car, created in 1908 (the twentieth in an alphabetical sequence of Ford cars, beginning with the first Model A in 1903; a second Model A appeared in 1927), became an icon as "a motor car for the great multitude," which has never faded from American memory. Indeed, it is probably the most famous car ever built. Model Ts can still be spotted on the road being driven to antique car shows for exhibition.

The Model T made history even in its first year, selling what was then a record-breaking 10,660 cars. Five years later, the Ford Motor Company was producing half of all the cars in the United States, despite ample competition from the many other car companies that had sprung up in America and Europe, including Cadillac, Studebaker, Packard, Pierce-Arrow, and Mercedes.

The Model T was always black—Henry Ford saw no reason to turn it out in colors—and its many satisfied owners had given it a nickname, the "Lizzie." Introduced on October 1, 1908, the Model T was the culmination of Ford's desire to build a reliable car "so low in price that no man . . . will be unable to own one." Without the extras, the Model T cost $260, or $400 with them. By 1913 the demand for the car was so intense that Ford, searching for ways to increase production, introduced the assembly line in his Detroit factory. The Model T, the first automobile to be mass-produced, easily outpaced its competitors. For twenty years, the company did not have to change anything in its essential design or engineering to sell it.

The competition caught up to Ford when other manufacturers started to add chrome, color selection, and yearly model changes. The concept of the model year seems to have originated in the 1920s with General Motors which started producing a new model every year to lure buyers. This often involved advertising claims and newness more than real change in car performance, but it equated status with the new and meant Ford also had to come up with new models. The pressure to be new was intense. The introduction of the Edsel model in 1957, named for family member and then president, Edsel Ford, which carried the collective hopes of the Ford Company, was a major flop. Consumers did not like the way the over-designed car looked.

Following its patriotic performance in manufacturing aircraft engines, bombers, and tanks during World War II, Ford continued restyling its vehicles but still found itself losing money. Finally, in a special ceremony held at the Waldorf Astoria in New York City, Ford introduced a new model for 1949 that propelled the company back to second place among car makers and set a standard for future automotive design. The 1949 Ford had independent front suspension and a one-piece body that incorporated the fenders. The back quarter windows opened.

Henry Ford did not live to see it, but his oldest grandson, Henry Ford II, would lead the company into worldwide prominence by the 1950s, with plants and offices in thirty countries. The company went public in the 1950s, and in the mid-1960s introduced another famous car, the Mustang, powered with a Ford Falcon engine and designed to appeal to younger, sportier tastes. Ford sold 100,000 Mustangs in its first 100 days of production. The Ford Thunderbird, introduced in 1955, went up against the Corvette brought out by Chevrolet two years earlier and beat it handily in sales.

Today, the Ford Motor Company is ranked second in the Fortune 500 list of the largest U.S. industrial corporations, based on sales. Globally, the company is represented in more than 200 nations on six continents as the world's largest producer of trucks and second-largest producer of cars. Its sports utility vehicles, including the Explorer, pickup trucks like the Silverado, and minivans fuel the American craze for new and powerful ways to get on the road. The company again has a family member in top management; William Clay Ford, Jr., a great-grandson of Henry Ford, is now chairman.

References

Doody, Alton F., and Ron Bingaman. *Reinventing the Wheels*. Cambridge, MA: Ballinger, 1988.
"Our Company Heritage." Ford Motor Company. November 21, 2000. <http://www.ford.com/.>
Shook, Robert. *The Ford Motor Company*. New York: Prentice Hall, 1990.

Mary Cross

The Hershey Bar

Milton S. Hershey, the founder of the Hershey Chocolate Company, has been called the Henry Ford of chocolate. Like Ford, he did not initially advertise his product. Launching their fledgling businesses at the beginning of the century, both men depended for sales on word of mouth and the free publicity generated by their popular products. The Hershey Chocolate Company did not begin to advertise until 1970, seventy-six years after its founding. Even without advertising, the Hershey bar had long attained iconic status. The company, enjoying its lead among American candy companies, could pitch the Hershey bar as the "Great American Chocolate Bar" with no exaggeration.

Hershey had been an astute entrepreneur in the candy business, and when it became clear that the future did not lie in the caramels he had been manufacturing in Lancaster, Pennsylvania, he switched to chocolate in 1886. By 1894 he was in the business of selling cocoa and baking chocolate from the Hershey Chocolate Company in a town that would someday be called Hershey, Pennsylvania. The invention of the milk chocolate Hershey bar in 1900, and selling it for a nickel, launched another American success story. Like Henry Ford, Hershey recognized that pricing a product so that everyone could afford it could be extremely profitable.

In 1907 the Hershey kiss, said to have gotten its name from the smacking sound the kiss machine made, was invented, and the Hershey almond bar came out in 1908. Sales of chocolate consistently defied economic turndowns, including that of 1929. People wanted some pleasure even in tough times. During World War I, Hershey developed Field Ration D to supply high energy on the battlefield. Soldiers found they could use Hershey bars as barter, so strong a symbol was it of America.

A Mennonite with a fourth-grade education, Hershey was a generous man. Childless himself, he felt a special mission to help children. With profits from the chocolate company, he founded the Milton S. Hershey School for Boys (now coed) for children who were orphaned or had only one parent. He built up the dairy farms all around Hershey to house the boys, who lived as part of a family and helped in the dairy to produce the milk the company needed for milk chocolate. They were housed and educated for free. The school is the richest orphanage in the world.

Meanwhile, Hershey had designed and built a little utopian town around his chocolate factory, building houses for his workers on streets named after cocoa-producing locales like Granada and Aruba, a community center, a bank, a hotel and inn, a theater, a department store, golf courses, swimming pools, a sports arena, a zoo, a museum, and an amusement park. The town of Hershey had its own water and sewage systems, its own telephone and electric companies, and its own cemetery.

During the years when it did not advertise, Hershey Chocolate got its name in the news anyway. It owned a hockey team, the Hershey Bears, staged tryout productions of Broadway-bound shows, hired celebrity golf pros, held major tennis tournaments, and brought in big-name bands for dances and concerts. The town, which smelled like chocolate all day long, became a popular tourist destination.

When Hershey finally decided to advertise, it hired Ogilvy and Mather in 1969 to introduce the Great American Chocolate Bar, a campaign that ran on television from 1970 to 1972 but increased sales 30 percent. Hershey, which had had no marketing department all those years, did not advertise heavily again until the 1980s. Today, with such brands as Reese's Peanut Butter Cups (bought in 1963 from a hometown rival) to market along with Almond Joy, Kit Kat, Krackel, Mr. Goodbar, York Peppermint Patties, and Twizzlers, as well as varieties of cocoa and ice cream toppings, the Hershey Foods Corporation spends more than $200 million a year on advertising to keep pace with its close competitor, Mars M&Ms, which currently leads the field.

References

Brenner, Joel Glenn. *The Emperors of Chocolate: Inside the Secret World of Hershey and Mars.* New York: Random House, 1999.

"History of Chocolate." Hershey Foods Corporation. April 4, 2001. <www.
    hersheys.com/consumer/history>.
Morton, Marcia, and Frederic Morton. *Chocolate, An Illustrated History*. New York:
    Crown Publishers, 1986.

Mary Cross

Ivory Soap

At the turn of the century, people felt little social pressure to take a bath every day, perhaps because taking a bath was such a chore. Indoor bathrooms were rare until the late 1880s. Water for the bath had to be carted indoors, heated, and poured into a suitable tub, then carried out again and dumped. No wonder baths were mainly a Saturday night affair.

In addition, most soap was homemade. Housewives made their own soap out of lye from wood ashes and cooking grease, or they bought a chunk from huge slabs at the grocer's. There was no difference between soap for clothes and soap for skin unless one bought an expensive European soap. Any store-bought American soap was essentially a by-product of candle making, the main business, for example, of a profitable company started by two Cincinnati brothers-in-law, William Procter and James Gamble.

Their sons, educated at Eastern universities, eventually took over the business and saw the future as soap, not candles. More frequent washing was being encouraged by the arrival of house plumbing, public waterworks, and an awareness of hygiene brought on by a "cleanliness" movement at the end of the 19th century. In trying to reproduce the pure castile soaps then being imported from Europe, James Gamble and a chemist came up with a formula in 1878 for P & G White Soap, designed with a notch in the middle so it could be used whole for the laundry or divided into smaller cakes for the bath.

The name White Soap, though it distinguished the soap from the standard lye-yellow cakes, was a bit bland, and the brothers searched for a new name. The next year, a cousin, Harley Procter, supplied it one day in 1879 after church, or so the story goes. He had been listening in church to the 45th Psalm with the line, "All thy garments smell of myrrh and aloes and cassia out of ivory palaces," and he said he was struck with the purity denoted by the word "ivory." The new soap henceforth was called Ivory. Cousin Harley, obsessed by purity, is said to have also come up with the slogan, "99 and 44/100 Per Cent Pure," after some calculation of the impurities in the soap (0.56 percent alkali, carbonates, and mineral matter). The slogan has become part of the language.

THE "IVORY" is a Laundry Soap, with all the fine qualities of a choice Toilet Soap, and is 99 44-100 per cent. pure.

Ladies will find this Soap especially adapted for washing laces, infants' clothing, silk hose, cleaning gloves and all articles of fine texture and delicate color, and for the varied uses about the house that daily arise, requiring the use of soap that is above the ordinary in quality.

For the Bath, Toilet, or Nursery it is preferred to most of the Soaps sold for toilet use, being purer and much more pleasant and effective and possessing all the desirable properties of the finest unadultered White Castile Soap. The Ivory Soap will "float."

The cakes are so shaped that they may be used entire for general purposes or divided with a stout thread (as illustrated) into two perfectly formed cakes, of convenient size for toilet use.

The price, compared to the quality and the size of the cakes, makes it the cheapest Soap for everybody for every want. TRY IT.

SOLD EVERYWHERE.

The first advertisement for Ivory Soap showed that the soap cake could be divided for use on the skin as well as on the laundry. © The Procter & Gamble Company.

One thing neither he nor the brothers had calculated was that Ivory Soap would float. When orders started to come in for "more of that floating soap," they tried to figure out what had happened. Apparently, the stirring process in one cycle of soap making had accidently been allowed to go on so long that it aerated that batch of soap. From then on, Ivory Soap was deliberately whipped and aerated, and a second slogan, "It Floats," was born.

Cousin Harley was put in charge of sales, and he busied himself making a brand out of Ivory, with an identifiable checkerboard wrapper and the two slogans that were to beat down the competition for decades. He began to advertise in magazines, emphasizing the purity and safety of the soap, even for babies. He advertised first in religious magazines which were the first in the United States to include paid advertising. Then he bought the page inside the back cover of publications like *Harper's Monthly*, *Century*, and *Ladies' Home Journal*. He hired famous artists to illustrate the ads, including Maude Humphrey, Humphrey Bogart's mother and a well-known painter of children. Illustrations of the "Ivory baby," first portrayed by another artist in 1887 ("Safe enough to use on . . ."), were to prove so popular that they were offered "suitable for framing" in return for a soap wrapper. The Ivory baby became a virtual brand image of the soap; by the 1930s, famous photographers were taking the pictures. Never repeating an ad after it ran, Procter & Gamble used a wide variety of thematic illustrations to keep its name in the public eye. In 1933 the company sponsored the long-running radio soap opera *Ma Perkins* to promote its Oxydol laundry soap. Its first television commercial was for Ivory Soap.

"Advertising has been a factor—an important factor—in the success of Ivory Soap," one 1911 Ivory ad appearing in the *Saturday Evening Post* said. Advertising is "evidence of a manufacturer's faith in the merit of an article," and "continuous advertising is proof of the public's confidence in it." The ad noted that "Ivory Soap has been advertised, continuously, for more than thirty years." Indeed, Procter & Gamble, thanks to Cousin Harley, had gotten into advertising with a head start on its later competitors—soaps like Sapolio, Woodbury's, Packer's, Peet's, and Pear's. With Ivory Soap, the company was one of the first to create an identifiable brand name instead of a generic company name. It had also created an insignia that was instantly recognizable. Growing out of a star drawn by a wharfhand on one of the Procter & Gamble Star brand candle crates, the symbol of the crescent moon and thirteen stars (for the thirteen colonies) was trademarked in 1882 and branded every product including, later, Hires Root Beer, Joy and Tide detergents, Crest toothpaste, Head & Shoulders shampoo, Crisco, and Charmin bath tissue, to name just a few.

In 1982, rumors begun by a competitor alleged that the stars in the symbol were the mark of the devil. So virulent were the rumors that, after three years of battling unsuccessfully to defeat them, Procter & Gamble dropped the emblem from its products and replaced it with a simple P&G logo.

With its long commitment to advertising, Procter & Gamble has led the pack in advertising dollars spent for thirty of the past thirty-seven years and has remained within the top three (with General Motors and Philip Morris) for the forty-four years that *Advertising Age* has kept count. In June 2001, Procter & Gamble made its biggest acquisition ever when it entered the hair color market by buying Clairol for $5 billion.

References

Endicott, R. Craig. "Marketing elite." *The Advertising Century: Advertising Age,* Special Issue (Spring 1999):128.

Hobson, Katherine. "P&G Gets a Hot New 'Do'." *U.S. News & World Report.* June 4, 2001: 44.

Lief, Alfred. *"It Floats": The Story of Procter & Gamble.* New York: Rinehart, 1958.

Morgan, Hal. *Symbols of America.* New York: Viking Penguin Books, 1986.

"Procter & Gamble History." November 20, 2000. <http:www.pg.com>.

Sivulka, Juliann. *Soap, Sex, and Cigarettes: A Cultural History of American Advertising.* Belmont, CA: Wadsworth, 1997.

Mary Cross

Kellogg's Corn Flakes

The health food craze of 1990s, accompanied by advertising claims for the benefits of fiber and low fat, was actually nothing new to the American 20th century. As early as 1898, the Kellogg brothers were running a health spa in Battle Creek, Michigan, where they advocated a diet of grains, fruits, and nuts for their patients. Will Keith Kellogg (W. K.), who helped his brother, Dr. John Harvey Kellogg, run the Battle Creek Sanitarium, virtually invented the corn flake while experimenting with grain products. When a batch of dried-out dough went through the rollers and came out as flakes instead of a sheet, he baked them and produced the crisp, ready-to-eat cereal that he called "corn flakes."

Kellogg's invention revolutionized breakfast at the turn of the century and invited competitors, forty-two of them at one point—all in Battle Creek—to capitalize on corn flakes. W. K. Kellogg formed his own company, the Battle Creek Toasted Corn Flake Company, in 1906 and added malt flavoring to distinguish his cereal from the others. He put his signature on every box with the message, "The Original Bears This Signature" (and it still does). He gave out 4 million free sample boxes of corn flakes in the first year and spent most of his working capital to take out a full-page ad in the *Ladies' Home Journal*. This marketing effort worked so well that by 1908 the company was unable to keep up with customer demand. A new advertisement urged, "For thirty days, please stop eating Toasted Corn Flakes" (so other people could have a chance). In 1909 Kellogg sold more than a million cases of his corn flakes.

He offered premiums with the cereal. When he realized that the cereal box on the breakfast table offered space for advertising, his company was the first to print nutrition messages, recipes, and product information on the box itself. In 1914 Kellogg's began to sell cereal in Canada; international sales now include 160 countries. In 1916 Kellogg began to produce All-Bran, a high-fiber cereal which, by the end of the century, could still capitalize on health news.

Kellogg doubled his advertising budget after the Wall Street crash in 1929 and, despite the downturn of the Great Depression, the company prospered. He had introduced Rice Krispies the year before and used the slogan "Snap! Crackle! Pop!" to promote the "sound appeal" of the cereal on a 1930s radio show. Later, on television, Snap, Crackle, and Pop became little animated elves who still appear on the cereal boxes and in the commercials.

During World War II, the company made the now-famous K-rations, a highly concentrated, cereal-based food for the military, and positioned itself in the 1950s to capture the then-burgeoning baby boom market. The advertising agency Leo Burnett helped Kellogg launch a raft of new sweetened cereals and bought up Saturday morning children's television hours to promote them with such characters as the enduring Tony the Tiger for Frosted Flakes, voted the second most recognized icon of the 20th century by *Advertising Age* (after the Marlboro man). The paintings of Norman Rockwell were used in print ads and on corn flakes boxes, along with the slogan, "The Best to You Each Morning."

Though W. K. Kellogg died in 1951 at the age of 91, his concern with health and nutrition continued as the backdrop for the company's advertising. Special K cereal, launched in the 1970s, was aimed at women, with a low-fat, vitamin-rich appeal. In the 1990s, the company called a new generation to corn flakes with the slogan, "Try them again . . . for the first time."

References

Bruce, Scott, and Bill Crawford. *Cerealizing America*. Winchester, MA: Faber and Faber, 1995.

"Company FAQs." Kellogg Company. <http://www.kellogg.marketlocator.com/>.

Mary Cross

Kodak Cameras

The original Kodak camera, first marketed in 1888, operated on the same principle as today's disposable cameras. The film, with 100 exposures, was preloaded, and when all the pictures had been taken, the entire camera was turned in for developing by sending it to the Kodak factory in Rochester, New York. For the first time, Americans could afford to own a portable camera and take their own pictures. "You press the button," Kodak ads said; "We do the rest." Kodak sold 2,500 cameras in the first year.

The slogan was written by George Eastman, the founder of the company, who wrote much of the advertising copy and who understood the power of advertising early on. The little eight-word phrase became one of the first advertising slogans to make it into popular culture. Like the 1980s slogan for Wendy's, "Where's the Beef?," it was on the lips of everyone from politicians to the man in the street. A Gilbert and Sullivan operetta, *Utopia*, used the line in one of its lyrics.

The slogan expressed what Eastman had in mind, making photography easy for the amateur. He had already demonstrated that dry photographic plates could work as well as wet ones and would not require instant developing. In 1885 Eastman had introduced the first roll film, doing away with the cumbersome glass plates previously grappled with by portrait photographers. Four years later, he produced a commercial version and was consulting with Thomas Edison in his development of the movie camera, eventually selling him celluloid film. When it was time to find a brand name for his successful products, Eastman made up one, saying that "Kodak" with its odd sound was unusual enough to stick in people's minds and would not be changed in translation to other languages. K was his favorite letter and the first letter of his mother's maiden name.

The Kodak camera, which sold for a pricey $25, was a leather-covered wooden box about half the size of a shoebox. For a viewfinder, it had a simple V carved into the top to line up the shot. Inside was the roll mechanism for the 100-exposure bromide developing-out paper. On the outside, there was a string to pull, a key to turn, and a button to push, a simple 1-2-3 operation that cocked the camera, set up the film, and took the picture. When all the film was exposed, the camera had to be

The basic Kodak camera was designed to make amateur picture taking easier.
Courtesy © Eastman Kodak Company. KODAK is a trademark.

sent back to the Rochester factory where, for $10, the company developed the film and returned the pictures and camera, reloaded with film. Commander Robert Peary took Kodak cameras with him on a Greenland expedition in the 1890s, where he took some 2,000 pictures, proving that the camera and its film could withstand even Arctic conditions.

In 1900 Eastman introduced an even simpler camera, the Brownie, which cost $1, plus 15 cents for the six-exposure film. It turned picture taking into a national pastime. By this time, Eastman had refined the design of his camera so that it was possible to remove the film in daylight. Photofinishing shops sprang up to develop the film. The Brownie Boy in the ads marketed the camera to children, but everyone used them. Eastman had taken the mystery out of photography, and his goal of aiming at amateurs and his policy of low pricing paid off. The company sold almost 250,000 Brownies in its first year.

Eastman was also working to supply plates and paper for the newly discovered X ray and to improve the processing of film. He began to provide benefits and pension funds for his employees, along with various dividends: a share in the company's profits and a savings and loan association to help employees save and finance the purchase of a home.

He kept the factory spotless, requiring that it be swept each day and sprinkled in the summer.

Over the years, the Eastman Kodak Company has kept its focus: to make picture taking easy for the consumer. The new company mantra is "Simple Is Smart," but "The No. 1 thing the brand has done an outstanding job with is emotion," Kodak Vice President and Marketing Manager Jude Rake told *USA Today*. Kodak's fall 2001 slogan, "Share Moments. Share Life," is being used in a campaign created with Ogilvy New York.

References

Collins, Douglas. *The Story of Kodak*. New York: Harry N. Abrams, 1990.

"History of Kodak." Eastman Kodak Company. April 1, 2001. <http:www.kodak.com/US/en/corp/aboutKodak/kodak History/milestones>.

Howard, Theresa. "Lights, Kodak, Action: New Ads a Hit." *USA Today*, August 27, 2001: 4B.

Watkins, Julian Lewis. *The 100 Greatest Advertisments: Who Wrote Them and What They Did*. New York: Dover Publications, 1959.

Mary Cross

Lydia E. Pinkham's Vegetable Compound

So we'll sing of Lydia Pinkham,
   Savior of the human race,
She sells her Vegetable Compound,
   and the papers publish her face.

—Folk ditty

The vogue for patent medicines peaked in the late 19th century but came to a virtual standstill when the first Food and Drug Act, passed in 1906, required disclosure of their contents. Nonetheless, their blockbuster advertising and marketing strategies had already taught merchants how to hawk their wares and paved the way for the growth of American advertising. By the turn of the century, patent medicine advertising was providing one-third of the advertising profits made by American magazines and newspapers, as well as half of the revenues of the existing ad agencies.

In the early 1900s, Lydia E. Pinkham's Vegetable Compound was one of the most trusted, well-known patent medicines. Originally concocted by Mrs. Pinkham on her kitchen stove, the compound was packaged and advertised to women as a cure for "female complaints." Remarkably, it

is still sold today, joining the current New Age vogue for herbal reme-
dies. The compound then was more than 18 percent alcohol in which
was dissolved a concoction of dogwood, licorice, dandelion, and other
herbs first cooked up by Lydia Estes Pinkham in 1875. Pinkham, who
lived in the same town (Lynn, Massachusetts) as suffragettes Susan B.
Anthony and Elizabeth Cady Stanton, marketed her compound as "The
Greatest Medical Discovery Since the Dawn of History," and she urged
women to "reach for a vegetable instead of a sweet." (Lucky Strike cigarettes echoed this slogan forty years later in their pitch to women:
"Reach for a Lucky instead of a sweet." See "Lucky Strikes" cigarettes
entry in Chapter 5.)

Patent medicines were drugs sold without prescriptions, but the patent
was not a real one; the word seems to have been purloined from the
British "patent of royal favor" given by the British crown to goods it
deemed worthy. American patent medicines had no such imprimatur,
but their claims were royal, offering to cure everything from headaches,
heartburn, indigestion, cramps, and colic to "lassitude," "coated tongue,"
and nightmares. A large part of the cure was the alcohol content of these
drugs, sometimes up to 40 percent. This meant that women who would
never set foot in a saloon could take their tonic at home in their own
parlors with all due propriety.

Perhaps the popularity of Mrs. Pinkham's Vegetable Compound owed
something to its alcohol content, but she was also an astute advertising
woman. She wrote her own copy, bought advertising space in newspapers and women's magazines, and used abundant testimonials collected
from satisfied customers. Her grandmotherly face appeared on every
package. Her trade cards (cards handed out to advertise the product),
now collectibles, promised "a positive cure" for ovarian troubles and the
"Change of Life," as well as "headaches, nervous prostration, general
debility, sleeplessness, depression, and indigestion." The advertising
copy claimed that the product would "under all circumstances, act in
harmony with the laws that govern the female system." The remedy was
an amazing success for almost fifty years.

Advertisements for Lydia E. Pinkham's Vegetable Compound invited
women to write to Mrs. Pinkham for advice, stating that "Any woman
... is responsible for her own suffering who will not take the trouble"
to write. Though Mrs. Pinkham died in 1883, such ads continued to run
until 1905 when the Ladies' Home Journal did an exposé, including a picture of her tombstone, asking how she had been able to dispense advice
for the twenty-two years since her death. Her daughter-in-law, Jennie
Pinkham, explained that she was answering the mail, although a journalist for Collier's Weekly reported that instead the company was using a
form letter and a squad of typists. It did not seem to matter to the cus-

tomers, who made the late Mrs. Pinkham one of the most famous women in America.

In 1906, however, Congress passed the first Pure Food and Drug Act, requiring patent medicines to disclose their alcohol content. Though Mrs. Pinkham was an advocate of the temperance movement, the revelation that her compound—and that of many other patent medicines—had an alcohol content much higher than beer raised public suspicions. Limericks and ditties mocking the Vegetable Compound became popular. The Food and Drug Act also required that any claim for cures be authenticated, forcing many patent medicines off the market. Pinkham's Vegetable Compound, however, was simply reconstituted with a lower alcohol content and kept on selling.

In 1968 the family sold the company to Cooper Laboratories, which continued to market the tablets and liquid. Today, it is sold by Numark Laboratories in drugstores and herbal shops. The ingredients, except for the alcohol, include some of the same ones—dogwood, licorice, and dandelion—that Pinkham simmered on her own stove.

References

Burton, Jean. *Lydia Pinkham Is Her Name*. New York: Farrar, Straus, 1949.

Margolin, Victor, Ira Brichta, and Vivian Brichta. *The Promise and the Product: 200 Years of American Advertising Posters*. New York: Macmillan, 1979.

"The Name That Launched a Million Bottles." Vanderbilt Medical Center. <http://www.mc.vanderbilt.edu/biolib/hc/nostrums/pinkham.html/>.

Mary Cross

Quaker Oats Cereal

At the beginning of the century, cereal makers made some of the same health claims for their products as cereals makers today. Though they lacked the scientific evidence of later cereals, cereal companies of the 1900s advertised their wares as aids to digestion, strong blood, and mental acuity. The early claim that wheat and oat fiber were vital to health and digestion did have some merit. Nutrition studies conducted later in the century showed their role in preventing cancer and lowering cholesterol. Quaker Oats, like Kellogg's, made much of the differences between people who ate their cereal and those who did not, claiming oatmeal built children up "symmetrically" and put off old age in their elders. Quaker claimed in one early ad that a "poll" taken among prisoners in four prisons revealed that fewer than 2 percent of them had grown up eating oatmeal.

The Quaker Oats story began in the 19th century with a German miller, Ferdinand Schumacher, who ground flour and animal feed in his Akron, Ohio, mill. When one day he ground up some of the feed oats to make porridge for breakfast, some of the neighbors were shocked, but Schumacher founded his own oatmeal company and soon was shipping barrels of oatmeal to Cincinnati, New York, and Philadelphia.

Another miller, Henry Parson Crowell of Ravenna, Ohio, joined Schumacher in 1901 along with a third miller, Robert Stuart of Cedar Rapids, Iowa, to form what would soon be the Quaker Oats Company. Crowell took the oatmeal out of the barrels and packaged it in two-pound boxes, adding a picture of a Quaker he had found in an encyclopedia. Upright and proper, the Quaker was portrayed holding a paper on which the word "Pure" was clearly legible, possibly borrowed from a then-current picture of William Penn.

Crowell believed in the power of advertising and free samples. He put the Quaker's picture advertising the oats on barnsides and silos as well as in newspapers, hired home economics students to cook oatmeal outside grocery stores, and handed out free bowls of oatmeal at county fairs. Trains with special "Quaker cars" brought the brand to America's small towns. Supposedly, someone even tried to paint the Quaker on the White Cliffs of Dover. The red, blue, and yellow colors on the oatmeal box were chosen by Crowell, who also put premiums of china, silverware, and glasses inside the box with two pounds of oatmeal poured over them.

Early in the century, Quaker hired the Lord & Thomas advertising agency (later Foote, Cone & Belding) to produce a campaign for its new puffed cereals. Copywriter Claude Hopkins, one of the ad world's eventual hall-of-famers, worked on the campaign, and wrote the famous line, "shot from guns" (metaphorically speaking, in the manufacturing process) for Puffed Wheat cereal, the name he gave to Quaker's Wheat Berries cereal. Hopkins was so good at what he did that Quaker kept him on its account for the next thirty years.

References

"History of Quaker Oats." Quaker Oats Company. <http://www.quakeroats.com/>.

Marquette, Arthur F. *Brands, Trademarks, and Good Will: The Story of the Quaker Oats Company.* New York: McGraw-Hill, 1967.

Mary Cross

Uneeda Biscuit

The National Biscuit Company has always had a penchant for unusual names: Oreos, Fig Newtons, Oysterettes, and Uneeda Biscuit, the name

The Uneeda slicker boy was on every
box of Uneeda Biscuits and he still is.
Courtesy of Nabisco.

that launched the company in the cracker business in 1898 and propelled
its sales to 100 million boxes by 1900. Founder Adolpus Green, a Chicago
lawyer who helped merge three big bakeries (New York Biscuit, American Biscuit, and United States Baking) into the National Biscuit Company, had tried out many names for his crackers: Bekos, Trim, Dandelo,
Verenice, Nabisco, and Fireside. He took them to an advertising agency,
N. W. Ayer & Son, where a copywriter, Henry N. McKinney, came up
with Uneeda. Green added the British term for cracker, "biscuit," to de-
note a more upscale product.

The square, puffy soda crackers themselves were meant to be a classier
version of the kind people were used to buying from the big cracker
barrels in most grocery stores. They were packaged for freshness in a
special box with an airtight liner ("In-Er-Seal" said the box), with a picture of a little boy in a yellow slicker carrying the package in the rain.
The boy, Gordon Stille, was the 5-year-old nephew of another N. W.
Ayer copywriter. The slicker boy became famous and so did the crackers.

The unique personality, name, and packaging of Uneeda Biscuit were
actually brilliant advertising strategies that later advertising experts
would preach as gospel. The name itself spawned many less successful
imitators, including Uwanta beer, Itsagood soup, and Ureada Magazine.

A slogan with a rhyme, "Lest you forget, we say it yet, Uneeda Biscuit," made it easy to remember. Green added an unusual logo to the biscuit box: the Byzantine cross over a circle which had been the printer's mark of a 15th-century Venetian printer, Nicolas Jenson. Printed in red on a white background, it is still the Nabisco trademark.

In 1900 the National Biscuit Company launched the world's first million-dollar ad campaign, putting its name on billboards and streetcars. Founder Green decided in 1901 to shorten the company name and coined the name Nabisco which he had imprinted on a new product that year, Sugar Wafers. The name was soon shortened to NBC, but in 1941, deferring to the broadcast station, the company dropped the acronym and returned to the name Nabisco.

There would be many other names to add to Nabisco's rosters. Oreos, the chocolate sandwich cookie, was introduced in 1912 with a name from the Greek word for hill (the cookies were shaped as a mound). In 1913 the company introduced Mallomars, which started out with jelly layered with marshmallow. Nabisco bought the Shredded Wheat company in 1928 and continued to manufacture the cereal as well as its Triscuit Wafers. In 1934 Nabisco introduced what would become the largest-selling cracker in the world, Ritz Crackers.

Today, Nabisco is a $8.27 billion company with operations in Latin America, Europe, Asia, the Middle East, and Canada as well as the United States. Its major brands include Oreos and Chips Ahoy! cookies, Ritz and Premium crackers, Snackwell's, Planters nuts, Life Savers candies, A-1 steak sauce, Grey Poupon mustard, and Milk-Bone dog snacks. The company's headquarters are located in Parsippany, New Jersey.

References

Cahn, William. *Out of the Cracker Barrel: The Nabisco Story, from Animal Crackers to Zuzus.* New York: Simon and Schuster, 1969.

Sivulka, Juliann. *Soap, Sex, and Cigarettes: A Cultural History of American Advertising.* Belmont, CA: Wadsworth, 1997.

Mary Cross

2

Icons of the 1910s

The 1910s began placidly enough. Prosperity, population growth, and peace embued the prewar period with a general feeling of well-being. It was a time known as the Progressive Era. William Howard Taft had been president since 1908; Teddy Roosevelt had declined to run for a third term. Cars were now all over the road, some 5 million strong in 1910, along with horse and buggies, and roadways were being built and improved. Electricity and indoor bathrooms, though hardly universal, were making life more liveable for Americans, as was an increase in people's purchasing power and the increasing availability of consumer goods. Chain grocers like Piggly Wiggly started to make their appearance in 1916, and the department stores made store-bought items and clothes more accessible.

The first transcontinental phone call, from New York City to San Francisco, went through in 1915, and D. W. Griffith's film *The Birth of a Nation* (1915) was drawing large crowds. Health products like aspirin were widely advertised and sold, wearing cosmetics like rouge and powder became more acceptable for women, and many kinds of candy and snack foods as well as soda drinks were on the grocer's shelves. Americans had more leisure activities, motoring among them, though the flat tires, the muddy roads, the breakdowns, and the outfits including goggles could make the Sunday drive a headache. Fewer Americans were farming and more of them were moving to the cities. In 1916 America had a population of 100 million people, nearly half of whom lived in urban areas.

The sinking of the *S.S. Titanic* in 1912 and the assassination of Archduke Francis Ferdinand of Austria in 1914, though not related, were events that presaged and precipitated major social change to come. There were other clouds on the horizon. In 1913 the Sixteenth Amendment to the U.S. Constitution gave the federal government the power to tax personal income. In 1919 the sale, consumption, and transportation of liquor were prohibited by the Eighteenth Amendment.

Though the United States did not enter World War I (1914–1918) until 1917, it was clear at home that a war was going on in Europe. The casualties and the carnage were shocking; worse was to come when American soldiers became involved. President Woodrow Wilson, elected in 1912 and again in 1916, was well known for his reluctance to enter the war. German U-boats, however, which were sinking transatlantic ships, were costing American lives and damaging export business. In 1917 Wilson declared war on Germany, joining England in the fight. At the same time in Russia, Czar Nicholas II was forced to abdicate, and the Bolsheviks took control.

World War I changed everything. There was a sense that an abyss had opened up endangering the safe and stable lives of Americans, and the values and culture of the country underwent startling upheavals. Ernest Hemingway, who served as an ambulance driver during the war, wrote that words like glory, honor, and courage seemed obscene in the light of the horrors of war. The very meaning of life had changed.

The advertising world was changing as well. Agencies had moved into the business of demographics and research to target their customers better, and the improved distribution of goods throughout the country made it possible to run national campaigns. Improved transportation and roadways made billboards and barnsides valuable media for advertising. Print media proliferated. Even the government started to advertise. During World War I, recruitment ads and posters and the selling of Liberty Bonds took up advertising space. Patriotism ran high. Manufacturers, not without self-interest, linked their products to the war effort in their ads. Kodak, for example, encouraged people to send snapshots from home to the boys overseas, and doughboys (what infantry men were called in World War I) sang the praises of pancakes in Aunt Jemima ads.

The war brought many women out of the house and into the workplace; they worked as stretcher bearers and ambulance drivers and in factories. They bobbed their hair and donned knickers (pants or underwear that ended at the knee) and overalls. By the time the war ended, women's fashions reflected women's new independence; it was the end of the Gibson Girl look, the eight-button shoes, the corset, and skirts to the ground. In 1920 women finally got the vote with the passage of the Nineteenth Amendment to the Constitution.

Advertisers took notice. The lady of the house had already been targeted as the major purchaser of household goods, but now the ads played to her vanity and desire for social status. Car ads pictured well-dressed women at the wheel, and cosmetics, soap, deodorant, and household cleaners were sold on similar images of beautiful, privileged women. Cosmetics entrepreneurs Elizabeth Arden and Helena Rubenstein were already in business, selling "hope in a jar," and Emily Post published her book of etiquette (1915) to guide milady in the proper conduct of her social life. By 1937 the book had gone into five editions. Though the days of the flapper were still to come and though nothing had really changed about her gender role (in 1914 Congress designated the second Sunday in May as Mother's Day), the advertising pitch to a "new" woman was already in place.

References

Evans, Harold. *The American Century*. New York: Knopf, 1998.
Green, Harvey. *The Uncertainty of Everyday Life 1915–1945*. New York: HarperCollins, 1992.
Norris, James D. *Advertising and the Transformation of American Society, 1865–1920*. Westport, CT: Greenwood Press, 1990.
Stern, Jane and Michael Stern. *Encyclopedia of Pop Culture*. New York: HarperPerennial, 1992.

Mary Cross

Cadillac

It was not until Henry M. Leland, an arms maker and mechanic, went into the automobile business that cars no longer had to be hand-cranked, an onerous job which involved compressing gas fumes enough to spark and ignite a piston. Charles F. Kettering of Dayton, Ohio, invented the electric self-starter in 1912, and Cadillac launched Kettering's career when Leland installed it in the cars he and the Cadillac Motor Car Company (acquired by General Motors in 1909) were manufacturing. They had already produced the first closed-bodied cars on the market in 1910 with the Fisher Body Company.

Cadillac's first car in 1903, the Model A, had a single-cylinder engine with a copper water jacket and sold for $750, more expensive than Henry Ford's Model T would be six years later at $260, but aimed at the luxury market Cadillac would consistently target. The car had been built with the help of former Ford workers laid off when the first Ford Motor Company was temporarily disbanded, and Henry Ford was briefly involved with Cadillac during that period, helping to start the company. The fancy Cadillac Model D appeared in 1905, a four-cylinder touring car with a wooden body covered by an aluminium skin.

Cadillac, named after the founder of Detroit, Le Sieur Antoine de la Mothe Cadillac, whose coat of arms it adopted and trademarked in 1906, aspired to be "the standard of the world," as its slogan proclaimed. Though it was eventually recognized as setting the standard, Cadillac was not the first motor car in the United States. Brothers Charles and Frank Duryea of Springfield, Massachusetts, had put the first gasoline-powered car on the road in 1893; theirs was the only organized output by 1896, a total of thirteen cars. Henry Ford built his first car in 1896, although he did not offer one for sale until 1903. Between 1904 and 1908, more than 240 car companies got into the business; most of them were out of the picture by 1910.

Cadillac's cars, innovative from the beginning, used standardized rather than the hand-fitted parts used by other auto makers. In England, the Royal Automobile Club, skeptical of Cadillac's standard parts, took three of its cars apart in 1908 and reassembled each with parts from the others. The reassembled cars ran so well on on a 500-mile test course that the club awarded a coveted trophy to Cadillac.

By 1915 many models later, Cadillac could boast of "The Penalty of Leadership" in an advertisement that ran only once, in the *Saturday Evening Post*, but has become one of the advertising world's most famous. It was written by Theodore MacManus, the star copywriter for General Motors. "In every field of human endeavor," the ad began, "he that is first must perpetually live in the white light of publicity. Whether the leadership be vested in a man or in a manufactured product, emulation and envy are ever at work." The Cadillac that came out that year, the Model 51 touring car, would indeed inspire envy with its V8 engine (eight cylinders, arranged in a V-shape) designed by Leland and priced at $1,975 for the luxury market, almost eight times more than the cost of a Ford Model T, which was priced for the working man.

Cadillac had established itself so well as a standard that during World War I its cars were chosen as the official U.S. Army cars and shipped overseas to the front. When the war started, Henry Leland wanted Cadillac to make airplane engines, but the company declined, and he left Cadillac in 1917 to found the Lincoln Motor Company. During World War II, General Douglas MacArthur rode in a Cadillac staff car, and many tanks were powered by Cadillac V8 engines. Cadillac continued to advertise during the war even though its cars would not be available until the fighting stopped. One ad showed a woman with the word "Cadillac" floating above her head and the words, "I know what I'll buy first."

In 1927 General Motors hired a designer, Harley Earl, who established the first styling department in a car company and who that year designed a "Companion car to Cadillac," the LaSalle, a smaller version also named after a French explorer. Earl and General Motors President Alfred P. Sloan introduced the concept of the model year, with annual changes as small as extra chrome or colors, and caught manufacturers like Henry

The PENALTY OF LEADERSHIP

IN every field of human endeavor, he that is first must perpetually live in the white light of publicity. ¶Whether the leadership be vested in a man or in a manufactured product, emulation and envy are ever at work. ¶In art, in literature, in music, in industry, the reward and the punishment are always the same. ¶The reward is widespread recognition; the punishment, fierce denial and detraction. ¶When a man's work becomes a standard for the whole world, it also becomes a target for the shafts of the envious few. ¶If his work be merely mediocre, he will be left severely alone—if he achieve a masterpiece, it will set a million tongues a-wagging. ¶Jealousy does not protrude its forked tongue at the artist who produces a commonplace painting. ¶Whatsoever you write, or paint, or play, or sing, or build, no one will strive to surpass, or to slander you, unless your work be stamped with the seal of genius. ¶Long, long after a great work or a good work has been done, those who are disappointed or envious continue to cry out that it can not be done. ¶Spiteful little voices in the domain of art were raised against our own Whistler as a mountebank, long after the big world had acclaimed him its greatest artistic genius. ¶Multitudes flocked to Bayreuth to worship at the musical shrine of Wagner, while the little group of those whom he had dethroned and displaced argued angrily that he was no musician at all. ¶The little world continued to protest that Fulton could never build a steamboat, while the big world flocked to the river banks to see his boat steam by. ¶The leader is assailed because he is a leader, and the effort to equal him is merely added proof of that leadership. ¶Failing to equal or to excel, the follower seeks to depreciate and to destroy—but only confirms once more the superiority of that which he strives to supplant. ¶There is nothing new in this. ¶It is as old as the world and as old as the human passions—envy, fear, greed, ambition, and the desire to surpass. ¶And it all avails nothing. ¶If the leader truly leads, he remains—the leader. ¶Master-poet, master-painter, master-workman, each in his turn is assailed, and each holds his laurels through the ages. ¶That which is good or great makes itself known, no matter how loud the clamor of denial. ¶That which deserves to live—lives.

Cadillac Motor Car Co. Detroit, Mich.

Copyright 1914, Cadillac Motor Car Co.

This advertisement, written by T. F. MacManus, first appeared in the January 2nd edition of THE SATURDAY EVENING POST in the year 1915. Many consider it one of the greatest advertisements ever written.

"The Penalty of Leadership" ad for Cadillac ran only once, in 1915, but has been famous ever since for its advertising claims. Courtesy of D'Arcy Masius Benton & Bowles.

Ford, who had not changed his Model T in twenty years, off guard. By the 1950s, General Motors had more than 1,200 designers working to design new exteriors for its cars every year. The famous tail fins on the 1948 Cadillac were one of those new designs. Harley Earl had admired the look of the Lockheed P-38 fighter plane and emulated it in the design for fins for Cadillac. Dealers parked these Cadillacs with their backs to the showroom windows and left the lights on overnight to show off the tail fins. The tail fin design exerted an influence beyond the car world for years to come.

References

Bayley, Stephen. *Harley Earl and the Dream Machine*. New York: Alfred A. Knopf, 1983.

Hendry, Maurice D. *Cadillac, Standard of the World: The Complete Seventy-Year History*. New York: Automobile Quarterly Publications, 1973.

Kinzer, Stephen. "From Brainwash to Carwash: Creating a National Passion." *New York Times*, February 6, 2001: C2.

Olcutt, Teri. "The History of Cadillac." *About.com*, 25 July 1998. 2 June 2001 <http://www.vintagecars.about.com>

Varian, Hal R. "Economic Scene." *New York Times*, December 14, 2000: C2.

Watkins, Julian Lewis. *The 100 Greatest Advertisements: Who Wrote Them and What They Did*. New York: Dover Books, 1959.

Mary Cross

Cracker Jack

Cracker Jack supposedly got its name when an early customer sampled the popcorn, peanut, and molasses confection and proclaimed, "That's a crackerjack!" In the popular parlance, it was a hit. The Chicago brothers who had mixed up the concoction, Frederick William (F. W.) and Louis Rueckheim, went right out and got the name trademarked.

F. W. Rueckheim, a German immigrant, had been working on a farm but went to Chicago in 1871 where he sold popcorn from a stand on Federal Street to workers cleaning up after the great Chicago fire in 1871. Business was so good that Rueckheim sent for his brother in Germany, and together they formed a company, F. W. Rueckheim & Bro., to buy candy equipment and produce marshmallows and other confections. They introduced their new candy popcorn at the first World's Fair in Chicago, the Columbian Exposition, in 1893. By 1896 Louis Rueckheim had discovered a way to keep the molasses-coated popcorn, then sold in large tubs, from sticking together, a method that is still secret. In 1899 the brothers and their new partner, Henry Eckstein, began selling Cracker Jack in boxes, using a waxed paper lining, a "Triple Proof Package that keeps out moisture, germs and dust," according to later ads. Cracker Jack sold for a nickel a box until the 1950s when the price went up to 10 cents.

The product was indeed a crackerjack, and by 1908, Cracker Jack was being immortalized in the lyrics of a popular song, "Take Me Out to the Ball Game," with the line, "Buy me some peanuts and Cracker Jack." Written by two men who had never been to a baseball game, Jack Norworth and Albert Von Tilzer, the song gave Cracker Jack an association with a great American pastime. One hundred years later, it celebrated its centennial, in 1993, with a commemorative set of baseball cards.

The Cracker Jack boxes included coupons that could be redeemed for prizes, but the company, now known as Rueckheim Bros. & Eckstein, began in 1912 to offer "a prize in every box," small wooden or porcelain toys and dolls, baseball cards, booklets, watches, and other trinkets that today, 17 billion prizes later, are valuable collectibles.

In 1919 F. W. Rueckheim put a picture of his grandson Robert in a sailor suit with his dog Bingo on the boxes as "Sailor Jack" (during World War I, the company had used red, white, and blue stripes on its boxes). He hired the N. W. Ayer advertising agency and started advertising nationally with the slogan, "The more you eat, the more you want," a slogan still in use.

Although the company produced other confections, including Campfire marshmallows, Cracker Jack was its biggest selling item, and the company name was changed in 1922 to the Cracker Jack Company. Radio advertising began after World War II in 1945, and the first television ads for Cracker Jack appeared in 1955, sponsoring the show *On Your Account*.

The Borden company of Columbus, Ohio, bought the brand in 1964 and improved production by moving from batch coating to a continuous cooking process. Borden introduced several new versions of Cracker Jack, including Cracker Jack popcorn and Butter Toffee-flavored Cracker Jack. A fat-free version was introduced in 1995. Cracker Jack was sold to Frito-Lay in 1997, which ran the first television advertisement in fifteen years for Cracker Jack during the Super Bowl game in 1999. New versions of Cracker Jack developed by Frito-Lay now include Cracker Jack clusters and "Nothing But Nuts" butter toffee peanuts.

References

Carlinsky, Dan. "A Prize in Every Box." *Modern Maturity*, April/May 1981: 34–35.

"How Cracker Jack Began." <http://www.angelfire.com/mt/crackerjack/beginning.html/>.

Mary Cross

Maxwell House Coffee

The slogan "Good to the Last Drop" and the trademark overturned coffee cup, which appeared in its advertising, made Maxwell House Coffee the most popular coffee brand in the United States in the early part of the century. The name is said to have come from the Maxwell House Hotel in Nashville, Tennessee, where the special coffee blend was introduced to guests in 1892. The famous slogan is supposed to have originated when President Theodore Roosevelt, dining in the area in 1907, was served a cup of the blend. He pronounced the coffee "good to the last drop" and asked for a second cup. The company, then the Nashville Coffee and Manufacturing Company, added the now-famous slogan to its ads in 1907 and has used it for almost ninety-five years since.

Joel Cheek, a traveling salesman from Kentucky, had blended and brewed the coffee himself on his mother's kitchen stove in the 1870s. In 1892, by blending coffees from Columbia, Mexico, and Brazil, he believed he had found the best blend, and he gave twenty pounds of it to the Maxwell House Hotel to serve to their customers. Six months later, the hotel granted his request to name the coffee after the hotel. At first, he sold the coffee regionally, but the slogan gave it a much broader consumer awareness by the 1910s, and the coffee was soon sold all over the country. By 1914 Joel Cheek was a wealthy man. He and his sons, and eventually a partner, managed the burgeoning business until 1928 when it became part of the Postum Company, later General Foods.

The idea of ground coffee originated during the Civil War. Usually, coffee was available only as beans, green ones at that, which had to be roasted. A grinder had to be handy, a difficult proposition on the battlefield. Initially the solution was to harden coffee pulp into blocks which could be broken up and boiled. Pregrinding the beans, blending them, and packaging them was the next step.

Tea was easier to make, and Sir Thomas Lipton was selling his packaged teas from England to Americans by the end of the 19th century. At the same time, another tea company, Salada, found American markets receptive to its teas, and the Great Atlantic & Pacific Tea Company had been selling tea to Americans since 1859.

Still, Americans were big coffee drinkers. Even during the Great Depression and the repeal of Prohibition, coffee sold well. By the 1930s, Maxwell House was developing instant coffee, first shipped in 1942 during World War II to the troops and in 1946 to consumers who increasingly made convenience foods like instant coffee popular. Later innovations included freeze-dried instant and decaffeinated coffees like Brim and Maxwell House Decaffeinated, introduced in the 1970s and 1980s as consumers became more health conscious. As people began to grind their own beans once again in the 1980s, seeking special coffees, companies like Maxwell House responded with espressos and private blends.

Maxwell House was the first coffee company to advertise on the radio. Its advertising agency, Benton & Bowles, developed a radio show in 1932, *Maxwell House Showboat*, inspired by the Jerome Kern musical and the Edna Ferber novel, which brought the brand national attention. The first television commercials, with the syncopated perking coffeepot, created by David Ogilvy, appeared in the 1950s. The so-called coffee wars among Maxwell House and competitors Folgers and Nestle in the late 1970s were waged mainly in television commercials at a time when the coffee crop failed in Brazil and coffee consumption was in decline in the United States.

Today, Maxwell House faces a new generation of coffee drinkers and their $2 lattes from Starbucks. Its advertising response, now managed by Ogilvy & Mather, revived the "Good to the Last Drop" slogan in the mid-1990s and capitalized on Maxwell House's history, reviving some of the old commercials. The company is now owned by Kraft General Foods.

References

Pendergrast, Mark. *Uncommon Grounds: The History of Coffee and How It Transformed Our World*. New York: Basic Books, 1999.

Sivulka, Juliann. *Soap, Sex, and Cigarettes: A Cultural History of American Advertising*. Belmont, CA: Wadsworth, 1997.

Mary Cross

The Michelin Man
(Michelin Tires)

Although he originated in France, the iconic Michelin man became American early in the century and has appeared in Michelin tire ads in U.S. media for more than eighty years. In early ads, he even wore an Uncle Sam hat. His real name is Bibendum, a moniker devised out of the Latin verb "to drink" because, as one of Michelin's founders said, "The tire drinks obstacles." Bibendum, 100 years old in 1998, has slimmed down from his thirty-tire shape to appeal to Asian and North American markets. Michelin North America, which has incorporated the tire division of B. F. Goodrich, has U.S. headquarters in Greenville, South Carolina.

By 1908 the Michelin brothers of France had established themselves in the United States at Milltown, New Jersey, and published their first ad, in the *Saturday Evening Post*, in the same year. Bibendum was shown refunding money to the purchaser of Michelin tires because, "If you buy a Michelin Universal and hand your dealer the same sum that you've been paying for other good tires, you'll get back a substantial sum in change."

The company was founded in 1889 by Édouard and André Michelin in France when they developed an inflatable bicycle tire sold on the "tire drinks obstacles" slogan. In 1897 they decided to move into the nascent automobile market and found an artist named Maurice Rossilon (known professionally as O'Galop) who drew the picture they used on their first poster: Bibendum, made out of tires, with a raised champagne glass full of nails and broken glass proclaiming, "Nunc est bibendum . . . À Votre Santé" (Now we can drink to your health) and the tagline, "Michelin tires drink obstacles."

Michelin, which handled its own advertising until the mid-1980s, took a humorous approach in its advertising, portraying Bibendum as a bon vivant with a cigar and a drink in his hand, and around the world as an Eskimo, a Venetian gondolier, a Spanish matador, and an American cowboy. Political correctness has caught up with him today; not only is he slimmer, he abstains from alcohol and tobacco. Capitalizing on the Michelin man's appeal to children, the company made Bibendum toys and games available. Moreoever, Michelin's "long-standing use of the image of a baby next to a tire—once ridiculed by gearheads—has connected with safety-conscious consumers," according to *Adweek*.

Doyle Dane Bernbach (DDB), the advertising agency that created the groundbreaking 1960s Volkswagen campaign, has handled the Michelin account in the United States and five other countries for the past seventeen years. DDB copywriter Barry Greenspan wrote the slogan "Michelin. Because So Much Is Riding on Your Tires," and art director Jack Mariucci came up with the baby-in-a-tire (like a playpen) image to go with it, an image that has become as enduring as Bibendum himself. The "baby" campaign ran throughout the 1980s into the 1990s, using eight different babies (all girls). DDB recently produced an admired television spot showing a mother-to-be at a baby shower receiving Michelin tires as a gift. But Bibendum, the Michelin man, is still the company's trademark character, voted one of the 20th century's top ten icons by *Advertising Age*.

The Michelin Man, Bibendum, became an instantly recognized symbol of the tire company. Courtesy of Michelin North America.

References

McMains, Andrew, and Kathleen Sampey. "Kicking the Tires: Shops Circle Michelin's $35 Mil. Account." *Adweek*, February 26, 2001: 6.
"Michelin Baby Hoops It Up in New Advertising." 17 April 2001. <www.michelin.com>.

Mary Cross

Morton Salt

The umbrella girl who graces the Morton Salt box got her start in the company's first advertising campaign in 1911 in *Good Housekeeping*. Like later icons Betty Crocker and the Breck Girl, her image underwent a number of makeovers to keep up with the times. The Morton Salt girl's appearance was updated in 1921, 1933, 1941, 1956, and 1968. She began actually appearing on the blue salt boxes in 1914, walking in the rain holding a huge umbrella in one hand and an open package in the other, its contents of salt pouring out.

Three years earlier in 1911, Morton Salt had begun adding an anti-caking element, magnesium carbonate, to its salt so that Morton Salt would pour even in damp weather. This innovation was captured in the slogan, "When It Rains it Pours," a revision of an old proverb, "It never rains but it pours." The ad agency, N. W. Ayer & Son, came up with a number of versions for Morton to consider, including, "Even in rainy weather, it flows freely," but the company wanted something shorter. Eventually the agency produced the short slogan which has become part of the language.

Morton Salt was founded as Richmond & Company, agents for Onondaga Salt, in Chicago in 1848 by Alonzo Richmond from Syracuse, New York. His company had done well supplying salt throughout the California Gold Rush in 1849 and the Great Chicago Fire of 1871, but in 1886 Richmond sold a major share of the company to Joy Morton, who renamed the company after himself. Morton expanded the business to produce some of the chemical byproducts of salt, to explore for new salt mines, and to merge with or acquire other companies.

By the 1920s, the company had introduced iodized salt to help prevent goiters which were then common, and developed a sealant, Liquid Polysulfide Polymer, from synthetic rubber which became an important technology in the aerospace industry. Other products included Morton Pellets, a recharging agent for home water softeners. The acquisition of salt and chemical companies in the United States, Canada, the Bahamas, and England made the company international and moved it into the dyestuffs, adhesives and coatings, airbags, and pharmaceutical markets.

The Morton Salt umbrella girl has been given six makeovers since she first appeared in 1911 in a *Good Housekeeping* advertisement. Used by permission of Morton International, Inc., Chicago, Illinois, 60606.

After merging with Norwich Pharmacal in 1969, Morton Salt entered the household cleaning business with Fantastik spray cleaner, Spray 'n Wash laundry stain remover, and Glass Plus glass cleaner from its Texise household products group. This business was sold to Procter & Gamble and Dow Chemical in the 1980s. Morton Salt merged with Thiokol, makers of synthetic rubber, airbags, and rocket propulsion systems in 1982, a merger that involved the company in the Challenger Space Shuttle for which Thiokol had made solid rocket boosters. In the aftermath of the shuttle explosion, Morton Salt lost nearly a quarter of its aerospace division revenues.

Meanwhile, Morton Salt had developed Morton Salt Substitute and Morton Lite Salt in the face of new health and diet concerns. As the Food and Drug Administration began to advocate low-sodium diets in the 1970s, consumption of table salt began to decline, though Morton Salt continued to hold the largest share of the salt market.

The familiar round blue box with the umbrella girl has been so distinctive that Morton Salt has had to advertise its table salt products very little. The company still promotes the old-fashioned uses of salt with recipes for curing meat and for canning and pickling and offers new seasoning mixes, smoked sugar cure salts, sausage and meatloaf mixes, popcorn salt blends, and kosher salt among its products. Its "Morton Salt Tips" campaign in women's magazines in 1993, engineered by DDB Needham, Chicago, offered ideas for using salt as a household helper, for example, removing red wine stains or rust.

Still based in Chicago, Morton Salt celebrated its 150th anniversary in 1998. By then, the company owned salt and coatings companies in France, Germany, Italy, and the Netherlands, making it the largest salt company in the world. It was acquired by a Philadelphia chemical company, Rohm and Haas, Inc., in 1999.

References

Margolin, Victor, Ira Brichta, and Vivian Brichta. *The Promise and the Product: 200 Years of American Advertising Posters*. New York: Macmillan, 1979.
"Morton Salt History." Morton Salt Company. <http://www.mortonsalt.com/mile/prflmile.htm/>.

Mary Cross

Mr. Peanut
(Planters Peanuts)

In 1916 the fledgling Planters Peanut company in Suffolk, Virginia, offered a prize of $5 for the best idea for a trademark for the company. A 14-year-old boy, Antonio Gentile, submitted a drawing of a man with a peanut body that became the company logo. Mr. Peanut, soon outfitted with a monocle, top hat, spats, and cane in the manner of turn-of-the-century haberdashery, became a ubiquitous figure in the company's early advertising and has been a valuable icon for the Planters Nut and Chocolate Company then and for its present owner, Nabisco, today. A Mr. Peanut statue on Main Street and a museum in Suffolk memorialize his impact on the city.

The founder of Planters was from Venice, Italy, an immigrant named Amedeo Obici who came to America in 1889 when he was just 12. By 1906 he owned a peanut roaster and was in business in Wilkes-Barre, Pennsylvania, with his brother-in-law, Mario Peruzzi, selling salted Virginia peanuts in 5-cent bags, which came to be known as the "Nickel Lunch." They moved the company to Virginia in 1913 and set up their factory in the middle of Virginia's plentiful peanut farms.

Mr. Peanut first appeared in 1918 in a full-page *Saturday Evening Post* ad, the first time a peanut brand had been advertised nationally. Obici put Mr. Peanut's picture in every ad, including a Times Square billboard, and on every peanut package thereafter. He produced promotional figures of Mr. Peanut that became collectibles and spawned fan clubs. Every flea market worth its salt still has a few of these for sale. In the 1920s, the company began offering premiums in exchange for redeemed Mr. Peanut packages, a program that continued well into the 1960s and 1970s. Premiums included everything from ashtrays to golf bags and wristwatches as well as kid-friendly banks and dolls.

Mr. Peanut has helped Planters prosper, with a 38 percent share of the nut business in the 1990s. The company was bought in 1960 by Standard Brands, merging with Nabisco Holdings Corporation in 1979. The Nabisco and R. J. Reynolds merger in 1989 made Planters part of RJR Nabisco and one of its fastest growing businesses. One of the reasons is that the 85-year-old icon keeps up with the times, wearing Rollerblades in one 1990s ad and, impersonated by an actor, touring the country on a tandem bike. The advertising agency Foote, Cone & Belding created a 1997 campaign to bring the brand to younger consumers with the slogan, "Relax. Go Nuts." One television spot in the campaign showed an eager beaver carving Mr. Peanut's picture into a tree trunk to show a band of peanut-eating hikers that everyone likes Planters. Mr. Peanut was back on a billboard in Times Square in 1998.

References

Dotz, Warren, and Jim Morton. *What a Character! 20th Century American Advertising Icons*. San Francisco: Chronicle Books, 1996.
Morgan, Hal. *Symbols of America*. New York: Viking Penguin, 1986.

Mary Cross

Smith Brothers Cough Drops

One of the more famous American trademarks is the picture of the two bearded Smith brothers on their cough drop box. William and Andrew Smith, sons of James who invented the cough drop mixture on his Poughkeepsie, New York, kitchen stove in 1847, put their pictures on pharmacy glass jars as a mark of identification. When competing cough drop makers started to borrow their name (Schmitt, Smyth), the brothers began labeling their pictures with the words "Trade" (William) and "Mark" (Andrew), designations that can still be seen on today's Smith Brothers boxes. Thus the idea of the trademark was literally translated. To ensure that only genuine Smith Brothers cough drops were sold, the

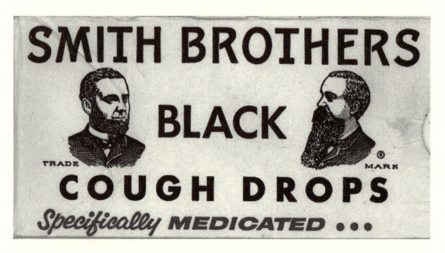

The Smith Brothers, William and Andrew, labeled their pictures "Trade" and "Mark" to fend off imitators of their cough drops. Courtesy of F&F Foods.

brothers switched from pharmacy jars to boxes in 1872, creating one of the first factory-filled packages, and put their pictures on them.

The first known advertisement for Smith Brothers was in a Pough-keepsie, New York, newspaper in 1852 for "Cough Candy," under the signature of William Smith. In 1919 an ad for Smith Brothers announced that "A Cough is a Social Blunder," the cougher "a public menace." The ad advised, "Have a box with you always," but stressed (truth in advertising) that Smith Brothers cough drops were not a cure for colds, just the cough. And, the ad said, the drops contained "Just enough charcoal to sweeten the stomach."

The company advertised continuously, in print and on barns and billboards, always with the bearded brothers identifying the product. Five generations of Smiths carried on the business, advertising with the same pictures of the brothers and simple copy ("Don't Let Those Beards Fool You"). The ad agency Ruthrauff & Ryan, which had specialized in copy for patent medicines and mail-order business, handled the account until some of its account executives split off and took the Smith Brothers with them to Sullivan, Stauffer, Colwell & Bayles in 1946. The agency was bought up in the merger mania of the 1970s as part of Interpublic which includes McCann-Erickson.

The Smith family continued as sole owners of the company until 1964, when it was acquired by Warner Lambert. Today the company is the property of F&F Foods of Chicago. Though the more than 150-year-old brand is seldom advertised, Smith Brothers Cough Drops are still sold with the bearded brothers on the box.

References

Fox, Stephen. *The Mirror Makers: A History of American Advertising and Its Creators.* New York: William Morrow, 1984.

"Smith Brothers, Then . . ." F&F Foods. <http://www.fffoods.com/gallery. htm/>.

Watkins, Julian Lewis. *The 100 Greatest Advertisements: Who Wrote Them and What They Did.* New York: Dover Books, 1959.

Mary Cross

Uncle Sam

The World War I U.S. Army recruiting poster depicting a stern-faced Uncle Sam was the work of artist James Montgomery Flagg. It is perhaps the most famous depiction of the avuncular figure ever drawn, though versions appeared early in the 19th century in political cartoons. The image was used in other advertising throughout the 20th century, touting everything from hot dogs to laxatives.

The recruiting poster came out in 1916 as the country was being dragged into the European war between England and Germany, but the idea of Uncle Sam had originated, according to legend, during another war, the War of 1812, when a meat packer in Troy, New York, Samuel Wilson, began shipping barrels of beef stamped with the initials U.S. to the war effort. Soldiers called the beef Uncle Sam's (after U.S.), and Sam Wilson became known as Uncle Sam, although, a clean-shaven man, he bore no physical resemblance to the eventual bearded image.

The first published recognition of this association appeared in the *New York Gazette* on May 12, 1830. Editorial cartoons of the 1830s and 1840s portrayed the image of a star-spangled Uncle Sam wearing striped pants and a tall hat. During the Civil War, Uncle Sam is said to have started to look more and more like Abraham Lincoln: tall, angular, and bearded. The image was adopted by the Union side.

Wilson, who died in 1854, was buried in Troy. His grave is marked today with a bronze plaque and an American flag on a thirty-foot flag pole. In 1961 the 87th Congress passed a resolution saluting " 'Uncle Sam' Wilson of Troy, New York, as the progenitor of America's national symbol of 'Uncle Sam.' " The city of Troy, now the official home of Uncle Sam, commissioned a monument to "Uncle Sam" Wilson, and holds a parade and celebration every year on Wilson's birthday, September 13.

The artist of the Uncle Sam poster, James Montgomery Flagg, himself proclaimed the poster the most famous image of Uncle Sam. Flagg, born in 1877 in Pelham Manor, New York, a commercial illustrator and portrait painter, was known for his pictures of buxom girls. When he was just 12, he sold his first picture to *St. Nicholas* and later did illustrations for *Harper's Weekly, Life* magazine, and *Cosmopolitan*. Flagg, who lived until 1960, wrote an autobiography in 1946, *Roses and Buckshot*.

Flagg's lithograph of Uncle Sam was first reproduced on the cover of *Leslie's Weekly* on July 16, 1916, with the words, "What Are You Doing for Preparedness?" Four million copies of the poster were printed and distributed between 1917 and 1918. Flagg went on to do forty-six other images for the war effort. He presented a copy of his famous poster to President Franklin Roosevelt during World War II, and it was used once again to recruit soldiers. In 1998 it made a reappearance, recruiting for the U.S. Air Force.

References

Ketchum, Alton. "The Search for Uncle Sam." *History Today* (April 1990): 20–26.
————. *Uncle Sam: The Man and the Legend*. New York: Hill & Wang, 1959.
"The Story of Uncle Sam." <http://www.sprynet.com/~nascar90/thestory. htm.23>.
Uncle Sam entry. <http://www.brittanica.com>.

Mary Cross

Woodbury's Soap

The famous Woodbury's Soap phrase, "A Skin You Love to Touch," first appeared in an advertisement created by the J. Walter Thompson agency in the *Saturday Evening Post* in May 1911. Though records have been lost, the phrase apparently originated as the title of a skin care booklet produced by the company. In 1915 the phrase was used again in a full-page *Ladies' Home Journal* ad and became one of the most well-known advertising taglines, used continuously in Woodbury Soap ads well into the century.

The soap itself was one of the first brands to advertise itself as a facial soap, invented by John Woodbury who trademarked a picture of himself in 1891 as a logo for his soap. The picture, showing just Woodbury's face, became a vaudeville joke as "the neckless head," but it did what logos are supposed to do: made the soap wrappers and advertisements instantly recognizable as Woodbury's. Early ads claimed the soap was effective against wrinkles, pimples, warts, and freckles, but soon Woodbury's positioned the soap as a beauty product rather than a cure, a clever move that propelled its sales in the early part of the century and made Woodbury's one of the first to advertise on the basis of sex appeal, capitalizing on women's fear of social disapproval. Some readers of the

Ladies' Home Journal claimed to be so shocked by the first ad in 1915 that they canceled their subscriptions.

Helen Lansdowne Resor was the copywriter who wrote the 1915 *Journal* ad for Thompson, seven paragraphs of copy describing the benefits of Woodbury's—"the most famous skin treatment ever formulated"— and how to use it, working the lather into the skin, "always with an upward and outward motion," and rinsing with warm, then cold, water followed by a rub with a piece of ice. There was a special offer: for 10 cents, a week's supply of Woodbury's and a copy of the painting in the ad, a handsome couple in evening dress painted by Alonzo Kimball. Sales of Woodbury's in the decade afterward jumped to six times the 1915 level.

Another advertisement in the same era shocked readers of women's magazines when a full page ad for Odorono deodorant in a 1919 *Ladies' Home Journal* discussed the delicate subject of underarm odor. "Within the Curve of a Woman's Arm," the headline read. "There's an old offender," the copy went on. "You may offend without knowing it." Though more women canceled their *Journal* subscriptions, the ad, written by James Young of J. Walter Thompson, increased Odorono sales 112 percent that year.

The cosmetic industry and cosmetic advertising were gaining momentum in the teens of the century, and World War I liberated opinion about women's appearance. Florence Nightingale Graham had already opened a New York beauty salon (she changed her name to Elizabeth Arden when it became successful), and women were already bobbing their hair and using lip rouge, trends that reached their height in the flapper days to come when lipstick began to appear in a bullet-shaped tube. Many soaps and beauty creams appeared on the market, including Cashmere Bouquet, advertised initially as a "handkerchief perfume," Palmolive, and Pond's Cold Cream.

In later campaigns, the famous Woodbury phrase became, "The Skin You Love to Touch," with pictures of Woodbury debs at their coming out parties and weddings. Like the Pond's Cold Cream slogan, "She's Beautiful, She's Engaged, She Uses Pond's," the Woodbury campaign implied that soap and marriage went together. But the ads gave full instructions on how to use the soap, not on how to get a man.

References

Fox, Stephen. *The Mirror Makers: A History of American Advertising and Its Creators.* New York: William Morrow, 1984.

Watkins, Julian Lewis. *The 100 Greatest Advertisements: Who Wrote Them and What They Did.* New York: Dover Books, 1959.

Mary Cross

Wrigley's Spearmint Gum

William Wrigley, Jr., bought the Chicago Cubs (who now play in a ball-park named Wrigley Field) with the money he made selling five-cent packs of chewing gum. He had started out in 1891 selling Wrigley's Scouring Soap for his father, but when he realized the gum packs they were giving away as premiums were more popular, he began marketing chewing gum. Wrigley's Spearmint gum, named for a kind of mint with a spearlike flower, was introduced in 1893 and replaced his first brands, Vassa and Lotta Gum. It bore the same arrow and spearmint leaves on the wrapper that it does today. Wrigley invented a foil wrapper to keep each stick fresh and wrapped the whole package in cellophane. It was a hit.

In 1914 he introduced Doublemint gum in a green wrapper branded with a white double arrow, reversing the colors from the white with green Spearmint wrapper. By the 1930s, Doublemint was being advertised with pictures of twins drawn by artist Otis Shepard. The slogan, "Double your pleasure, double your fun," was added in 1960. It was one of the most successful advertising campaigns ever. The slogan was recognized in *Advertising Age*'s special issue, "The Advertising Century," as ranking seventh out of the ten best of the 20th century. In 2001 the Williams sisters, tennis champions Venus and Serena, are the "twins" in the new "Distinctively Doublemint" campaign.

Indeed, Wrigley believed strongly in the power of advertising and from the beginning had insisted on using streetcars and outdoor billboards as well as newspapers and magazines to advertise his products. One of his billboards, in Times Square in New York City, was fifty feet high, sporting little spearmen and fountains at either end of the 200-foot-wide expanse. Wrigley's marketing philosophy was, "Tell 'em quick and tell 'em often." In 1918 an ad for, by then, all three Wrigley's gums (Juicy Fruit was introduced in 1893) advised consumers, "Chew it after every meal" to help digestion, keep teeth clean, and steady the nerves. For sixty years, Wrigley sold just these three brands, all at 5 cents a pack. In 1972 the company reluctantly raised the price to 10 cents and added two sticks to the original five-stick pack.

His competitors at the turn of the century had included Beeman's Pepsin ("Cures Indigestion and Sea-Sickness"), Chiclets, and Adams' Tutti-Fruiti. Adams' Black Jack chewing gum, orginating in 1875, was the oldest flavored chewing gum in America until it was taken off the market in 2001. The six largest gum companies merged in 1899 to form "the chewing gum trust," which Wrigley declined to join. Later competitors included Trident and Dentyne, marketed by Warner-Lambert (now Pfizer), in terms of dental hygiene. Wrigley ads tended to emphasize fun and relaxation.

Chewing gum was not new to America. New England Indian tribes were said to have chewed resin from spruce trees and to have introduced it to the colonists. Long before that, the ancient Greeks chewed resin to clean their teeth and improve their breath. In the 1860s, chicle from the sapodilla tree of tropical rain forests was imported to the United States and became the basis of modern chewing gum, being softer and holding flavor longer than resins. Today, Wrigley's chewing gum is made with a gum base including a resin derived from pine trees grown in the southeastern United States, along with sweeteners and flavoring like fresh spearmint, grown for Wrigley on fifty-three square miles of farmland around the country.

The Wm. Wrigley Jr. Company went international early, opening plants in Canada in 1910 and Australia in 1915. It became the leading manufacturer of chewing gum, a position it continues to hold. During World War II, the company was unable to obtain enough ingredients to make the gum and took its three brands off the consumer market for two years. Instead, Wrigley sent all its regular products to the armed forces overseas. Even though civilians could not buy it, Wrigley's continued to advertise the gum with the slogan, "Remember This Wrapper." By 1946, after the war, the gum with the famous wrapper was once again available. Chewing gum, recognized for easing tension and keeping people alert, is still standard issue in armed forces field and combat rations. During the Gulf War in 1991, the Wrigley Company supplied gum to U.S. troops in Saudi Arabia.

In the 1970s, Wrigley expanded its brands to include Freedent, Big Red, and Hubba Bubba ("the only bubble gum that won't stick to your clothes"). It added Extra, a sugarfree gum, in 1984. Newer brands include the company's first pellet gum, Eclipse, and an antacid chewing gum, Surpass. Wrigley is creating a new division to deliver health care, like cavity prevention and cold relief, in a chewing gum. In 2001 the company commanded 50 percent of the world market in chewing gum against rivals like Pfizer's Dentyne, Chiclets, and Trident and Hershey Foods' Carefree and Bubble Yum. The Wm. Wrigley Jr. Company is now headed by the fourth-generation William Wrigley, Jr.

References

Barboza, David. "A New Heir Has New Plans at Old Company." *New York Times*, August 28, 2001: C1.

Margolin, Victor, Ira Brichta, and Vivian Brichta. *The Promise and the Product: 200 Years of American Advertising Posters*. New York: Macmillan, 1979.

"The Story of the Wrigley Company." William Wrigley Jr. Company. May 18, 2001. <http://www.wrigley.com>.

Mary Cross

3

Icons of the 1920s

The images of the 1920s that have come to define the decade are, like all stereotypes, grounded in a certain reality but are only partial representations of a complex age. The flapper, the hip flask, and the speakeasy (illegal drinking clubs) represent the decade as a period of reckless living associated with the overturning of traditional sexual mores, flouting of the law, and organized crime. Alongside the images of the jazz age one can also place the tabloid newspaper, the motion picture, and other forms of mass entertainment like the sporting event. Figures like aviator Charles Lindbergh, screen star Rudolph Valentino, and baseball sensation Babe Ruth became the focus of a celebrity culture promulgated by the popular press. But the 1920s was also a period in which the patterns of domestic life and family were set for the next generation and the patterns of economic life took on a shape that would not change appreciably—except for the interruption of the Great Depression—for several decades.

Warren G. Harding, elected president in 1920, ran on a platform of a return to "normalcy" after the national mobilization of America's participation in World War I, but what was "normal" after the war was not exactly the same as what was normal before it. In the last years of the 'teens, America had changed. The shift from an agrarian, rural society to an increasingly urban and industrial society, already under way in the last decades of the 19th century, proceeded apace. More and more people were living in urban areas; small towns were being depopulated. The ease of mobility was enhanced by the spread of automobiles and the new roads built to accommodate them. The growth of mass industry, temporarily diverted to the war mobilization between 1917 and 1919, provided increased job opportunities and increased wages so that working people could, for the first time, enjoy the products they made.

While remnants of labor unrest and dissatisfaction persisted in some areas of the economy into the early years of the decade, workers were doing better and living better than ever before. Leaders of Big Business, depicted in the writings of the early 20th-century muckrakers as rapacious, greedy, and exploitative, came to be seen as pioneers of enlightened and scientific management spreading the blessings of "a full dinner pail" to a wider segment of the populace. To be sure, some of this change of image was due to the work of the men (and some women) employed in the advertising agencies and public relations agencies which, in the 1920s, assumed a greater influence in shaping the social consciousness: the "apostles of modernity," as advertising historian Roland Marchand calls them.

The shift to modernity was not an untroubled one, however. The general drift in society toward increasing prosperity and stability was accompanied by heightened racism, nativism, and social conservatism. Race riots and deportations of aliens punctuated the opening years of the decade (which actually may be said to have begun in 1919 with the end of World War I). Legislation restricting immigration was passed on an emergency basis in 1921 and then permanently in 1924. The Ku Klux Klan reemerged as a potent social force. Religious fundamentalists lobbied state legislatures to pass laws restricting the teaching of the theory of evolution, leading to the well-publicized trial of a high school teacher, John Scopes, in Dayton, Tennessee, in 1925. Scopes, who volunteered to challenge the state law, lost his case, and other states followed Tennessee in passing similar legislation which remained on the books for years afterward.

Political corruption reached into the highest realms of government during Harding's administration. The head of the Veteran's Bureau, the secretary of the interior, and even the attorney general were accused of embezzlement or accepting bribes and kickbacks in a number of unrelated cases, which led to several suicides of public figures. The leasing in secret of the government's oil reserves at Teapot Dome and Elk Hills to private speculators came to symbolize the whole complex of scandals, the stress from which may have led to Harding's premature death in 1923.

Although under Harding's successor, Calvin Coolidge, the scandals abated and the economy entered an unprecedented period of prosperity, the decade came to an end with the collapse of the stock market in October 1929. This ushered in a period of economic depression and dislocation that would not really end until the mobilization for World War II.

The advertising of the 1920s is only a partial representation of the times. The social unrest was, of course, not directly depicted (although the Colt Firearms Company ran ads in major periodicals, selling their pistols as the best form of home protection against unnamed threats). Because the manufacture, transportation, and sale of alcoholic beverages became illegal in 1920 with the passage of the Eighteenth Amendment to the Constitution and the Volstead Act, which defined it, one of the decade's key products was not advertised. Drinking did continue, despite national efforts to stop it. It may be argued that the allure of drinking alcoholic beverages may have been enhanced by its being outlawed— at least for a certain segment of society that defined itself as standing against mainstream values.

Many of the products the advertising agencies were selling were not new in the 1920s. Soaps, canned goods, household cleansers, appliances, and automobiles had for the previous two decades been the chief focus of advertisements in the mass circulation magazines, on billboards, and on advertising cards. The new products of the 1920s were the radio set, the talking motion picture, the mass-produced cigarette, and the chain store.

What was new was the way in which these new and older products were presented to the readership of advertisements and, increasingly, the listeners to radio, which by the decade's end had become a major vehicle for advertising. Advertising agencies used the techniques of the new psychology (behaviorism and psychoanalysis) to understand the motivations and needs of their target audiences and to shape their messages accordingly. Increasingly advertising appealed to fears and emotions rather than rational choices. The newly emerging middle classes, one step removed perhaps from the working class, were perceived to be bundles of anxieties, socially unsure, to whom the products were sold as talismans bestowing grace and social acceptability. Men looking for jobs who could be rejected for an unkempt appearance were exhorted to use soap and change their "linen." Women, newly enfranchised by the Nineteenth Amendment and increasingly members of the workforce, needed to preserve their youth and vigor; products such as Lysol disinfectant and sanitary napkins could help along with a myriad of beauty aids. Stay-at-home wives needed the help of canned goods and other prepared foods to please their husbands and to put on sumptuous dinners for the ever-demanding boss or for the ever-scrutinizing social circle. Modern life was celebrated in advertising, although its stresses needed the respite provided by cigarettes and sweets, its ills needed the relief offered by a panoply of medicines and home cures.

As the historians of advertising (Marchand, Ewen, Lears) stress, advertising in the 1920s acclimatized people to the new mass society and made self-indulgence acceptable. The traditional American values of independence, self-reliance, and frugality were being replaced by the values of an increasingly collectivized life and the imperative to consume at the same time that the advertising industry continued to invoke those traditional values to sell their products.

References

Allen, Frederick Lewis. *Only Yesterday: An Informal History of the Nineteen-Twenties*. 1931. Reprint, New York: Harper and Brothers, 1957.

Ewen, Stuart. *Captains of Consciousness: Advertising and the Social Roots of the Consumer Culture*. New York: McGraw-Hill, 1976.

Goldberg, David J. *Discontented America: The United States in the 1920s*. Baltimore, MD: Johns Hopkins University Press, 1999.

Lears, T. J. Jackson. *Fables of Abundance: A Cultural History of Advertising in America*. New York: Basic Books, 1994.

Marchand, Roland. *Advertising the American Dream: Making Way for Modernity 1920–1940*. Berkeley, CA: University of California Press, 1985.

Sklar, Martin J. *The United States as a Developing Country: Studies in U.S. History in the Progressive Era and the 1920s*. Cambridge: Cambridge University Press, 1992.

Smith, Page. *Redeeming the Time*. Vol. 8 of *The People's History of the United States*. New York: McGraw-Hill, 1987.

Martin Green

Burma-Shave

One of the most distinctive campaigns in the history of American advertising was the homespun campaign for Burma-Shave. Started in the late 1920s, this campaign picked up momentum in the 1930s and by the 1940s had become an icon of the national folkways, widely alluded to and instantly recognizable.

The campaign capitalized on the impact of the automobile on American mobility. Looking for a way to market a new shaving cream, one of the members of the family firm that concocted the product hit upon the idea of placing small signs along the side of a road near their hometown of Minneapolis. He placed several signs at intervals along the road, much like the signs he had seen alerting motorists to filling stations. The signs were plain text on painted boards, announcing the product's benefits and availability in local stores. The product was not named until the last of the series of four signs: "Shave the Modern Way/ Fine for the Skin/ Druggists Have It/ Burma Shave." The product's name was based on an earlier family-concocted product, a liniment called Burma-Vita, whose chief ingredients came from Southeast Asia.

Like many innovations, this simple campaign did not emerge full-blown from the head of its pioneer. First, he had to convince the head of the firm—his father, in this case—that the campaign made sense. Once sales began to move upward, the campaign spread, and its form changed. The number of signs in the series was increased to five or six, and the messages employed rhyme and folksy humor to increase attention. As in the original campaign, however, the delay in naming the product until the last sign continued. Soon, the signs—placed at intervals of 100 paces along the road and easily read from a car going along at the sedate pace of from twenty-five to thirty miles per hour—became familiar to the growing numbers of motorists filling America's newly expanding highways, and their jingly humor became a national pastime. The rhyme scheme that came to typify the signs was added in 1929: "Your Shaving Brush / Has Had Its Day / Why Not / Shave the Modern Way / with Burma-Shave?" Later, humor was added: "The Bearded Lady / Tried a Jar / She's Now / A Famous / Movie Star / Burma-Shave." As an indication of how much cultural impact such advertising had, even Vladimir Nabokov's novel *Lolita* (1955) includes a scene on an American highway where the novel's hero, Humbert Humbert, recites—as if in response to what he sees as he drives—"The Bearded Woman read our jingle and now she is no longer single" (Part Two, Chapter 2).

By the 1930s, the company began to sponsor contests for new series of signs, making the composition of new rhymes and puns a new form of travel entertainment. At the height of the campaign, 50,000 entries were submitted and advertising agency copywriters had to be engaged to help in judging them. As the campaign matured, many of the sign series played on the early themes of the campaign. "Our Fortune / Is Your Shaven Face / It's our Best Advertising space / Burma Shave." Others employed some risque double entendre: "The Big Blue Tube's / Just Like Louise / You Get A Thrill / From Every Squeeze / Burma Shave." Yet others emphasized traffic safety: "Past / Schoolhouses / Take it Slow / Let the Little Shavers Grow / Burma Shave." (The name of the product was inconsistently spelled on the signs, with the hyphen sometimes present and sometimes absent.)

Beyond its distinctive advertising, the product itself was a pioneer in the field of men's grooming aids. As the fashion trends shifted from the hirsute look of beards, mutton chop sideburns, and moustaches to the clean shaven face of the 1920s, companies like the Gillette Safety Razor Company and others moved in to market products to make shaving an everyday part of men's lives. The advent of brushless shaving creams, of which Burma Shave was an early example, further enhanced the convenience and ease of daily shaving. The original Burma-Shave campaign emphasized the modernity of the product, its ease of use, and its economy: "No Brush / No Lather / No Rub-In / Big Tube 35 Cents." It also appealed to men's vanity as the company hinted that the product would make them more appealing to the opposite sex: "A Chin / Where Barbed Wire / Bristles Stand / Is Bound To Be / A No Ma'am's Land."

By the height of Burma-Shave's popularity in the 1950s, the company had 7,000 sign series in almost all the then forty-eight states, and its distinctive rhymes were echoed in graffiti spread by American servicemen in World War II. With the advent of the super highway and faster cars, the campaign began to die out, to become a part of American nostalgia for a simpler, less hurried past. The company itself—founded by the Odell family—was acquired by Philip Morris in the 1960s and folded into its American Safety Razor Products division. An attempt to resurrect the product in the 1990s on the basis of nostalgia was accompanied by a television advertising campaign that tried to update the Burma Shave wit. Showing an older man and young woman in a Corvette, the ad incorporated up-to-date signs emphasizing, in the words of one critic, "a touchy-feely refrain fresh from the 90s: 'You Don't Have A Care / You Don't Have A Worry / You've Reached The Point / Where You Don't / Have To Hurry / Burma-Shave'" (Lord). Constructing new Burma-Shave–style placards on the Internet has given further life to the campaign.

References

Appel, Alfred, Jr., ed. *The Annotated Lolita* by Vladimir Nabokov. New York: Vintage, 1991.

Larabee, John. "It Was the Rave, in Those '50s Days, It Won't Go Away: Burma Shave." *Detroit News*, January 10, 1996. <http://detnews.com/menu/stories/31520.htm/>.

Lord, Lewis. "A Hit / It's Not / If Its Wit / Is Shot." *U.S. News Online*, July 21, 1997. <http://www.usnews.com/usnews/issue/970721/21week.htm/>.

Morgan, Hal. *Symbols of America*. New York: Viking Penguin, 1986.

Rowsome, Frank, Jr. *The Verse by the Side of the Road: The Story of the Burma-Shave Signs and Jingles*. Brattleboro, VT: Stephen Greene Press, 1965.

Thomas, Marvin. "The Burma Shave Phenomenon." <http://www.mc.cc.md.us/Departments/hpolscrv/mthomas.html/>.

Waterman, Martin. "Feeling Nostalgic? Now You'll Rave! Here's the Story of Burma Shave." *Backwoods Home Magazine* 37 (1998). <http://backwoodshome.com/articles/waterman37.html>.

Martin Green

Camel Cigarettes

"A boon for a breathless age": A 1928 advertisement for Camel cigarettes, produced by the N. W. Ayer & Son advertising agency of Philadelphia, pictures an elegantly attired young woman holding a teacup in one hand and a cigarette in the other. The ad copy extols the virtues of a "really *good* cigarette" as the antidote to the "mad, merry whirl [of] Youth": "Bridge . . . tea . . . dinner . . . theater . . . shopping . . . settlement house . . . golf . . . correspondence." Long before the surgeon general's findings that cigarette smoking was a major health risk, the cigarette was a major icon of popular culture and the 1920s was its heyday. Camel cigarettes was one of the first brands to push its products through ingenious mass marketing campaigns.

"I'd Walk a Mile for a Camel" was a long-running tagline for this company that accounted for over 45 percent of the 75 billion cigarettes consumed in 1925. R. J. Reynolds, the makers of Camel, pioneered many provocative ad campaigns. Its introductory campaign in 1914, "The Camels are Coming," with a picture of a camel, teased the audience for weeks. Then the campaign announced, "Tomorrow there'll be more CAMELS in this town than in all Asia and Africa combined!" Finally it was revealed that Camels were cigarettes. Camels took over the market. Its flavor blend of North Carolina tobacco with burley, a light-colored tobacco, and Turkish tobacco was a hit.

The product's logo was modeled after Joe the Dromedary, a star of the Barnum and Bailey Circus. The name Camel had been chosen to give the cigarette the cachet of Middle Eastern tobacco, and an artist's sketch of the circus camel against a backdrop of desert palm trees and pyramids remains the image on the cigarette package.

While smoking had long been a part of men's lives, the widespread use of cigarettes in the 1920s was a recent innovation. According to advertising historian Michael Schudson, the habit of smoking cigarettes as opposed to pipes and cigars developed during World War I, when U.S. military officials provided tobacco rations in the form of cigarettes as supporting troop morale. "When Our Boys Light Up the Huns Will Light Out" was a popular slogan. Produced cheaply by technologies developed in the 1890s, the cigarette was an efficient and convenient format for troops at war. It was also more addicting than the traditional pipe and cigar smoking, and servicemen brought their habit home. Where once smoking cigarettes had been considered effeminate, it now became a sign of masculinity. It also became an icon of the liberated woman, and many of the cigarette advertisements, especially in the later 1920s, consciously targeted the woman smoker.

The newly liberated young women of the 1920s took to cigarettes long before the advertisers began targeting them, according to Michael Schudson in *Advertising, the Uneasy Persuasion* (1984). College officials attempted to ban smoking by women students on many campuses but found themselves helpless against a growing social trend. When a 1926 ad for Chesterfield cigarettes depicted a woman sitting next to a man

A boon for a breathless age

Bridge . . . tea . . . dinner . . . theater . . . shopping . . . settlement house . . . golf . . . correspondence. . . . It's a mad but merry whirl. And sometimes even Youth likes to sit down and rest for a golden moment. . . . At which times a really *good* cigarette is like the Dawn of a New Day.

Second. GAE—18; C—4; A—4; L—4; T—4.
N. W. Ayer & Son, *Philadelphia.*

121

Advertisements for Camel cigarettes in the 1920s were aimed at women. Courtesy of R. J. Reynolds.

smoking and asking that he "Blow Some My Way," the hesitation that tobacco companies had felt about encouraging women's smoking went up in smoke.

Ads like the one for Camels emphasized cigarettes as a fashion accessory for the contemporary woman and as a symbol of women's new status (much like Virginia Slims would do decades later in the 1970s). The Marlboro brand, later associated with the rugged Marlboro man icon, was in the 1920s geared toward women with its slogan "Mild as May" and its depiction of elegantly attired women. Other ads directed toward women appealed to their consciousness about weight. "Reach for a Lucky Instead of a Sweet!" was one popular campaign slogan. In the 1920s, the woman's body image was transformed from the buxom stereotype of 19th-century motherhood to the lithe image of the flapper dressed in stylishly slim-line clothing. Beginning a trend that would be a constant until the surgeon general's reports were issued in the 1960s and 1970s, cigarettes were also touted for their health benefits. The mild blend of tobaccos, it was claimed, was better for one than other forms of smoking. Luckies' trademark tagline, "It's Toasted," suggested that its milder flavor reduced smokers' cough. Even doctors were said to endorse one or another cigarette brand.

Cigarette advertising became a mainstay of radio and later television advertising until it was banned in the 1970s. Until the 1990s it was still a feature of print advertising. In 1987 it introduced its cartoon icon, Joe Camel, which, because of its apparent appeal to children and teenagers, became the controversial symbol of efforts in the 1990s to ban most forms of cigarette advertising (see "Joe Camel" entry in Chapter 10).

References

The Advertising Parade: An Anthology of Good Advertisements Published in 1928. New York: Harper and Brothers, 1930.

Atwan, Robert, Donald McQuade, and John W. Wright. *Edsels, Luckies & Frigidaires: Advertising the American Way.* New York: Dell Books, 1979.

Lears, T. J. Jackson. *Fables of Abundance: A Cultural History of Advertising in America.* New York: Basic Books, 1994.

Marchand, Roland. *Advertising the American Dream: Making Way for Modernity 1920–1940.* Berkeley, CA: University of California Press, 1985.

Norris, James D. *Advertising and the Transformation of American Society, 1865–1920.* Westport, CT: Greenwood Press, 1990.

Schudson, Michael. *Advertising, the Uneasy Persuasion: Its Dubious Impact on American Society.* New York: Basic Books, 1984.

Martin Green

Frigidaire Home Refrigerators

In the 1920s, along with the automobile and enhanced methods of food manufacture and distribution came a revolution in home refrigeration, pioneered by a company whose brand name has become synonymous with the product line: Frigidaire.

Before 1915 home refrigeration, where it was available at all, was supplied by the icebox, an insulated cabinet in which a large block of ice provided the necessary cooling until it melted and needed to be replaced. The daily delivery of blocks of ice and the necessity of removing the pools of melted ice water were a familiar part of household routine for those fortunate enough to own an icebox. As late as the 1940s and 1950s, these iceboxes could still be found in many homes, particularly in rural areas of the country. Inventors in the 1910s began to experiment with mechanical methods of supplying continuous coolness to iceboxes. The first successful commercial electric household refrigerator, produced in 1913, was an air-cooled unit mounted on the top of an icebox.

In 1915 Alfred Mellowes, working in his backyard washhouse in Fort Wayne, Indiana, perfected a self-contained unit with a compressor located at the bottom of the cabinet. A year later, Mellowes had organized a company, the Guardian Refrigerator Company, to build and sell these machines, but his handcraft method of manufacture proved too slow and cumbersome for profitability. Rescue came in 1918 in the person of William C. Durant, the powerhouse behind the formation and success of the General Motors Company. Durant bought the Guardian company with his own money and came up with the product's distinctive brand name, Frigidaire. He later folded the company into the burgeoning General Motors family of automobile companies. With access now to the mass production methods of the auto industry, the refrigerator soon made its way into many homes. Despite a high price of $775 (later reduced by almost half), a million Frigidaires were purchased in the first ten years of the company's existence. Conversion kits were also available.

Advertising for the new refrigerators stressed the modernity of the device—although the bulky models displayed in the ads seem like dinosaurs in comparison to today's sleek models. Along with the electric washer-dryer and indoor plumbing improvements, refrigerators embodied the conveniences of modern living. Their success was also due to innovative financing plans that companies adopted to permit those with limited incomes to share in the cornucopia of new products being turned out by American industry. Easy credit terms were arranged so that consumers did not need to have the total purchase price to buy these technological wonders. As economic historian Martha Olney points out, purchases of major durable goods like appliances and cars began to absorb a larger share of household income in the 1920s (56), a pattern that continues today.

The Frigidaire Company dominated the field of household refrigeration for decades, pioneering additional applications for the technology, such as home freezers and domestic and industrial air-conditioning. The company later expanded its product line to include home laundry equipment, dishwashers, and food waste disposers. General Motors sold the Frigidaire Company in 1979.

References

Atwan, Robert, Donald McQuade, and John W. Wright. *Edsels, Luckies, and Frigidaires: Advertising the American Way.* New York: Dell Books, 1979.
"Frigidaire Historical Collection." Wright State University Libraries Special Collections and Archives. <http://libnet.wright.edu/staff/dunbar/arch/ms262.htm>.
"Frigidaire Home Products." *International Directory of Company Histories.* Vol. 22. Detroit, New York, and London: St. James Press [Gale], 1998: 216–18.
Olney, Martha. *Buy Now, Pay Later: Advertising, Credit and Consumer Durables in the 1920s.* Chapel Hill: University of North Carolina Press, 1991.

Martin Green

Great Atlantic and Pacific Tea Company (A&P)

A 1928 advertisement for the Great Atlantic and Pacific Tea Company (A&P), created by the Paris and Peart agency of New York, asks its (male) readers the rhetorical question: "Your Wife . . . Are the things she does important?" Her shopping was being touted as being the equivalent of the major business decisions the ad's male audience was making daily.

Women as household managers were the targets of many advertising campaigns in the 1920s, an age social historians point to as marking a major transition in the concepts of men's and women's social roles. The technology of household appliances and other labor-saving devices was making vast strides, and manufacturers of domestic goods and processed foods were flooding the major media of magazines and the developing broadcasting system with advertisements for a host of products that ostensibly made a housewife's work easier. Historian Ruth Schwartz Cowan has argued that, in fact, the new technology of the household was presenting women with new challenges and concerns that transformed household labor in new directions. Keeping pace with these innovations was the growth of new forms of retailing, especially the chain supermarket.

The comprehensive food market, as opposed to the individual shops of single-product merchants, was an outgrowth of two traditional forms of merchandising: the village marketplace and the country general store. The innovation of the supermarket also derived from the national distribution of processed foods that had been growing steadily since the late 19th century. Under one roof, the housewife could find everything from packaged foods to fresh produce, all organized in glittering aisles brimming over with a cornucopia of goods far beyond what women of a prior generation had found in the dreary precincts of the general store.

The Great Atlantic and Pacific Tea Company was among the first of the new merchandising form. Founded in 1859 in New York City as an outlet for bulk tea at cheaper than prevailing prices, the Atlantic Tea Company soon expanded to several stores throughout the city. By the time of the completion of the transcontinental railroad in 1869, the Atlantic Tea Company had added additional grocery products to the merchandise and changed its name to the now familiar A&P logo. Around the turn of the century, the company continued its expansion in both the range of merchandise and in the number of outlets. The combination of reasonable prices and sumptuous décor attracted customers nationally. The A&P pioneered such retailing practices as premium stamps and mail-order deliveries. New chains of markets soon followed the A&P example as did other national chain merchandisers. Such names as Grand Union, Woolworth's, J. C. Penney, Whelans, Walgreen, United Cigar, Kroger, Kresge, and Piggly-Wiggly were appearing in all the major cities.

In 1912, in response to declines in growth, the company launched a chain of "economy stores," which eventually outstripped the established shops in the chain. By the 1920s, in the new age of affluence following World War I, the company resumed some of the services ruthlessly cut in the economy plan and advertised to attract a more affluent clientele.

A history and analysis of the growth of national chain stores published in the early 1940s reported that the 1920s was the decade of greatest growth for the chains. Between 1921 and 1927, the number of chain stores increased from 27,000 to 100,000 and sales volume tripled (Nichols 83). Another study of about the same time cited census data that the number of chain stores had reached over 200,000 by 1929 and accounted for 14 percent of all retail sales (Beckman and Nolen 30). A&P's sales reached $400 million in 1925 and by 1929, just before the stock market crash, they reached the unheard of level of $1.05 billion (Walsh; Lebhar).

While the corner store still continued to exist—as it still does in many major cities—it was an endangered species under the advance of the mega-merchandisers whose convenience, efficiency, and affordability defined the modern lifestyle. Today, national retailers dominate the merchandising landscape. Along with many of the chains that have had continuous existence since the 19th century (like A&P), new merchants of everything from clothing (The Gap) to fast foods (McDonald's) to coffee (Starbuck's) have set up their shops from main street to the local mall.

References

The Advertising Parade: An Anthology of Good Advertisements Published in 1928. New York: Harper and Brothers, 1930.

Beckman, Theodore, and Herman C. Nolen. *The Chain Store Problem: A Critical Analysis.* New York: McGraw-Hill, 1938.

Cowan, Ruth Schwartz. *More Work for Mother: The Ironies of Household Technology from the Open Hearth to the Microwave.* New York: Basic Books, 1983.

Lebhar, Godfrey M. *The Chain Store—Boon or Bane?* New York: Harper & Brothers, 1932.

Marchand, Roland. *Advertising the American Dream: Making Way for Modernity 1920–1940.* Berkeley, CA: University of California Press, 1985.

Nichols, John P. *The Chain Store Tells its Story.* 2d ed. New York: Institute of Distribution, 1942.

Walsh, William. *The Rise and Decline of the Great Atlantic and Pacific Tea Company.* Secaucus, NJ: Lyle Stuart, 1986.

Martin Green

Listerine

In the early 1920s, consumers discovered, thanks to the creativity of advertising copywriters, that they might be suffering from a condition that they previously were unaware of: halitosis. The product that fought this horrible-sounding malady (actually, bad breath) had been around for a long time already, selling modestly since 1879 in plain brown paper–wrapped bottles. But Listerine, an all-purpose antiseptic owned by the Lambert Pharmaceutical Company, was about to enter the annals of advertising history and earn the status of a cultural icon.

The product was named to capitalize on the growing fame of Sir Joseph Lister, the 19th-century British surgeon who pioneered the development of sterile surgery. Lister used diluted carbolic acid as a dressing for wounds and surgical incisions and for sterilizing instruments. Lister was reported to be unhappy with the commercial exploitation of his name, but he could not do anything about it.

According to advertising historian Roland Marchand, as a result of the Listerine campaign in the 1920s, the profits of Lambert Pharmaceuticals "mushroomed," making it one of the most spectacularly successful campaigns at that time. Not only did the Listerine ads make Lambert a success, it created a whole new advertising style and approach. The copywriters emphasized the product as being a cure for one of a number of maladies that were increasingly being portrayed in advertising as barriers to social success. Overcoming the reticence for public discussion of matters of personal hygiene, the ad writers positioned themselves as kindly friends bestowing, as Marchand states, "sympathetic advice on how to triumph over the impersonal judgments of the modern world" (Marchand 19). The image of the world the advertisers created was one in which small matters could make a big difference in one's success in life. Dirty fingernails, soiled "linen," unpleasant body odors, or an unkempt appearance could make the difference in whether a man would be hired, promoted, or keep his job in the increasingly competitive world of modern business in which social graces were as important as knowledge and skill. For women, the road to matrimony—the sine qua non of women's lives—was studded with all kinds of barriers and traps, not the least of which was the need to be forever youthful and attractive even after marriage. Lysol, for example, familiar today as a household disinfectant, was also marketed in the 1920s and after as a feminine hygiene product for douching.

Listerine positioned itself as the answer to matrimonial success. The heroine of a 1923 ad for Listerine "had the advantages of education and better clothes than most girls in her set. She possessed that culture and poise that travel brings" (Marchand 19). Yet, this young girl, staring longingly into her mirror, "was often a bridesmaid, but never a bride," a slogan that has become proverbial. The reason, of course, was her breath—"a thing people simply will not tell you to your face." Men, too, could suffer from this condition, as another ad depicted a rising young businessman who is turned down for matrimony by his dream girl "and he never knew why." The specter of friends' gossiping behind one's back became the basis for another of the product's famous taglines: "Even your best friend won't tell you."

As Marchand argues, the Listerine ads, with their potent appeal to personal self-consciousness, reflected the growing trend in American popular culture to personal-interest stories and advice to the lovelorn columns that would give rise to the *True Confessions* genre of magazine. The reader of the ads is invited to relate to the figures pictured in the ad, and the ad copy provides soothing, scientific-sounding reassurance that the problems could be overcome.

The Listerine ads were a home-grown product. The company manager, Gerald B. Lambert—who joined the family firm in the early 1920s—recruited copywriters from the company's regular ad agency, Williams and Cunningham in Chicago, and challenged them to come up with a way of spurring Listerine's modest sales. Lambert modestly claimed that the use of the word halitosis, which they discovered in some early medical literature, came about casually as he and his ad writers tried to figure out how the product could be used and how they could overcome the social stigma of referring publicly to intimate matters of personal hygiene. The ad agency itself felt that the campaign was not going to be successful, but Lambert had extreme confidence in his idea and got his board to agree to a major increase in ad spending as soon as product sales increased. The budget rose from a modest $100,000 year to over $4,000,000. He later spun off a wholly owned subsidiary ad agency to develop new campaigns.

The Listerine ads spurred other ad writers to find new names for commonplace (and long-standing) "problems" for which their products were cures: in addition to "bromodosis" (sweaty foot odor) and "acidosis" (sour stomach), creative copywriters created "homotosis" (lack of attractive home furnishings). The owners of Listerine were also inventive in finding new products and new applications for the old one. A toothpaste was developed that the company claimed made brushing easier and faster ("a dentifrice for busy people, for tired people—even for lazy people," proclaimed a 1927 ad in the *Saturday Evening Post*). The original Listerine could, they claimed, fight loose dandruff (the disease with the aristocratic sounding name of Epithelial Debrism) and prevent sore throats, colds, and the Asian flu. For years these claims—especially those relating to cold and flu prevention—were generally unchallenged, until the 1970s when the Federal Trade Commission, after an investigation, required Warner-Lambert (the merged company that now owned the brand) to undertake a $10 million disclaimer campaign.

References

Lambert, Gerald B. "How I Sold Listerine." *Fortune*, September 1956: 111+.

Marchand, Roland. *Advertising the American Dream: Making Way for Modernity 1920–1940*. Berkeley: University of California Press, 1985.

Ogilvy, David. *Ogilvy on Advertising*. New York: Vintage, 1985.

Room, Adrian. *NTC's Dictionary of Trade Name Origins*. Rev. ed. Lincolnwood, IL: NTC Business Press, 1991.

"Warner-Lambert." *International Directory of Company Histories*, vol. 1. Detroit: St. James Press [Gale], 1988: 710–12.

Martin Green

Packard Automobiles

In the 1920s, sociologists Robert and Helen Lind began to study the changing face of small-town America. One of the strongest trends they discovered during their study was the impact of the automobile on social life in their typical American small town, "Middletown," in reality, Muncie, Indiana. The automobile was just about twenty years old in the early 1920s, but it was already dominating life in America, changing the way people commuted to work, spent their leisure time, and spent their household budgets. It was also having an impact on sex education, especially after the "closed car" became standard, allowing young couples a private place to conduct their intimate relationships. A 1932 report published in *Passenger Car Industry* boasted: "In the eighteen years between our first report [1914] . . . and this report, the automobile industry has made a greater contribution to the pleasure, the health, and the efficiency of the human race than any other industry has ever done in the span of a single generation" (11).

While Henry Ford was to a large degree responsible for the way in which the automobile became such an important part of American life, the Packard automobile and its distinctive advertising may be a better icon of the 1920s. Ford certainly dominated the lower priced market with his fabled Model T "Tin Lizzie," a spartan, workaday vehicle whose low price ($260) made it affordable even to the workers who produced it. According to Jane and Michael Stern, by 1920 "half of the eight million cars on the road were Model Ts" (14). Packard, on the other hand, was a luxury car, selling for close to $5,000 when the average worker earned approximately $1,400 a year. While Ford mass produced cars on the assembly line "in any color as long as it's black" and was slow to offer alternative models, Packard emphasized the range of its models, its commitment of handcraftsmanship, and the power and luxury of its automobiles, appealing to upwardly mobile executives and those already arrived in the upper class. Packards were on display at most public events and parades, carrying presidents to their inaugurations or triumphant heroes, like Charles Lindbergh, through ticker tape parades. It symbolized the power and prestige of business and the comfortable life of the era of Warren Harding and Calvin Coolidge.

The Packard Company was founded in 1899 by brothers James W. and William D. Packard in Warren, Ohio. Before the advent of such monolithic companies as General Motors and Chrysler, the industry was populated by a host of startup companies, many of which were swallowed up or merged into the conglomerate firms. Packard remained independent for over fifty years. The company, which moved to Detroit in the early 1900s, succeeded early in producing technically advanced cars that appealed to the successful and wealthy. The company's slogan, "Ask the Man Who Owns One," signified their confidence in the reliability and quality of their machines, and their advertising emphasized the durability of the cars.

Advertising heavily in the *Saturday Evening Post* and other periodicals,

PACKARD

Only through high intent and steadfast will to achieve are obstacles overcome—the heights attained

Packard has always aspired high and had but a single goal. Thirty years ago Packard chose the difficult, distant peak of perfection as its aim.

From that original intent—to build only the finest motor cars to a single standard of highest quality—Packard has never deviated. It has sought broader patronage not by building to a price, but by producing better cars.

Step by step through the years, Packard cars have been refined, improved—in beauty of design and in excellence

of engineering. Facilities for their manufacture and distribution have been increased and bettered many fold. Supremacy has been attained, but Packard still constantly seeks to make its cars more nearly perfect.

Packard offers its clientele today incomparably finer and more luxurious vehicles at prices which are but the natural result of increased public favor. For as Packard has prospered, it has shared its success with those discriminating motorists who buy its cars.

ASK THE MAN WHO OWNS ONE

In the 6th series, the Packard family crest appeared on the radiator shell. Packard introduced the speedster, a modified standard eight produced for 2 years. The above ad appeared in July 1929, although the 6th series was introduced in the fall of 1928.

Packard advertisements stressed the power and luxury of the car, appealing to the upwardly mobile consumer. Courtesy of Packard Motor Car Company.

the company stressed its commitment to quality and engineering refinement. A 1923 ad proclaimed that its new Single Eight model offered "such an abundance of power as to dwarf the ability of any other in the world." A 1926 ad boasted that "[t]he top speed of Packard cars is too great for safe use anywhere off the speedway." A 1929 ad depicted a man of classic features purposefully gazing up a rugged mountain juxtaposed against a picture of a new convertible four-door speedster model. The copy reaffirmed the company commitment to continue to "build only the finest motor cars to a single standard of high quality." Throughout the ad series, produced by a Detroit agency, Austin Bement, Packard vehicles were shown in scenes of upper class life, like horse shows, or juxtaposed against airplanes and dirigibles, capitalizing on the company's reputation as a producer of airplane engines.

These themes continued throughout the 1930s and 1940s, even after the company's advertising was taken over by Young and Rubicam and even though the company attempted to stem the effects of the Great Depression through marketing lower-priced vehicles. The company weathered the Great Depression and World War II (when its engines powered many U.S. aircraft), but it began to decline in the late 1940s and ceased production of its signature vehicle in 1956 after a merger with Studebaker.

References

Griffith, Gwil. *Packard: A History in Ads 1903–1956*. Timonium, MD: Privately printed, 1970.

Lynd, Robert S., and Helen Merrell Lynd. *Middletown: A Study in Modern American Culture*. New York: Harcourt Brace & Co., 1929: 251–63.

The Passenger Car Industry: A Report of a Survey Made by Charles Coolidge Parlin, Manager, and Fred Bremner, Assistant, Curtis Publishing Company Commercial Research Division. Philadelphia: Curtis Publishing, 1932.

Schroeder, Otto. *Packard: Ask the Man Who Owns One: The Life and Times of That Proud Car . . . Portrayed by Pithy Advertising from the Great Magazines*. Arcadia, CA: Post-Era Books, 1974.

Sklar, Robert, ed. *The Plastic Age (1917–1930)*. New York: George Braziller, 1970.

Stern, Jane, and Michael Stern. *Auto Ads*. New York: Random House, 1978.

Martin Green

Prudential Insurance Company

During the 1920s, insurance companies like Prudential advertised with graphic depictions the dire consequences and guilt of doing without insurance. One 1925 Prudential ad pictured "The little grey lady" at a factory sewing machine who knows only "a merciless cycle of toil" because "a husband, a brother, a son has failed in his imperative duty" to provide life insurance and give old age "the comforts and consideration it so richly deserves." Her "needle-scarred fingers tremble more and more" and "the lines on that pitifully beautiful old face grow deeper," as the little grey lady toils on. Other Prudential ads of the 1920s told of the mortgage "lapse," picturing the family left behind and facing foreclosure or, by the 1930s, picturing children in an employment line, missing school because they had to find work.

Other insurance companies in the 1920s, like the Travelers, the Hartford, and Metropolitan Life, had their own versions of what could happen without insurance. The Hartford Fire Insurance Company ran a series picturing a black-hooded "fire demon" who would "Look On and Smile" at fires or warn, "Some Day Fire Will Get You." The Travelers pictured tired widows and scolded their dead husbands. Metropolitan Life did a public health campaign on the dangers of syphillis.

It is difficult to advertise insurance, which does not have an actual physical product to sell, and companies relied on these attention-getting tactics to make their wares known. They also used important, recognizable logos and advertised them frequently to make their names familiar. At the bottom of every Prudential ad was the company's iconic logo, a picture of the Rock of Gibraltar, framed in a circle with the words, "The Prudential has the strength of Gibraltar" seemingly carved into the stone (some tourists, allegedly, were surprised when they actually visited Gibraltar and did not find the words engraved on it). The idea was, of course, that Prudential was solid as a rock.

The image, which has been with us for more than 100 years, has long been an icon of American advertising, thanks to the J. Walter Thompson advertising agency which first suggested it to Prudential in 1896. According to one story, a copywriter at the agency, Mortimer Remington, got the idea as he was riding the train past a local landmark, Snake Rock, on his way from Newark, New Jersey (Prudential's headquarters) to New York City. The biggest rock he could think of was Gibraltar, and the company first used the image in an ad in *Leslie's Weekly* on August 20, 1896. Since then, the logo has undergone several changes; the most recent occurred in 1984 with a total streamlining that has transformed the romantic rock into a geometric set of stripes, sans slogan.

Prudential continued to advertise the dangers of being uninsured through the 1920s and into the Great Depression, then mostly to keep the policyholders it had from letting their policies lapse. Later, it shifted its tone though never its focus on its solid-as-a-rock reputation. A successful campaign of the 1960s and 1970s, for example, used the slogan, "Own a Piece of the Rock" (later, "Get a Piece of the Rock"), emphasizing the cash value of owning an insurance policy. Prudential's rock has remained its consistent advertising theme throughout the century, and Prudential itself continues to be the biggest insurance company in America.

References

Morgan, Hal. *Symbols of America*. New York: Viking Penguin, 1986.
Watkins, Julian Lewis. *The 100 Greatest Advertisements: Who Wrote Them and What They Did*. New York: Dover Books, 1959.

Mary Cross

RCA Radio

A 1926 ad for the new RCA Radiola "Super Heterodyne" portable radio set promises, "And you shall have music wherever you go." Costing $225, this bulky machine was among the earliest sets that liberated radio listeners from the confines of the home and enabled them to take the benefits of radio with them to the seashore or the countryside—the primitive ancestor of the boom box and the Walkman.

Radio was one of the primary icons of the 1920s—a technological marvel that changed the way in which people received news and entertainment and the way in which they participated in the wider culture. Radio broadcasting opened up a truly national experience for perhaps the first time in American history. The ordinary citizen could hear the voices of political leaders and other celebrities and participate vicariously in political conventions, sporting events far from home, and other events of national significance. The Radio Corporation of America, with its Art Deco modernistic lightning bolt RCA logo, was for most of the 1920s and after the dominant manufacturer of sets, and its subsidiary, the National Broadcasting Company (NBC), was the leading purveyor of programming.

While early radio pioneers like Guglielmo Marconi, Reginald Fessenden, Lee de Forest, and Edwin Armstrong experimented with broadcasts of music programming on an occasional basis before 1910, it was David Sarnoff, an employee of the American Marconi Company and later leader of RCA, who proposed in 1916 a "radio music box" to bring culture to the masses. Sarnoff's vision was dismissed by his employers who regarded radio as an extension of the telephone and telegraph, and it was not until 1920 that broadcasting as we have come to know it developed. The first regularly scheduled broadcasts were initiated by a Westinghouse engineer in the spring of 1920. Westinghouse executives and a local department store manager saw the possibilities of stimulating sales of radio sets and launched station KDKA in Pittsburgh on November 2, 1920. Soon other stations were launched, including WEAF in New York City, owned by the American Telephone and Telegraph Company (AT&T).

In 1922 AT&T executives came up with the concept of selling airtime to anyone who had a message to broadcast, and commercial radio was born. Although AT&T claimed a monopoly on "toll broadcasting" or "radio telephony," as they called it, they soon dropped out of broadcasting in favor of RCA, a company in which AT&T was one of the founding partners along with General Electric, Westinghouse, and the United Fruit Company. RCA's broadcasting division, the National Broadcasting Company, was launched in November 1926 and soon had two national networks in operation. RCA also bought out the Victrola Company, a manufacturer of record players, and acquired its familiar—and iconic—logo of Nipper the dog listening to "His Master's Voice" on a loudspeaker.

Early radio sets were simple but crude devices that could be put together by individuals. They were low in fidelity and difficult to tune precisely. Armstrong developed the "superheterodyne" tuning system that led to increasing precision (he later pioneered FM technology that increased the fidelity of sound). Radio sets became prime consumer goods, usually encased in fancy cabinetry, which became the centerpieces of people's living rooms. Soon, the "portable" set liberated listeners to hear their programs anywhere. In 1928 the radio industry sold 2,631,000 sets and racked up revenues of $650,550,000 (*Broadcast Advertising*, April 1929: 7). By the end of the 1920s, the radio audience had grown from 75,000 in 1922 to 35,000,000. Advertising revenues had also grown, but not in similar exponential fashion. Between 1927 and 1929, broadcast ad revenues had risen nearly sixfold from $3,832,510 to $18,729,571 (*Broadcast Advertising*, December 1929). Nonetheless, a government study showed that few stations were yet making a profit.

Early radio advertising was far from the style that most people recognize today. Broadcasters and public officials alike expressed reluctance to turn the home into a "public square" where vendors hawked their wares. Although the sponsors owned whole programs directly (*The Cliquot Club Eskimos* and *The A&P Gypsies*), mentioning specific products and retail prices was taboo. Shows were initially dignified and serious (the music was mostly light classics; announcers often wore evening attire when they broadcast). Soon more popular entertainment forms, exemplified by the comedy of *Amos 'n' Andy* and the crooning of Rudy Vallee, began to dominate the airwaves, and commercials became more direct after the stock market crash of 1929, when, as historian Erik Barnouw states, "resolute salesmanship seemed needed" (*The Sponsor*). The growth of other networks competing with NBC also contributed to the change in culture.

With the advent of television in the 1940s, radio seemed doomed to become a backwater of popular culture. The development of FM technology, available since the 1930s, and the increased mobility of equipment provided by transistors and printed circuits, helped radio rebound with new formats in the 1950s.

References

Barnouw, Erik. *The Sponsor: Notes on a Modern Potentate*. New York: Oxford University Press, 1978.

———. *A Tower in Babel*. Vol. 1 of *History of Broadcasting in the United States*. New York: Oxford University Press, 1966.

Broadcast Advertising: An Independent Magazine Devoted to Advertising by Radio. Vols. 1, 2, April 1929–January 1930.

Douglas, Susan. *Inventing American Broadcasting 1899–1922*. Baltimore, MD: Johns Hopkins University Press, 1987.

Lewis, Tom. *Empire of the Air: The Men Who Made Radio*. New York: HarperCollins, 1991.

Martin Green

The *Saturday Evening Post*

A struggling and undistinguished magazine acquired by Cyrus Curtis in 1897, the *Saturday Evening Post*, became an icon of American popular culture by the turn of the century and continued as such until its demise as a weekly in the 1960s. In the 1920s, it was at the height of its commercial and cultural ascendancy, spreading its message of American values to a wide readership. As a vehicle for advertising, then in rapid expansion in the 1920s, the *Saturday Evening Post* represents the crucial role of the magazine to 20th-century American advertising.

With growing readerships, magazines soon became the favored vehicles for advertising. Popular magazines had seen an unprecedented growth in the 1890s, when a combination of changes in the technology of printing and in government postal regulations made possible the publication and distribution of periodicals at a cheap price. In this Curtis and his two flagship publications, the *Saturday Evening Post* and *Ladies' Home Journal*, led the way. Curtis believed that *Saturday Evening Post*, a weekly magazine directed at a broad audience, had great potential as an advertising medium. Advertisers agreed: *Saturday Evening Post* received support as well as credit from the N.W. Ayer advertising agency, a neighbor in Curtis's hometown of Philadelphia. Although *Saturday Eve-*

ning Post initially lost money, by the early 20th century, under the editorship of George Horace Lorimer, it was rivaling *Ladies' Home Journal* in sales and advertising space, and it continued its growth through the years of World War I.

The *Saturday Evening Post* was initially pitched at the up-and-coming young (male) business executive although later its content was designed to appeal to women as well. The *Post's* ads for itself mainly appealed to young boys and men to become sales agents for the magazine. The company paid premium rates to writers and paid at the moment of acceptance, attracting such major talents as Jack London, Frank Norris, Mary Roberts Rinehart, Kenneth Roberts, and F. Scott Fitzgerald among many others. Its colorful covers, drawn by Norman Rockwell and other illustrators, came to define mainstream America.

After the recession of early 1920s in which the *Post's* revenues sagged, the magazine rebounded. Contents were likewise burgeoning. According to historian Jan Cohn, "By 1926 the yearly contents had grown to 20 serialized novels, 16 novelettes, as well as 437 short stories and 421 articles. The average number of pieces per issue had risen to 16.5 and a really large issue of over two hundred pages carried as many as 22 or 23 stories, articles, and serial installments." Advertising accounted for as much as 61% of the pages, helping the Curtis Company to achieve earnings of $21,534,265 in 1929 (Cohn, 165, 166).

The magazine's politics and social values were in keeping with the general conservative tendencies of mainstream America in the 1920s. Focused on success in business and supportive of Republican policies, the magazine campaigned in favor of restricting immigration and against unions and decried the avant-garde in the arts. In keeping with its editor's traditional values, the magazine also editorialized against consumerism (while supporting consumerism through its advertising) and speculative finance.

Critics were not lacking. Radical novelist Upton Sinclair, author of *The Jungle*, wrote in 1927:

From the point of view of the literary business man, these Curtis publications are perfection. They read your manuscripts promptly, and pay the very highest price upon acceptance. So they are the goal of every young writer's ambition, and the most corrupting force in American letters. Their stuff is as standardized as soda crackers; originality is a taboo, new ideas are treason, social sympathy is a crime, and the one virtue of man is to produce larger and larger quantities of material things. They have raised up a school of writers, panoplied in prejudice, a lynching squad to deal with every sign of protest against the ideas of the plutocracy. (quoted in Cohn, 175)

Even with the competition of new media such as radio and sound motion pictures, magazines in the 1920s continued to appeal across a wide spectrum of readers. The *Saturday Evening Post* itself stood up to the other media and prospered for another fifty years before a radical decline in readership led to its demise in 1982.

References

Cohn, Jan. *Creating America: George Horace Lorimer and The Saturday Evening Post.* Pittsburgh: University of Pittsburgh Press, 1989.

Elson, Robert. *Time, Inc.: The Intimate History of a Publishing Enterprise, 1923–41.* New York: Atheneum, 1968.

Goldstone, Tony, comp. *The Pulps: Fifty Years of American Pop Culture.* New York: Chelsea House, 1970.

Heidenry, John. *Theirs Was the Kingdom: Lila and DeWitt Wallace and the Story of the Reader's Digest.* New York: W. W. Norton, 1993.

Janello, Amy, and B. Jones, eds. *The American Magazine.* New York: Abrams, 1991.

Peterson, Theodore. *Magazines in the Twentieth Century.* 2d ed. Urbana: University of Illinois Press, 1972.

Tebbel, John, and Mary Ellen Zuckerman. *The Magazine in America, 1741–1990.* New York: Oxford University Press, 1991.

Wood, James Playsted. *The Curtis Magazines.* New York: Ronald Press, 1971.

Martin Green

Wonder Bread

"The greatest invention since sliced bread" is an old cliché that has a grain of truth in it. The advent of the packaged loaf of sliced bread was a major innovation in the food revolution that marked the early years of the 20th century. Wonder Bread, although probably not the first such product, is surely the icon of this product type.

Developed by a baking company in Indianapolis, Indiana, in the early 1920s, Wonder Bread was a local marketing success and then captured a share of the national market when the company was acquired by the Continental Baking Company in 1925. (The company was sold to Interstate Industries in the 1970s.) Its name and the distinctive yellow, blue, and red balloons on its package were inspired, according to company legend, when the company's vice president saw a sky full of colorful balloons at a balloon race at the Indianapolis Speedway. Like the "Camels are Coming" campaign for Camel cigarettes, in which the nature of the product was kept secret until the climactic moment, the makers of Wonder Bread ran teasing ads about a new "wonder" soon to appear in town, revealing at the end of the campaign that the product was white bread: "A new delight with every bite, / Both morning, noon and every night."

The original version of Wonder Bread was not, however, sliced. That was an innovation of the 1930s. Rather, its chief selling point in the 1920s seems to have been that it was "slo-baked" and the product of a spotless bakery. When the product went national after 1925, the company sponsored radio programs featuring a singing quartet dressed in spotless white uniforms (although no one at home could see them on the radio) who sang the praises of their product baked in "pans . . . polished and shining bright." Later, the nutritional value of the bread for children became its major selling point. The slogan "Builds Strong Bodies 8 Ways" was introduced in the 1940s, then modified as "Builds Strong Bodies 12 Ways!" in the 1950s: 1. muscle, 2. bones and teeth, 3. body cells, 4. blood, 5. appetite, 6. growth, 7. brain and energy, 9. red cells, 10. vitamin B12, 11. protein digestion, 12. tissue respiration (Wonder Bread advertisement).

American food habits were changing in the 1920s, like so many other aspects of the consumer culture. Convenience, efficiency, and nutrition were the buzz words of the time as scientific knowledge was combined with marketing skill by growing food-processing companies. According to historian Harvey Green, "[b]etween 1914 and 1929, capital investment in the food industry more than tripled, making it the largest American manufacturing industry," and "growers and [food] manufacturers . . . became the second largest purchasers of newspaper advertising in the 1920s" (160). Canned goods, processed meats, and packaged breads, and later frozen foods became staples of the American diet.

Prior to the 1920s, baking bread was a common element of housework in middle-class and working-class homes. Time consuming and demanding of attention, bread baking was an easy target for replacement by modern mass manufacturing methods. The traditional home-baked loaf was a dense, crusty product, usually made from rye or whole-wheat flours. The new manufactured breads were made of bleached flour, and their whiteness was a sign of their supposed purity and freshness. As early as the 1830s, food reformers, like Sylvester Graham, had criticized the bland products of bleached flour, but they gained popularity nonetheless, especially in middle-class homes where white flour signified refinement. For working-class families struggling into the middle classes in the early years of the 20th century, the white loaf was a sign of social mobility and assimilation into American society. As Graham had recognized, processing flour robbed it of its natural nutrients, so it was logical for bakers like Continental to put the vitamins back in artificially. By 1939, according to Harvey Green, four times as much "white pan bread was produced (7.2 billion pounds) as rye or whole wheat or hearth breads (1.7 billion pounds)" (160–61), and the soft loaf of bland white bread became, for better or worse, an international symbol of American eating habits.

References

Green, Harvey. *The Uncertainty of Everyday Life 1915–1945*. New York: HarperCollins, 1992. Reprint, New York: HarperPerennial, 1993.

Levenstein, Harvey A. *Revolution at the Table: The Transformation of the American Diet*. New York: Oxford University Press, 1988.

Wonder Bread advertisement. *Advertising Age: The Advertising Century*, Special Issue (Spring 1999): 102.

"Wonder Bread History." <http://www.wonderbread.com/>.

Martin Green

Icons of the 1930s

Reflecting the depressed economy, 1930s ads looked and sounded different. Print ads were cluttered with narrow margins, using up the white space which, in 1920s, was left lavishly empty. (Lavish white space, paid for but not used, connoted wealth and luxury in the advertising business.) There was a shrill sound to ad headlines and an alarming look of bad news about the black-and-white photographs that replaced color in the advertisements. Copywriters turned to scare tactics to stress the urgency of buying their products, inventing new "diseases" and conditions that could be cured only by purchasing what they were selling. Insurance companies and mouthwash manufacturers alike depicted in graphic terms the dire predicaments people could find themselves in without the proper insurance or breath freshener. When the consumer neglected to buy the right product, old ladies could end up in the poorhouse, children could suffer, and husbands could lose their jobs, according to the ads.

The handmaidens of business, the advertisers of the 1920s, were supposed to perform two tasks. First they were to educate the huddled masses—teaching newly arrived immigrants good nutrition and basic hygiene—to brush, polish, and bathe. Simultaneously, they were to fuel the American economy by convincing consumers to buy the right products in the right amounts. In 1926 President Calvin Coolidge himself had commended advertisers for their brilliant public service.

During the Great Depression, however, American business itself became suspect. And the most suspicious part of that dubious enterprise, as well as the most dispensable, was the advertiser. After advertising budgets hit their absolute low in 1933, new agencies and new strategies were developed that led to new products that would save companies—as the Plymouth did for Chrysler—or raise their market share—as Ritz Crackers did for Nabisco in 1934.

Some techniques were clearly in place well before the stock market crash of 1929. The emergence of highly imaginative diseases, invented by the ad agencies, and treatable only by buying a certain product, was hardly new. The symptoms, treatments, and the diseases themselves were often quite original and made use of new technology. For example, it would take the team of modern, well-scrubbed well-draped surgeons pictured in the ads to deal with the effects of "poisonous" toilet paper.

The hard-sell, tabloid techniques—pages loaded with images, the techniques of true story magazines, and comic strips right out of comic books and into advertisements—initiated in the 1920s were standard practice in the 1930s. Ads printed in columns like news items could be read as news stories which their new formats resembled. The cartoon strip became incorporated into ads, with bland, recognizable plain folk substituted for the cartoon characters.

Advertisers spent less, which meant black-and-white print ads rather than color ads in magazines. They took tried and true methods, that is, the so-called "true stories" which worked so well in magazines (soap opera–style stories that were popular until the real, radio soap operas began), and wrote some stories of their own into their ads. Comic strip stories touted products. Advertisers also made good use of radio. Whole shows stood behind one brand. The advertised product figured in the show, used by characters in soap operas or appearing in the punch line in comedy shows like Jack Benny's. Never was brand identity clearer or loyalty higher.

Old established companies had to roll out new appeals and do it on the cheap. Prudential Insurance had to shift strategies. Instead of marketing new policies by appealing to the guilt of the wage earner, they focused on keeping their policyholders from letting their policies lapse. "Children of the Lapse," read one Prudential ad in 1930, picturing a forlorn group of children in an employment office looking for work and "deprived of full-time schooling" because their deceased parents had let their life insurance lapse.

The biggest boon for advertisers came in 1934 with the repeal of Prohibition. Suddenly, liquor could be promoted, but careful handling was required, lest the puritanical but powerful minority triumph a second time. Beer and liquor went their separate ways. Ads for liquor took the high road, featuring elegantly dressed men and women. Beer rolled out a wagon full of kegs but pointed out that good fathers hurried home after the stress-reducing brew to their waiting families.

Certainly, as Roland Marchand points out, advertisers appealed to a dream: Ritz and Philip Morris touted an image of elegant living. Some, like Elsie, Betty Crocker, and Charles Atlas, served as sources of information. Thousands of highly personal letters poured in asking advice from these fictitious company figures. Companies had to hire help to answer them all, but they themselves had created the consumer anxiety and need for advice, using what Marchand calls "scare copy" advertising, which makes the advertiser look like the caring friend of the consumer, allaying fears and curing diseases.

Deep suspicions about business and advertisers remained after the Great Depression, and the first consumer movements were under way. Through the efforts of President Franklin D. Roosevelt and thanks to the muckrakers, government regulatory agencies of the Federal Trade Commission and the Pure Food and Drug Administration came into existence. The Consumers Union was born to test products and supply concrete information to the public. The Pure Food, Drug, and Cosmetic Act of 1938, the Wheeler-Lea Amendment to the Federal Trade Commission Act, the advertising regulatory sections in the Security and Exchange Commission, the Post Office laws, and the Alcohol and Tobacco Tax Division of Internal Revenue Service began to put the advertising business under surveillance. After a decade of hyperbolic headlines, shrill come-ons, and not always reliable claims, advertising had created a cautious consumer who would have to be wooed back with a new strategy. It was on its way, and it was called television. (See Chapter 5, "DuMont Television").

References

Lears T. J. Jackson. *Fables of Abundance: A Cultural History of Advertising in America*. New York: Basic Books, 1994.

Marchand, Roland. *Advertising the American Dream: Making Way for Modernity 1920–1940*. Berkeley: University of California Press, 1985.

Marjorie Keyishian

Betty Crocker
(General Mills)

Betty Crocker, the fictional spokeswoman for General Mills products since 1921, has undergone seven makeovers in her lifetime, appearing younger and less wrinkled each time. The current Betty Crocker, a product of computer morphing, is a thirty-something brunette. She looks like a professional woman who has just come home after work to cook a meal. An icon of domesticity long before Martha Stewart, Betty Crocker now has her own Web site, seven test kitchens, and a publishing record of 200 different cookbooks.

In her first incarnation, in 1936, Betty Crocker was portrayed as a respectable, motherly type with a touch of grey in her hair. She was mod-

The image of Betty Crocker has been updated seven times since she was first created to give a friendly face to the company. Courtesy of the General Mills Archive.

eled after the women in the company's Home Service Department and named Betty because it sounded friendly and wholesome (Crocker was the name of a former director of the company). But Betty Crocker, as the voice of the popular *Betty Crocker Cooking School of the Air*, was already familiar to the public. She had been talking to customers on the radio for the forerunner of General Mills, the Washburn Crosby Company, answering mail, and giving out recipes.

In the 1930s, however, her chief role was to give a friendly face to the company, which by then had been consolidated into General Mills in Minneapolis. The housewife's friend during the difficult period of the Great Depression, she offered budget-friendly recipes and personal, womanly advice about cooking, even though initially, the torrents of mail received by the company were actually answered by a man, the director of advertising, Samuel C. Gale (most of General Mills's advertising was handled in house). Her radio show, *The Betty Crocker Cooking School of the Air*, on NBC featured the voices of thirteen different women as the voice of Betty Crocker over regional networks. The show ran for thirty years, from 1927 to 1957. During World War II, she advised women how to survive rationing and published a cookbook, *Your Share*, on the subject. By the 1940s, she was nearly as well known as Eleanor Roosevelt, the best-known woman in America at that time.

Betty Crocker's signature (in the handwriting of one of the Home Service Department women) appeared on every product, and the famous red spoon logo appeared along with it on Betty Crocker cake mixes beginning in the 1950s. Instead of the coupons for Oneida flatware she offered in bags of flour at the end of the 1920s, today Betty Crocker has her own cooking catalog and her name on 250 food products.

References

"Betty Crocker." General Mills. <http://www.generalmills.com/explore/history/BC_hist/>.

Enrico, Dottie. "Top 10 Advertising Icons." *The Advertising Century: Advertising Age*, Special Issue (Spring 1999): 44.

Marchand, Roland. *Advertising the American Dream: Making Way for Modernity, 1920–1940*. Berkeley: University of California Press, 1985.

Mary Cross

Charles Atlas Dynamic Tension System

Angelo Siciliano was a 97-pound weakling whose family came from southern Italy to the lower East Side of Manhattan in 1903. The boy, who could not speak English, transformed himself from a bullied immigrant to a model of masculinity, able to protect himself and teach others the techniques he used to transform themselves into powerful and beautiful males. He earned $100 a week by modeling for sculptors like Gertrude Paine Whitney and Arthur Lee; he modeled for seventy-five statues around the world.

Siciliano incarnated the great American dream of transforming oneself into something else. In 1921 he entered and won Benarr Macfadden's Most Beautiful Male Contest. The prize, $1,000, was the most he had earned until then. In 1922 he won the Madison Square Garden contest for male physical perfection sponsored by Benarr Macfadden, and he was crowned the "World's Most Perfectly Developed Man." Macfadden ended the contests, which had run since 1903, because he said Siciliano would win them all.

Siciliano saw a bust of Hercules on a school trip to the Brooklyn Museum and took it as an inspiration for his own personal perfection. He changed his name to Charles Atlas in honor of another mythological muscle man whose name was as familiar to him as that of a Coney Island hotel, the Atlas. The system of isometric exercises he developed involved setting one part of the body against another. He marketed the system for five dollars to several thousand people, but it took the teamwork of Charles Atlas and Charles Roman, an advertising copywriter making $35 a week, to develop the campaign that made Charles Atlas a household name. Together, they marketed his program of daily exercise, a healthy low-fat diet, and clean living worldwide. Atlas inspired awkward teenagers and the middle-aged to remake themselves.

Charles Roman renamed Atlas's system "Dynamic-Tension," and he wrote simple and direct copy ("In seven days, I'll prove to you I can make you a man!") which appealed to young men around the world. He designed the cartoons that appeared in magazines and comic books, beginning in 1928, which told the story of Mac, based on the autobiography of Atlas, the 97-pound weakling who, when he was 16, took a beautiful young lady to the beach. At the beach, in one of the most well-known insults of all time, a handsome bully kicked sand in Mac's face and walked away with the distinctly disloyal young woman. Later, after developing muscles using the Dynamic-Tension method, the young Atlas became a 180-pound hunk of perfection. After ripping phone books in half, he beat up the bully and reclaimed the girl.

The simple story, appearing in just about every magazine and comic book (even today, in *Marvel* and *Dark Horse* comics), and the frequent appearances of Charles Atlas, naked to the waist, wearing white trunks, and orchestrated by Charles Roman, did the job. By 1937 Charles Atlas had sold half a million courses. He was a worldwide celebrity, a brand name.

Charles Atlas was his own best spokesperson. In 1939 he pulled a railroad car carrying 72 tons 112 feet down the track. He went to Sing Sing prison where he bent an iron cell bar. The headline read, "Man Breaks Bars at Sing Sing. Prison Inmates Cheer. No One Escapes."

Atlas lived modestly with his wife and son, Charles, Jr., and daughter, Diana. On the few occasions when he went to a night club, El Morocco, he drank milk and tried to get the other patrons to switch from alcohol, stop smoking, and embrace traditional family values.

To respond to letters generated by ads in 400 comic books, Atlas employed nearly thirty women to open and sort the mail he received, mostly from small-town boys who wrote for advice. Four times a year, he awarded a prize to the one who had made the most progress. He lived to be eighty, fit as ever in old age. His perfect measurements never changed. His partner, who practiced the method and took over the business, survived to the age of ninety-two.

At the end of the 1930s, Atlas was accused of false advertising by a weight lifter who convinced the Federal Trade Commission to investigate Atlas. The government vindicated the Atlas method. Making use of the new technology, Atlas appeared on television, in ads, and in person in the 1950s and 1960s, demonstrating his perfect physique nearly to the end of his life. He died in 1972.

A Southern entrepreneur, Jeffrey C. Hogue, bought Charles Atlas, Ltd., and its archives in 1997 from cofounder Charles Roman. Hogue is using the Internet to target new customers and fuel an expansion of the company, headquartered in Harrington Park, New Jersey.

References

"Charles Atlas Biography." *A&E Biography* video. <http://www.charlesatlas. com/>.

"History of Charles Atlas." Charles Atlas, Ltd. <http://www.charlesatlas. com/>.

Rowsome, Frank, Jr. *They Laughed When I Sat Down: An Informal History of Advertising in Words and Pictures*. New York: McGraw-Hill, 1959.

Stancavish, Don. "Charles Atlas Plan Updated for the Web." *Bergen Record*, September 7, 2000. <http://www.bergen.com/biz/atlas/>.

Marjorie Keyishian

Chrysler Plymouth

"Give the public something better and the public will buy," Walter Chrysler is supposed to have said. His brand of car, the Plymouth, which was better and cheaper, competed successfully with the two titans, Ford and General Motors, and saved Chrysler during one of the company's most difficult periods. Featured in the center of the ad is a photograph of Walter Chrysler. Defying the Great Depression, he claimed, "We Couldn't Have Done It in Any Other Year."

Walter Chrysler had just completed construction of the tower of the Chrysler Building in New York City, in 1929, which resembled nothing so much as Walter Chrysler's handmade tools, which are still on display at the Walter Chrysler Museum in Auburn Hills, Michigan. A craftsman who respected his workers, Chrysler acquired the Dodge company to take over their manufacturing plants. He hired J. Sterling Getchell, an agency established in the 1930s, to market the Plymouth, a brand new line of cars designed to appeal to the low end of the market, the biggest market for cars in the United States. The success of the car and the marketing campaign meant that Chrysler would become one of the Big Three auto makers. So strong was customer loyalty that the Plymouth survived to nearly the end of the twentieth century.

Chrysler coined "floating power" to describe the rubber engine mounts that were its engineering advance. The Sterling Getchell Agency came up with the powerful "Look at All Three" motto, which advised potential buyers that Chrysler supplied more machine for fewer dollars than Ford or General Motors.

For the first time, an advertisement boldly compared a product to its chief competitors. The agency is credited with breaking new ground, using photographs instead of paintings as illustrations. Chrysler himself agreed to spend hours modeling for the commercial photographers, starting a movement for down-to-earth shirtsleeves and overalls advertising. Here was the CEO Walter Chrysler, himself, in shirtsleeves, his foot up on the bumper of a new Plymouth, giving the public the lowdown. Plymouth ads, thanks to Getchell, told the story in sequential photographs which starred the common man and personalized the company. Even Eleanor Roosevelt was said to drive a Plymouth.

The Plymouth combined low price with high quality and used parts interchangeable with the new six-cylinder De Soto, another Chrysler car which had exceeded marketing expectations. In 1930 Walter Chrysler decided that Dodge, DeSoto, and Chrysler dealers would all carry the low-end Plymouth. Those 10,000 dealers now had a price leader able to carry their higher priced lines through lean times.

In 1932 a redesigned Plymouth, sporting a radiator that looked like a stylized harp, had a redesigned engine that put out fifty-six horsepower, more than Chevrolet's or Ford's forty. Promotions included a $300 ticket that entitled the buyer to a plane ride in exchange for taking a demonstration ride in the new model, as well as a 6,228-cross-country ride in a stock Plymouth sedan that took five days, twelve hours, and nine minutes and set a new transcontinental record.

Chrysler spent millions to develop the new model even as sales fell.

He made use of new advertising methods and his decision paid off: by 1936 sales were three times higher than they had been in 1929. The combination of good craftsmanship and effective marketing successfully carried the company through the difficult decade. In 2001 the final Plymouth, a Neon, went to Darrell Davis, the Chrysler vice president for parts and service operations, who added the car to his collection of vintage automobiles.

References

Curcio, Vincent. *Chrysler: The Life and Times of an Automotive Genius*. New York: Oxford University Press, 2000.
Mannered, Michelins. "Let US Remember the Dear, Departed Plymouth." *New York Times*, July 6, 2001: F1.

Marjorie Keyishian

Coca-Cola

The most famous Coca-Cola slogan, "The Pause That Refreshes," was written by D'Arcy Advertising creative director Archie Lee in 1929. The campaign, which was launched just before the stock market crash in October 1929, made the slogan virtually synonymous with Coca-Cola over the next thirty years and set sales records. The strategy was to make the act of drinking Coca-Cola a central part of being an American. To that end, even Santa Claus, portrayed by artist Haddon Sundblom, was shown in 1930s ads and calendars and on trays drinking a Coke as he paused from his labors. Sundblom's Santa with the slogan, "Thirst Knows No Season," and "The Pause That Refreshes" campaign helped Coca-Cola sales remain strong throughout the Great Depression and well beyond.

Coca-Cola was actually invented as a "brain tonic" in the 19th century. John Pemberton, an Atlanta pharmacist and Civil War veteran, was looking for a cure for his headache. He mixed up a carmel-colored concoction and took it over to Jacob's Pharmacy to try it out with carbonated water. It tasted good enough to sell. The drink was a hit with customers at 5 cents a glass, and Pemberton's bookkeeper, Frank Robinson, named it "Coca-Cola," writing out the name in his own Spencerian-style handwriting, the same script used on the trademark today. The exact mixture, involving a coca leaf (the raw ingredient of cocaine) and a kola nut (high in caffeine) was a secret in 1886 and still is. Fewer than ten people know the formula, which is kept in a vault at a Georgia bank. Coca-Cola was dogged by rumors that the drink contained cocaine, and initially the original one did, but investigations conducted by chemists in 1905 and later found none.

The first ad for Coca-Cola ran in the *Atlanta Journal* in May 1889. The copy read: "Delicious/Refreshing/Exhilarating. The new and popular drink containing the tonic properties of the wonderful coca plant and the famous cola nuts, on draught at the popular soda fountains at 5 cents per glass."

Pemberton, who did not realize what a bonanza his invention would prove to be, sold the still-secret formula in 1893 to Asa Griggs Candler who proceeded to market Coca-Cola avidly. He gave away coupons for free tastes, installed clocks and chandeliers bearing the Coca-Cola name in pharmacies, and hired the first celebrity spokesperson for Coca-Cola, a music hall performer named Hilda Clark who was featured in advertisements. Candler opened coke syrup plants in Chicago, Dallas, and Los Angeles, and he was dismayed when another entrepreneur, Joseph Beiderman, wanted to buy the rights to bottle the drink and make it portable (up until then, the coke syrup was mixed at the soda fountain with carbonated water). Beiderman won the right to bottle Coca-Cola in 1899, and began bottling Coca-Cola in six-ounce bottles with a stopper in the top. It looked like a patent medicine and, in fact, was sold as a medicinal tonic. The label instructions told users to add a tablespoon to a wine glass of water for "relief of headache and nervous afflictions." The so-called hobble skirt bottle design, familiar today, was introduced in 1916. Raymond Loewy, a well-known industrial designer, once declared that the two most perfectly designed containers ever made were the Coke bottle and the egg.

Touted as "The Ideal Brain Tonic" in 1893, Coca-Cola has had thirty-two different slogans over its lifetime. It was "Delicious and Refreshing" in 1904 when Coke began running national magazine ads and put the name on trays and calendars. In 1906 Coca-Cola hired D'Arcy Advertising of Saint Louis who handled the account for years and created its greatest slogan, "The Pause That Refreshes." McCann Erickson took over the account in the 1970s, creating such slogans as "I'd Like to Teach the World to Sing," "It's the Real Thing," and "I'd Like to Buy the World a Coke."

In 1963 the Coca-Cola company offered a diet cola named Tab, targeting a market of 28 percent of Americans who were dieting and pitching it mainly to young women. When, six years later, the Food and Drug Administration outlawed the cyclamate sweeteners in diet drinks, Coke pulled Tab off the market. It reemerged in the 1970s in a McCann Erickson campaign, "The Beautiful Drink for Beautiful People," but Coke cut into its own market with the introduction of Diet Coke in the early 1980s.

The decision to change the taste of Coca-Cola and introduce New Coke in April 1985 is regarded as the company's biggest marketing blunder.

The idea was to make the soft drink sweeter, the better to compete with its main rival, Pepsi, which was winning the cola wars. Although initially sales of New Coke went up as everyone rushed out to try it, the reformulation set off weeks of protests and angry letters and phone calls from frustrated consumers. By July of that year, the company had "old" Coke back on the shelves, labeled "Coca-Cola Classic," and New Coke eventually and quietly disappeared. Coca-Cola executives said they had no idea of the depth of the emotional involvement customers had with the original Coca-Cola. It is an icon of popular culture and 20th-century American advertising for good reason.

References

Beverage World: Coke's First Hundred Years. Shepherdsville, KY: Keller International Publishing Corporation, 1986.

Gladwell, Malcolm. "Java." *New Yorker*, July 9, 2001.

Griggs, Robyn. "Coca-Cola Slogan Gives Pause." *Advertising Age: The Advertising Century*. Special Supplement, 1999: 36.

Oliver, Thomas. *The Real Coke. The Real Story.* New York: Random House, 1986.

Watters, Pat. *Coca-Cola: An Illustrated History.* Garden City: Doubleday, 1978.

Mary Cross

Elsie the Cow
(Borden's Dairy Products)

Elsie the Cow appears on almost all lists of successful icons, trademarks, and advertising campaigns. She is the ruffled-aproned wife/mother figure who lives in the kitchen of our imagination, smiling directly at us, milk and cheese in hand, offering good health and good taste. A fictitious, as well as real live cow, Elsie has been a popular advocate for health and nutrition.

Borden's Elsie was born in the 1930s. Originally, she was one of a number of cows who were combatants in the "milk wars," a pricing conflict between farmers and dairy processors for control of the industry. Advertisements pitching milk products as healthy foods appeared in medical journals and were so popular that doctors asked for posters that reproduced the cows for their offices.

Borden's began placing newspaper ads featuring Elsie, and in 1938 a radio commentator named Rush Hughes read a letter "written" by Elsie on the air. Listeners were delighted and began sending fan mail to Elsie. The company, recognizing her potential, hired correspondents to answer those letters. She began appearing in national consumer magazine ad-

Elsie the Cow, dressed in her apron, was Borden's advocate for good health and nutrition. © 1951, Borden, Inc.

vertisements. The perfect woman of her time, she was a sturdy counter-balance to the willowy flapper with her debutante slouch; Elsie, with a twinkly smile, was the very incarnation of farm and family values.

The first living Elsie made her debut at the 1939 New York World's Fair. She was one of 150 cows who were employed to demonstrate an automatic milking machine, the "rotolactator." Sixty percent of the questions visitors asked was, "Which one is Elsie?" Borden's picked a beautiful seven-year-old Jersey cow named "You'll Do, Lobella." She was dressed up in an embroidered green blanket and milked separately twice a day, to the delight of spectators.

By the following year, the company had created a "boudoir" for Elsie, complete with paintings of her ancestors and tables made of churns, topped with lamps fashioned from milk bottles. She became a mother, joined by her daughter Beulah. The two were carted across the country to numerous fairs in their own home in a railway freight car.

A year later Elsie was portrayed, standing up wearing an apron. She became "an average young housewife." She acquired a husband, Elmer (later to become the logo cow on Borden's Elmer's Glue) and twins, a daughter and a son, Beauregard, whose name (after General Pierre Beauregard of the battle of Bull Run) was chosen in a contest which brought in over a million entries from consumers. Smiling confidently at readers, Elsie was pictured holding up trays with Borden milk and cheese products, wearing ruffled aprons over her skirts and a necklace of daisies. She developed recipes and was very willing to send them to consumers.

In a national survey conducted in the late 1960s, Elsie was named the best known, best loved trademark in the country. The first televised Elsie ad, an animated cartoon, appeared in 1971. Retired from 1973 to 1993, she returned as a corporate mascot for Borden, Inc., in March 1993, powered by Ketchum PR of New York who designed a billboard campaign in ten cities that promoted her reappearance: "Guess Who's on the Mooove." In 1994 the campaign won the Silver Anvil Award in advertising.

By 1997 Borden had become primarily a chemical company and sold its dairy business to Mid-American Dairymen, which changed its name to the Dairy Farmers of America (DFA). DFA has rights to the Elsie and Borden trademarks which are used on DFA products. The milk wars controversy, which led to Elsie's creation in the 1930s, has long ended. She remains a potent icon in the dairy industry, although she no longer represents the company. In tribute to her iconic stature, the *New York Times* named her "America's Cow" in 2000 ("Elsie Remains Lovable Trademark"), and, according to *Advertising Age*, she is one of the ten most successful icons of the 20th century. For over seventy years, Elsie has promoted wholesome dairy products, health, and nutrition in a way no ordinary cow could do.

References

"Elsie Remains Lovable Trademark." Borden, Inc., press release, August 1984.
Enrico, Dottie. "Top 10 Advertising Icons." *Advertising Age: The Advertising Century*. Special Supplement, 1999: 46.

Marjorie Keyishian

Fleischmann's Yeast

From the middle of the 19th century, Fleischmann's Yeast had produced a product useful in most households, the dependable ingredient that makes bread rise. When home baking declined as women joined the workforce and sliced, packaged, white bread became more popular, Fleischmann's had to reinvent itself. The first reinvention, the "Yeast-for-Health" campaign, capitalized on the vitamin fad sweeping the country after World War I. Taking advantage of the public's new faith in science, Fleischmann's claimed that, though hard on the taste buds, the yeast would fill the body with potent vitamins. A refinement in the 1920s focused on the "water soluble" vitamin B contained in Fleischmann's. Advertisements appeared in a dozen magazines, including the *Ladies' Home Journal* and *Literary Digest*, advising readers to "Start the Day Right." The campaign, which feature the visual icon, the yellow Fleischmann's package, was successful enough by the end of the 1920s to have sold a hundred million cakes more than had sold in 1918.

In 1929 consolidation or absorption of the Royal Baking Powder Company, E. W. Gillette Company, Ltd., of Canada, the Widlar Food Products company, and Chase & Sanborn, Inc., into Fleishmann's Yeast formed a corporation named Standard Brands.

J. Walter Thompson generated a new health problem for its 1930s Fleischmann's Yeast campaign, "intestinal fatigue," which invoked national concern for both better personal hygiene and regularity, for "internal as well as external cleanliness." One ad warns the vigilant housewife: "*Many men are failures because of INTESTINAL FATIGUE*: She has a sure cure at hand, the trusty yeast that once she kneaded into the family loaf to make it rise." Despite protests made by the American Medical Association, the agency ran ads featuring paid testimonials by European doctors about the benefits of Fleischmann's Yeast. The white-haired, white-coated doctors informed consumers how the pressures of modern civiization had produced this newly labeled disease.

Fleischmann continued to promote its name by using the most potent new medium, radio. Rudy Vallee, a well-known singer, hosted the *Fleischmann Hour*, a musical variety show set in a club. While strolling among the tables, Vallee would pretend to overhear conversations, many of which were straightforward commercials about Fleischmann's Yeast.

Fleischmann's overall advertising strategy in the 1930s belonged to the burgeoning trend of acquiring internal as well as external cleanliness. Now the contents of the handy packet could fight constipation as well as build better bodies. One black-and-white ad introduces five groups of "People You Might Know," including a hunter, a mother with four children, an elegant young woman, and a gardener, all of whom have used the yeast to "correct clogged intestines." The ad was part of a candid man-in-the-street campaign.

Fleischmann's laboratories were built on an American chemist's 1935 discovery that Vitamin B1 cured beriberi (a disease of the central nervous system caused by the lack of thiamine in the diet), intensifying efforts to develop strains of yeast containing vitamin B1. By the end of the decade, Hi-B1 yeast, claiming to reproduce the value of whole wheat in white bread, hit the market. Fleischmann's has continued its policy of successful reinvention. Briefly a part of Nabisco, Fleischmann's is now owned by an

Australian company that has refocused on its initial yeast product, using
a subtle new trademark and bringing out a rapid-rise yeast to take advantage of the burgeoning health and home baking market in America.

References

Fleischmann's Yeast. <http://www.fleishmann.com>.
Marchand, Roland. *Advertising the American Dream: Making Way for Modernity
     1920–1940.* Berkeley: University of California Press, 1985.

Marjorie Keyishian

Kotex Sanitary Napkins

The 1930s advertising climate, with its health and cleanliness concerns
and its new frankness about bodily functions, allowed products like Kotex sanitary napkins new commercial visibility. Instead of drawings, the
ads for Kotex in 1932 used photographs of women in body-hugging
gowns to demonstrate that no revealing lines would trumpet their condition to the world. The copy was frank and direct. A new product, the
sanitary belt to hold the bulky napkin in place, was promoted openly.
In the 1930s, Kotex brought out tampons as a modern alternative to
sanitary pads.

Kotex, a Kimberly-Clark product, was originally developed during
World War I from processed wood as an absorbent wadding and called
Cellucotton. Battlefield nurses noted that Cellucotton was far more effective in dealing with their menstrual periods than the material they
had been using. Until then, women had used and reused cloth rags to
deal with menstrual discharge. The first marketing agency to handle Kotex, Charles F. W. Nichols Company, came up with the name Kotex to
replace Cellunap, a contraction of "Cellucotton napkins."

Magazines had to be convinced to accept ads for sanitary napkins,
stores had to be willing to stock them, and women had to be persuaded
to buy them. The first ad, accepted by the *Ladies' Home Journal*, showed
a nurse attending to wounded soldiers, but the Nichols agency itself
decided the ad was inappropriate to run because it pictured men. Another campaign was launched in the *Journal* in 1921: one headline read,
"Simplify the laundress problem." Kotex, it claimed, "complete[s] the
toilet essentials of the modern woman." The first published Kotex ads
featured sophisticated women, elegantly dressed, draped over a stair
bannister.

The first Kotex sanitary napkins were sold in unmarked boxes. The
brand name was at one end of the rectangular box, under a small cross,

but no description told the public what was inside. One inventive druggist in Wisconsin, who found his customers squeamish about asking for Kotex, camouflaged the boxes in plain wrappers, placed them on his counter, and let women leave the money, no conversation required. Sales picked up. Later Kotex ads mentioned this marketing device.

Times have changed. People are not so squeamish about bodily functions. Advertising today talks freely about every bodily condition known, and the brand name of Kotex has become a generic name for an entire product category.

References

"About Us." Kimberly-Clark. <http://www.kimberly-clark.com/>.
Fox, Stephen. *The Mirror Makers: A History of American Advertising and Its Creators.* New York: William Morrow, 1984.

Marjorie Keyishian

Philip Morris Cigarettes

Advertising budgets dropped significantly during the Great Depression. In 1933, Alfred E. Lyon, then Philip Morris's vice president for sales (later president and chairman of the board) and Milton Biow, the advertising agency president handling the Philip Morris account, decided that the company needed a living trademark to do their advertising. They chose a real hotel bellman to incarnate the Philip Morris logo and to trumpet aloud the name of their little-known cigarette.

They auditioned midget Johnny Roventini, billed by his press agent as the smallest bellboy in the world, in the lobby of the Hotel New Yorker by offering him a dollar to shout out, "Call for Philip Morris." On April 17, 1933, on NBC's *Ferde Grofé Show*, Johnny Roventini created a voice for the company and the cigarette, a perfect B-flat, backed by the "On the Trail" section of Grofé's *Grand Canyon Suite*. These sound effects were a hit on the radio. Each of the many Philip Morris–sponsored radio shows, including *It Pays to Be Ignorant*, *The Kate Smith Show*, *This Is Your Life*, *The Rudy Vallee Show*, *Candid Microphone*, and *The Philip Morris Playhouse*, opened with "Johnny presents" and his famous "Call for Philip Morris."

Within five years, Philip Morris was fourth in sales in the country. The famous bellboy, who had signed a lifetime contract with the company, appeared in hundreds of magazine and newspaper ads, as well as store windows and counters, wearing the bellman's short red jacket, emblazoned with gilt buttons, and pillbox hat. He was earning more than

$50,000 a year at a time when that was a fabulous salary. He became so popular that Philip Morris had to hire and train an entire troupe of Johnny stand-ins to make "personal appearances" around the country.

The bellboy image conjured up the sophisticated world of hotel lobbies, nightclubs, and exclusive resorts filled with slinky women, well-clad men, and Scotch tinkling in crystal glasses when the Depression was at its deepest. The bellboy appeared everywhere: on farms, for holidays, wrapped in holly for Christmas, with turkeys for Thanksgiving, and, when war loomed, in uniform. In fact, the ads provide a kaleidoscope of yearly experiences, stretching through decades of American life. The only health issue addressed is the irritated throat soothed by Johnny's brand. NBC radio celebrated Johnny in 1959 with a special half-hour program celebrating his twenty-fifth anniversary.

The 47-inch tall, 59-pound Roventini moved onto the television screen when the Leo Burnett Agency of Chicago took over the account. He appeared on *Candid Camera* and with Lucille Ball and Desi Arnaz. In 1965, during the heaviest ad schedule of Philip Morris's television programming, Johnny was heard on *The Red Skelton Show*, *The Jackie Gleason Show*, *Hazel*, *Hogan's Heroes*, *Candid Camera*, and *CBS News* with Walter Cronkite.

When he retired in 1974, he was replaced by dancing cigarettes. Philip Morris currently produces nearly twenty brands of cigarettes, including Marlboro and Virginia Slims in America, and double that number of brands worldwide. A multibillion, multinational food company, it now includes Kraft Foods and Miller Beer, as well as tobacco, and despite lawsuits seeking redress for smokers damaged by tobacco, historically, it continues to make money for its stockholders.

References

Goodrum, Charles, and Helen Dalrymple. *Advertising in America: The First 200 Years*. Harry N. Abrams, Inc., New York, 1990.

Goodwin, Danny. "Johnny Celebrates 5 Years Calling for Philip Morris." *Old-Time Radio* web site. May 9, 2002. <www.old-time.com/commercials/philipmorris.html>.

Marchand, Roland. *Advertising the American Dream: Making Way for Modernity, 1920–1940*. Berkeley: University of California Press, 1985.

Marjorie Keyishian

Ritz Crackers

In 1934 the National Biscuit Company, RJR Nabisco, whose Shredded Wheat promised both health and regularity, introduced a buttery, rich new biscuit, the Ritz Cracker. The cracker was meant to appeal to people who wanted an inexpensive touch of luxury. In ads, Ritz Crackers were offered to members of elite golf clubs by waiters whose uniforms included white gloves, and they were served aboard an ocean liner, the *Queen Mary*. The cracker, selling for 19 cents a box, outsold, in just one year, every other cracker in the country. Five billion were baked in 1935, "forty crackers for every single American in 1935" ("The History of Ritz Crackers").

The McCann-Erickson advertising agency, who launched the product, described the crackers as "elegant or fancy." Full-page color ads recommended them to a public tired of the black-and-white ads so common during the 1930s. Despite the Great Depression and the long lines of the unemployed whose meals consisted of handouts from soup kitchens, the consumer was to "gently but firmly insist" that the tuxedo-clad waiter at an exclusive golf club stock the new buttery biscuit immediately.

As Roland Marchand points out, McCann-Erickson was selling a dream, and very successfully, too. In Europe, according to the company, young men took a box of their biscuits to present to their lovers instead of elegant chocolates. The cracker was served at the Waldorf-Astoria hotel in New York City and it still is.

Serving Ritz Crackers was a way to level the playing field. The hostess-housewife in her modest apartment could ply guests and family with the choice of butlers and stewards. The cracker nourished the new democracy of consumer goods, which made apartment dwellers the equals of millionaires.

Advertisers were shifting their strategy. In the past, copywriters could simply boast of the excellence of their product or they could point to the efficiency of their production line, which provided the finest merchandise for the lowest price. Now they began to study the consumer. Studies indicated that as many as 90 percent of their customers were women, who were characterized as being open to snob appeal, aware of social class, and terribly anxious to belong to the right one. The agencies produced ads for that audience. Those incredible numbers—five billion crackers in one year, or forty crackers for every single American—clearly indicate that some combination of cracker and advertiser worked.

The crackers continue to sell well, thanks to continuing careful connection to the audience. The company's own food center develops recipes, which are now available on line. Among the most popular is the recipe for a mock apple pie made entirely of Ritz Crackers, with not one slice of fruit.

To market Ritz Crackers to contemporary diet-conscious Americans, a "light" version with less fat is sold as well as the rich, buttery version that dominated the market in the 1930s.

References

"The History of Ritz Crackers." Department of Consumer Affairs, Nabisco Brands, n.d.

Marchand, Roland. *Advertising the American Dream: Making Way for Modernity 1920–1940*. Berkeley: University of California Press, 1985.

Marjorie Keyishian

Scott Tissues

A dramatic black-and-white photo in a 1930s ad features a white-gowned middle-aged male wearing surgical gloves. He is lecturing to an elegant, willowy young woman, facing upstage, hand over her heart, gazing at the two columns of text which warn her that harsh toilet paper can lead to "serious rectal trouble." According to the ad, which looks like a news article, Scott Tissues is the answer to the problem.

Another Scott Tissues ad, featuring a 1931 photo taken by noted photographer Edward Steichen, shows an operating theater where a draped patient is surrounded by gowned and masked surgeons and nurses. The text explains, "*. . . and the trouble began with harsh toilet tissues.*" Advertising in the 1930s creatively invented a number of dangers to health and helpfully suggested cures.

Throughout the decade, such advertisements appeared in a wide variety of magazines, including *Time, Good Housekeeping, Parents*, and *True Stories*. The hard sell came into its own, carrying the emotional freight of the true confession magazine. In one Scott Tissues ad, two well-dressed women discuss the "humiliating and extremely painful" consequences inflicted by harsh toilet paper. "Sixty-five percent of middle-aged men and women suffer from rectal disease," the ad declared. "Science finds Harmful Acids . . . *Mercury* . . . *Arsenic* in many brands of Toilet Tissue," another ad published in the *Saturday Evening Post* in January 1933 announced, offering Scott Tissue as the healthy way, the one way, to protect self and family from the dangers that lurk in other brands as well as scrap paper alternatives that cost nothing at all. Dramatic confrontations in Scott's 1930s ads also featured worried mothers and their suffering little girls, some of whom refuse to go to school where they are subjected to the harsh, bullying tissue. Photosequences featured two suffering infants and two smiling babies whose happy mothers were kissing their chubby little feet. Husbands, too, suffer in their three-piece suits.

Scott Paper was the first U.S. company to sell toilet tissue. Brothers E. Irwin and Clarence Scott of Philadelphia, who once sold paper products from a pushcart in 1879, decided to buy up tissue paper and package it for use when the indoor toilet began to appear. By 1939 they were the largest selling brand in the United States and remained so until the early 1970s when Procter & Gamble's Charmin took the lead. In 1956 Scott Paper was the first to advertise toilet paper on television, with the J. Walter Thompson agency handling the account. In 1995 the Scott Paper Company and Kimberly-Clark Corporation merged, recapturing the giant share of the market and challenging all competitors.

References

Marchand, Roland. *Advertising the American Dream: Making Way for Modernity 1920–1940*. Berkeley: University of California Press, 1985.

"Our History-Making Brand." SCOTT brand website. May 9, 2002. <www.scottbrand.com/history>.

Marjorie Keyishian

5

Icons of the 1940s

Perhaps more than any other single decade in the 20th century, the 1940s witnessed a fundamental transformation in American culture and society. Following the economic traumas of the Great Depression, the 1940s brought even greater upheavals to the country—World War II, postwar prosperity, and cataclysmic fears. The United States entered the decade as an isolationist nation; many of its leading politicians were committed to sheltering the country from the havoc being wrought in Europe and Asia. At the end of the decade, the country emerged as the world's greatest economic power, with primary responsibility for the governance and rebuilding of many shattered societies, including those that had been hated enemies only a few years before.

The country had weathered the Depression, and the economy was beginning to recover when the Japanese struck with a vengeance at Pearl Harbor on December 7, 1941. Suddenly, America was at war. Though all the deadly battles were taking place half a world away, thousands of Americans fought and died there. For those on the home front, beyond the emotional stress of having loved ones at risk, the main distress was deprivation of goods, particularly food and fuel.

With the war effort demanding a full commitment of large-scale manufacturing, auto assembly lines were devoted to jeeps, tanks, and army trucks. No consumer vehicles were built between 1942 and 1946. Those cars already on the road were subjected to gas rationing. The average driver got A ration books from which coupons could be torn for restricted amounts of gas; those who performed essential services got B ration books for more ample gas supplies. Coupon books restricted food purchases, and staples like butter and sugar were in short supply. Silk became vital for parachutes, not stockings, and women began to paint their legs to simulate hose, even drawing a dark seam up the back of their calves. Families grew their own vegetables in victory gardens and saved tin cans. Boy Scouts collected string and the inner foil wrappers of cigarette packs. The scarcity of the war years was purposeful and unified most of the population. All did their part.

With so many men in uniform, women were called upon to fill essential jobs in factories and encouraged to join the workforce by posters illustrating Rosie the Riveter, an iconic figure in her own right who symbolized women's role in the war effort. Although returning servicemen reclaimed their old jobs from women in many cases, a significant social transformation was under way by the end of the war. The men had seen the world in Europe, the Pacific, and North Africa; but the women had seen the possibilities of wage-earning employment. After the war, many veterans took advantage of the GI Bill to buy homes and seek a college education. By the mid-1940s, the American consciousness was being transformed; millions of its citizens had traveled, were educated, and were ready for work. For many of them, their experiences produced an illumination. The United States had taken its place at the center of the world, and they envisioned new possibilities.

Video technology, which had rarely left the laboratory before the war, reached the mass market, and people snapped up television sets despite their high cost. Television became a coveted necessity. Not only did people have entertainment right in their own living rooms, albeit on tiny screens and through fuzzy grey figures, but they were urged to buy an abundance of new products to consume—dishwashers, washing machines, frozen food, and new cars. Television and advertising enjoyed a symbiotic relationship: the programs attracted millions to sit quietly and watch commercials for products they wanted to buy.

By the end of the decade, the economy was flourishing and prosperity reigned, at least as it had never done for so many. In a few years, Americans had left the Depression and even the war behind. America had become a consumer culture like none the world had ever seen.

References

"American Cultural History: The Twentieth Century, 1940–1949." Kirkwood College Library. <http://www.nhmccd.edu/contracts/lrc/kc/decade40.html/>.

Gerdes, Louise I., ed. *1940s* (American Decades Series). San Diego, CA: Greenhaven Press, 2000.

Walter Cummins

Chiquita Banana

Even more popular than "Pepsi Cola hits the spot" in the 1940s was the Chiquita Banana song, an infectious tune with a Latin rhythm that raised the national awareness of that tropical fruit and, especially, the Chiquita brand. Bananas took on the aura of an exotic treat. People could hardly ignore the jingle that, at its height, received 376 plays each day on American radio stations after its 1944 introduction.

The tune, unlike other advertising songs, was both promotional and instructional. Rather than extolling the product's virtues or values, such as "hitting the spot" or "twelve full ounces," it explained when to buy bananas, how to use them, and how not to store them. A banana named Miss Chiquita, dressed up in a fruitbowl hat, gave the directions to a calypso beat: "I'm Chiquita Banana and I've come to say." She suggested then to use bananas when they are a deep yellow color to make everything from salads to pies, and never to put them in the refrigerator.

A Batten, Barton, Durstine & Osborn (BBDO) advertising agency team produced a jingle under the direction of Robert Foreman, with lyrics by Garth Montgomery and music by Ken MacKenzie. They banged out the tune on an old upright piano and shook a box of paper clips to simulate maracas. Soon after, artist Dik Browne, later creator of the "Hagar the Horrible" comic strip, drew Chiquita's cartoon image.

In the 1940s, many associated the visual figure of Chiquita, a smiling banana in flouncy dress, with popular movie star Carmen Miranda. In fact, in 1945, an actress named Elsa Miranda (no relation) was hired to play Chiquita on film and stage. Carmen, a transplanted Brazilian actress, had become a figure of affectionate caricature for her redundant movie roles of bouncy rhythms, comic accent, and outlandish headdress. The Chiquita song could have been written for her instead of her namesake.

Years later, by the end of the century, as the country became more sensitized to racial and ethnic stereotypes, both Carmen Miranda and Chiquita Banana were reevaluated for their negative impacts. A 1996 documentary, *Carmen Miranda: Bananas Is My Business*, exposed the debasing of Miranda, a serious actress and performer in her native country who endured miscasting and misuse by the American film industry. Beneath the professional pose of energetic joy, she suffered great unhappiness. The highest-paid woman in Hollywood in 1945, she was dead ten years later after an illness of severe depression. Criticisms of Chiquita, who was—of course—not a real person, raised claims of economic and political abuse.

Most prominent was the association of Chiquita and its parent corporation, the United Fruit Company, with the term "Banana Republic"—that is, a Latin American country essentially owned and ruled by an American organization that exploited its land and its people for the production of a single product, a cash crop. Exposés of worker abuse and environmental degradation spread through the media. The luscious fruit with its golden hue was transformed into a symbol of the Ugly American.

In the late 1990s, Chiquita became the subject of a journalistic scandal when, on May 3, 1998, the Cincinnati *Enquirer* published an eighteen-page supplement written by reporters Mike Gallagher and Cameron McWhirter that attacked the corporation's alleged abuses, such as provoking war, overthrowing governments, using banned pesticides, and bribing officials to buy land at bargain prices. The report's reliance on 2,000 illegally obtained taped voice mail messages led to the *Enquirer's* apology and a $10 million payment to Chiquita, along with a guilty plea by Gallagher for intercepting internal company communications.

The company, now known as Chiquita Brands International, Inc., celebrated its 100th anniversary in 1999, with the health virtues of bananas certified by the American Heart Association and a new set of lyrics to the Chiquita song which emphasizes good nutrition, vitamins, fiber, and energy—that is, bananas as the perfect food source.

References

Adams, Frederick Upham. *Conquest of the Tropics: The Story of the Creative Enterprises Conducted by the United Fruit Company.* New York: Arno Press, 1976.
Bauman, Jan. "Chiquita Banana." Marin Interfaith Task Force, September 1998. <http://www.thirdworldtraveler.com/Transnational_corps/Chiquita Banana.html/>.
"Chiquita History." <http://www.chiquita.com/>.
Lobe, Jim. "MEDIA-US: Journalist in Chiquita Banana Expose Pleads Guilty." <http://www.oneworld.org/ips2/sept98/01_00_002.html/>.

Walter Cummins

Du Mont Television

The Alan B. Du Mont Laboratories seemed ideally positioned for the great flourishing of television in the American home in the late 1940s. It manufactured sets to receive the broadcasts and provided the broadcasts themselves on the Du Mont Television Network. Such a convergence of content and technology motivated a number of multibillion dollar mergers of the 1990s. And yet, by the late 1950s, the Du Mont network and television set production were out of business.

Dr. Allen B. Du Mont provided the invention that made commercial television possible: a cathode ray tube that did not burn out in twenty-five hours. As a result, in 1939, he became the first manufacturer to offer television sets to consumers. With the coming of World War II, the market remained in limbo. When war broke out, there were only 7,000 television sets in the United States and seven stations broadcasting irregularly. In the immediate postwar years, with the growth of the industry, Du Mont enjoyed a reputation for high quality and innovation—for example, producing a picture-in-picture television through the ingenious arrangement of two tubes and a one-way mirror. It even developed a technique for color television that never went into production. This quality, however, came at a cost, and Du Mont lost significant market share when competitors GE and RCA began producing low-priced sets in large numbers.

Even before he began selling sets, Du Mont realized that the public would need available programming as a stimulus to buying. In 1938 he formed a partnership with Paramount Pictures to create a network of broadcast stations. That partnership, which became the source of his undoing, resulted from economic necessity, a quest for funds to finance his research. To obtain backing, he sold Paramount an interest in his company for $50,000.

Paramount, a moviemaking company, feared television as a threat to the film industry, and it became a deliberate competitor. It worked against Du Mont to build its own stations in major markets, effectively shutting out Du Mont from those cities because of a Federal Communications Commission rule, only recently abandoned, that prohibited any company from owning more than one station in a city. Because Du Mont and Paramount were linked, the FCC considered Paramount stations "Du Mont owned." Du Mont did obtain a license for a New York station in 1944 and one in Washington, D.C., in 1945. The two were linked by coaxial cable for the network's first broadcast, an announcement on August 9, 1945, that a second atomic bomb had been dropped on Nagasaki, Japan. The network added Pittsburgh as the home of its third VHF station, and there it stopped.

Despite Du Mont's lack of experience in broadcasting, with no previous history as a radio network, it boasted American's top show on the nation's first official television ratings in 1948: *The Original Amateur Hour*. An innovator in set design, Du Mont also could boast of several firsts in television programming: the first soap opera, the first scheduled children's show, and the first National Football League live game.

Despite all this potential, Du Mont failed not only because of limited funds for programming and media inexperience, but primarily because of frequency allocation concerns that led to a 1948 FCC freeze on new VHF stations that lasted until 1952. Only two such stations were allowed

Du Mont created television sets and the programming to go with them during the post–World War II years. Courtesy of Twentieth Century Fox.

in any market, and CBS and NBC already dominated in most. Du Mont was forced to resort to the UHF band at a time when few television sets could receive those stations. The early technological leader became a victim of a technological limitation. The Du Mont network disbanded in 1956. Only decades later did a major fourth television network, Fox, come on the scene, ironically making its mark with NFL football. In 1957 Du Mont Laboratories sold its television set business to the Emerson Company.

References

Hess, Gary Newton, *An Historical Study of the Du Mont Television Network*. New York: Arno Press, 1979.

"KTTV TV11." <http://r-vcr.com/~television/TV/TV11.htm>.

Sullivan, Neil. *Captain Video Book: The Du Mont Television Network Story*. Loose-strife Press, 1990.

"Thomas Goldsmith Du Mont Oral History." <http://www.ieee.org/organizations/history_center/oral_histories/transcript/goldsmith8.html/>.

Walter Cummins

DuPont Nylon Stockings

Among the deprivations the civilian population suffered during World War II was the stocking shortage faced by American women. Tradition-ally, they had worn silk hose, but silk became a vital material for military usage, such as in parachutes. Although nylon, a substitute fiber, was introduced to consumers in 1940, it was withdrawn from commercial sale to supply defense needs as tires and glider tow ropes, as well as parachutes.

The E. I. du Pont de Nemours and Company, known as DuPont, had actually developed nylon in the late 1930s and used its pavilion at the New York World's Fair in 1939 to publicize it. At the same time, it launched an advertising campaign, created by advertising agency Batten, Barton, Durstine & Osborn (BBDO), with the slogan, "Better Things for Better Living Through Chemistry," an image-building effort for the com-pany that actually built public demand for a specific product: nylon stockings. The stockings went on sale in May 1940 and were an imme-diate success—so great that supply could not keep up with demand.

Despite the fact that they were less comfortable to wear, nylons looked as good as silk and offered the added benefits of durability and practi-cality. DuPont, confident that it had a superior product, priced the stock-ings 10 percent higher than silk and still captured 30 percent of the hosiery market in less than two years. Then came the attack on Pearl Harbor and the diversion of all nylon to America's military effort. Women, now without either nylon or silk stockings, resorted to painting their legs with tones that emulated the look of stockings, even adding a dark seam line to the back of their calves.

Nylon was developed at DuPont specifically through the work in polymerization by Dr. Wallace H. Carothers, who is credited as the inventor of the fiber. The first testing took place in 1937 under the direction of a research chemist named Everett Vernon Lewis. Lewis, who later worked on the Manhattan Project for the splitting of the atom, claimed management's security precautions to keep nylon secret were tighter than those followed at Los Alamos. After initial problems with wrinkling and dyeing, DuPont was able to produce "full-fashioned hosiery excellent in appearance and free from defects" by the end of that year. Despite Du Pont's attempts at security (as today, protecting proprietary information by not publishing scientific papers on the work in progress, allowing no public relations statements, intimidating those who might try to leak information), word of the invention leaked out through articles in newspapers in 1938 that announced the new strong hoisery and spoke in awe of the scientific miracle of a new wonder fiber made from "coal, air, and water."

At war's end, women clamored for nylons as an important symbol of a return to peacetime and the fruits of new technological breakthroughs. In the winter of 1945, they lined up by the hundreds outside stores that could not fulfill their demands. Newspapers featured stories of women battling over the still scarce product; one headline said, "Women Risk Life and Limb in Bitter Battle over Nylons."

DuPont's advertising campaign and its slogan, "Better Things for Better Living Through Chemistry," continued after the war. The last four words of the slogan—often cited by critics in a cynical way—were used well into the 1970s before the campaign ended. Nylon, the greatest profit maker in DuPont company history, was the impetus for the development of more and better synthetics, including Orlon and Dacron in the 1950s. Today, with many others competing with fabrics such as Goretex and Coolmax, the technology of what people wear allows greater protection and comfort. It all started with nylon.

References

Handley, Susannah. *Nylon: The Story of a Fashion Revolution*. Baltimore, MD: Johns Hopkins University Press, 2000.

Hounshell, David A., and John Kenly Smith, Jr. "The Nylon Drama." In *American Heritage Invention and Technology*, 40–52. Cambridge: Cambridge University Press, 1988.

"Nylon: Miracle or Marketing?" <http://www.si.edu/lemelson/centerpieces/whole_cloth/u7sf/u7materials/sfEssaysmain.html/>.

"Nylon Stockings." <http://www.ideafinder.com/history/inventions/story062.htm/>.

Walter Cummins

Gillette Razors

"Look sharp, feel sharp, be sharp"—that slogan became ingrained in the consciousness of any American male with an interest in sports when it was introduced in the 1940s. The repetition of "sharp" linked the notion of a finely honed cutting edge with the slang connotation of stylish. Batten, Barton, Durstine & Osborn (BBDO), Gillette's advertising agency, developed the campaign. To go with it, Gillette sponsored boxing matches, the Friday night fights, first on radio and then on television in 1946, building the association of a close shave with masculine toughness and athletic skills.

Later in the 1940s, the weekly *Gillette Cavalcade of Sports* was one of the innovators of both the scheduled television sports series and of animation in a commercial, with a barbershop quartet singing an expanded version of the slogan with a parrot that squawked, "How're you fixed for blades?" In 1947 Gillette teamed with Ford to sponsor the first televised World Series in which the New York Yankees beat the Brooklyn Dodgers, paying a total of $65,000 for the rights. Gillette dominated both sports advertising and the razor market in the 1940s.

By that time, the Gillette safety razor had already been around for more than forty years. It was King Camp Gillette, the company's namesake, who came up with the concept of a disposable blade in 1895, but he did not file for a patent until 1901 and begin production until 1903. Before that invention, men shaved with a shaft of stainless steel that folded into a base and required frequent sharpening. The device was called by many a "cut-throat" because it had the appearance and potential of a lethal weapon.

King Gillette's brainstorm was a disposable blade that would be replaced rather than resharpened after a single use. Producing such a device—a small, thin piece of steel that could actually remove whiskers—proved a great technical challenge, one that delayed production and distribution for nearly a decade. Gillette needed an engineering adviser, William Nickerson, and financial backers to launch his company and its primary product.

Central to Gillette's original inspiration was the marketing strategy for which razors are famous—practically give away the razor, and make money from selling the blades. In his first year, Gillette did just that. Of the fifty-one razors and 168 blades he produced, he distributed a number of the razors to friends to whet their interest. Within just a few years, the Gillette Safety Razor Company was turning out thousands of razors and millions of blades.

At first the razors used a separate handle and clamp for fixing the blade, but Gillette created a one-piece unit in the late 1930s, with a handle base that unscrewed to open two wings for inserting and then clamping the blade. This was the razor promoted in the 1940s ads and commercials, the one that served as the standard for several decades. The "Look sharp, feel sharp, be sharp" campaign itself had set standards that BBDO tried to recapture in later campaigns to advertise Gillette's advances in razor technology. A new slogan, primarily for television advertising, was invented to market the Sensor razor in late 1989: "The best a man can get," introduced during a Super Bowl Game television broadcast. The campaign was a great success, as was the Sensor razor, and the slogan is used to advertise each new shaving product, including the three-blade Gillette Mach3.

References

Adams, Russell B., Jr. *King C. Gillette, the Man and His Wonderful Shaving Device.* Boston: Little, Brown, 1978.
"*Advertising Age*'s 50 Best Commercials." <http://adage.com/news_and_features/special_reports/commercials/years.1940.html/>.
"Razors." <http://homepage.dtn.ntl.com/paul.linnell/electricity/razors.html/>.
"Those Were the Days Archives." <http://www.440int.com/twtd/archives/sep30.html/>.

Walter Cummins

Lucky Strike Cigarettes

In the 1940s few, if any, would have even imagined that cigarettes were a health hazard. In fact, cigarette advertising carried endorsements from doctors and photos with a T-shape drawn over the mouth and throat of a smiling face to assure that cigarettes were beneficial to one's "T-zone" (ad-speak for "Taste Zone"). Cigarette rations were considered an imperative comfort for troops at war. Now in a time when tobacco makers, embarrassed by public exposure of secret internal documents and stung by multibillion-dollar liability settlements, remove cartoon figures from billboards and pull ads from youth-oriented magazines, it may be difficult to believe the ubiquity of cigarette advertising in the 1940s. The radio shows of such family favorites as Jack Benny and Fred Allen, for example, were proudly sponsored by Lucky Strikes.

Lucky Strikes, the dominant project of the American Tobacco Company, is responsible for two of the most memorable advertising slogans of the decade, if not the century. First, in 1942, the company proclaimed that "Lucky Strike green has gone to war." The decision to change the color of the pack that had been green since 1917 to white resulted from both patriotic and marketing pressures. Military needs placed a premium on green pigment, but customers also disliked the green pack. The slogan, however, emphasized that the company was doing its bit for the war effort.

An even more striking slogan emerged two years later, in 1944, with "L.S.M.F.T." Today those letters exist as a trivia question, but they also still can be found on the bottom of a Luckies pack. They stand for "Lucky Strikes Means Fine Tobacco." A typical radio commercial of the period would begin with an indecipherable rapid-fire tobacco auctioneer's chant punctuated by the cry of "Sold American!" Another voice would follow, delivering L.S.M.F.T. twice with a telegraphic urgency, then breaking the code and adding, "So firm, so round, so fully packed. So free and easy on the draw," in mellifluous tones. The double entendre of the phrase may have been coincidental, but it got the attention of many preadolescent boys. Those same boys also found humor in plays on the meaning of the letters, with inventions such as "Ladies' Seats Make Fine Targets." Some of their elders used them to make a political statement: "Lord, Save Me from Truman."

A 1999 study conducted by marketing expert James A. Nowakowski to "determine which is better: to use a lot of magazines with a few ad insertions (reach) or a lot of ad insertions in a few magazines (frequency)?" cites L.S.M.F.T. as an example to make the case for frequency: "Frequency, and nothing but frequency, drilled the 'L.S.M.F.T.' message into our collective consciousness, regardless of whether or not we smoked."

References

The American Tobacco Story. American Tobacco Company, 1960.

Bayley, Stephen. *The Lucky Strike Packet by Raymond Loewy*. Frankfurt am Main, Germany: Verlag Form, 1998.

"History 101—Lucky Strikes." <http://www.antiqueadvertising.com/history.html>.

Moilanen, Hanna, and Matti Pitkälä. "Cigarette Brands Sold in the U.S.A.," 1994. <http://www.uta.fi/FAST/US8/PAPS/cigaret.html/>.

Nowakowski, James A. "Frequency or Reach? Understanding the Better Choice in B-to-B Ad Strategy. Marketing to Mining." <http://www/mtm-marketing to mining-LSMFT.htm/>.

Walter Cummins

Pepsi-Cola

By the mid-1940s, a four-line jingle changed the fortunes of the Pepsi Cola Company from forty years of near failure as a soft drink company to a prominence as a contender to Coca-Cola in the public consciousness. In the early 1930s, the Great Depression led Pepsi to the second bankruptcy of its history, no advertising budget, frequent changes in ownership, and few prospects. A resurgence began in 1934 when, under the ownership of Charles Guth, Pepsi doubled the size of its bottles, from six to twelve ounces, and kept the price at five cents. Its competitors offered only six ounces for the same price. Sales rose and output increased.

But it was not until the 1940s that Pepsi became a household name, thanks to a jingle first broadcast in late 1939 which became known by its first line: "Pepsi Cola hits the spot." It pointed out that each bottle contained twice as much soft drink as its rivals'. The jingle was created by Alan Bradley Kent and Austen Herbert Croom-Johnson for the advertising agency of Lord & Thomas, one of several bidding for the account. Despite the conception, Lord & Thomas did not get the account. It went to Newell Emmett, and so did the jingle.

The fifteen-second tune was infectious; people sang and hummed it; a big band version was recorded for jukeboxes. In 1940 it had 300,000 spot plays on the radio, and that number rose in the following years. First known as "Nickel, Nickel," because those words were chanted as a background refrain and then "Pepsi Cola Hits the Spot," it was the first advertising jingle ever broadcast nationwide on radio. It came to be recorded in fifty-five different languages. By the end of World War II, Pepsi had a $4 million advertising budget and had passed both Royal Crown Cola and Dr Pepper in popularity.

Unfortunately for Pepsi, the postwar economy changed the company's fortunes toward the end of the decade; sales dropped $10 million in 1948 alone. The new prosperity made the message of "twice as much" counterproductive, giving Pepsi the impression of a bargain brand when the country was on a spending spree. The Newell Emmett agency was replaced by Milton Biow. After a brief fling with "more bounce to the ounce," by 1950, the cola had turned to a new image, one of low calories and slender women, "the light refreshment that refreshes without filling." For a brief time, even the jingle underwent a rewording for "modern folks who watch their weight."

In the second half of the twentieth century, the Pepsi image and its advertising experienced several transformations as the soft drink sought a new identity and a bigger share of the market. In the late 1950s, it was associated with elegant taste, served at sophisticated parties to men in tuxedos and women in smart gowns. Beginning with the mid-1960s, youth culture dominated, and the target audience became "the Pepsi Generation," reached by pop star singers (including Michael Jackson and Madonna in the 1980s). As Pepsi began to pull even with Coke in sales, it showed that the strategy was working. Admired today for its innovative advertising, Pepsi's success as a brand still owes much to that catchy radio jingle in the 1940s.

References

McDonough, John. "Encyclopedia of Advertising: Pepsi Cola Company." <http://www.fitzroydearborn.com/chicago/advertising/sample-pepsi.asp/>.
Stoddard, Bob. *Pepsi: 100 Years*. Los Angeles: General Publications Group, 1977.
"Walter S. Mack, Jr." <http://www.sodafountain.com/softdrnk/pepsi_wm.htm/>.

Walter Cummins

Smokey Bear

While most people remember his name as Smokey *the* Bear, Smokey Bear was the name the USDA (United States Department of Agriculture) Forest Service gave its fire-fighting icon in 1945 to help raise public awareness about preventing forest fires. This was serious business in the midst of World War II when timber was vital for gunstocks, battleship construction, and other building important to the nation's military effort. The Forest Service enlisted the aid of the War Advertising Council, a newly formed organization of professional advertising people who volunteered their talents, to create an advertising campaign that would alert American citizens to the urgency of preventing forest fires.

For its first ad in 1944, the council used the cartoon figure of Walt Disney's "Bambi" from the movie that was so popular at the time. This convinced them that a forest creature would get the point across most effectively, but they wanted one that was unique to the campaign. Smokey Bear, painted by a well-known artist of animals, Albert Staehle, seemed to have the right kind of appeal. In 1945 he appeared on his first poster, proclaiming, "Smokey Says—Care will prevent 9 out of 10 forest fires." An immediate hit, Smokey Bear soon filled billboards, print advertisements, and more posters. The result of the campaign was a significant decrease in the number of human-caused fires.

After the war, the Smokey campaign, now managed by the Foote, Cone & Belding agency, also began to reach out to children, and the cartoon figure evolved through a number of transformations, with Forest Service artist Rudy Wendelin responsible for many Smokey originals, including those for licensed products. Smokey Bear's most notable slogan, used first in 1947 and repeatedly thereafter was, "Remember, only you can prevent forest fires."

In 1950 a living version of Smokey came to the National Zoo in Washington, D.C. A bear cub who received public attention after surviving a blaze in the Lincoln National Forest, New Mexico, he became a popular zoo attraction. An official Smokey Bear song was released in 1952, and the U.S. Congress passed the Smokey Bear Act to ensure his longevity. By 1964 the U.S. Postal Service had to assign Smokey his own ZIP code (20252) because he received so much mail. Artist Chuck Kuderna drew the Smokey-in-a-forest-ranger's-hat image, familiar today, in 1965.

Smokey's slogan was so familiar that, by 1981, ads needed to use only the first two words: "Only you . . ." By 1984 Smokey was on a postage stamp. Yet, after decades as one of America's dominant symbols of concern for nature, Smokey Bear gradually fell out of favor, his message suddenly suspect. It turns out, experts now say, that a bit of burning has positive benefits, clearing out the dead wood and regenerating the landscape. Even the notion of preventing all forest fires has been called into question, despite the blazes of recent years that have devastated millions of acres in the Western United States during the summers of 2000 and 2001. Reflecting on the demise of Smokey Bear, environmentalist Charles Little wrote that "Smokey's ecological correctness quotient is low, as an increasing number of forest ecologists have been pointing out in recent years. We anthropomorphize at our peril."

Smokey Bear now has his own website, using the slogan, "Only You Can Prevent Wildfires," at www.smokeybear.com/.

References

Morrison, Ellen E. *The Smokey Bear Story*. Detroit, MI: Harlo Press, 1994.

"Ecological Fire Management Strategy." <http://www.mnr.gov.on.ca/MNR/temagami/AP1FIRE.html/>.

"The Enemy: Smokey Bear, Fire Prevention Policy Creates Tinderboxes in the Forests." *New York Times*, 21 August 2000: A8.

Little, Charles E. "Smokey's Revenge." *American Forests*. May/June 1993. <http:www.majbill.vt.edu/history/barrow/hist3144/readings/little.html/>.

"Smokey Bear—A 55-Year Career." <http://forestry.about.com/science/forestry/library/weekly/aa091398.htm/>.

"Smokey Bear—The First Fifty Years." Adapted from USDA Forest Service Publication FS-551. <http://www.odf.state.or.us/smokey/bearfaq2.htm/>.

"Summer of Fire and Ice: Business As Usual?" <http://www.cnn.com/SPECIALS/views/y/2000/09/dykstra.fires.sept7/>.

Walter Cummins

Spam

Today, the word "spam" means junk e-mail, unwanted messages broadcast to thousands of online addresses usually offering get-rich-quick schemes or pornography. In the 1940s, it meant a can of pink luncheon loaf that became a staple both for American troops and for civilians faced with meat rationing.

The basic ingredient of Spam is pig meat, a combination of pork shoulder and ham combined with water and sugar and preserved by sodium nitrate. J. C. Hormel created the product in 1937 but did not see it play a significant role in the American diet until the outbreak of World War II, when Hormel began providing 15 million cans of it to troops each week. Spam became a constant element of soldiers' diets—many GIs were said to be eating it two or three times a day—and it was made available to British and Soviet troops and civilians as well. By 1945 more than 100 million pounds of Spam had been shipped overseas to military forces or aid programs.

The product benefited from several virtues: it stayed fresh, uncontaminated, and edible packaged in cans that could be carried into foxholes and jungles. For those at home at a time when steak and roast beef were infrequent delicacies, it offered inexpensive nourishment, something to put on the plate for the evening meal after sizzling it in the frying pan.

The derivation of the name is debated. Carolyn Wyman, author of *Spam: A Biography*, claims that it came from "spiced ham." Other theories offer as the source "shoulder of pork and ham" or "seasoned pork and ham."

Although Spam can be found on most supermarket shelves today, abundance, variety, and fast food have made it an infrequent menu choice for Americans. Yet an estimated 120 million cans are sold worldwide annually, with the highest per capita consumption on the island of Guam, where typhoons often knock out power for cooking and refrigeration.

In its heyday, Spam became an object of affectionate mockery for soldiers and sailors frustrated with its inevitability in their diets. They called it "ham that didn't pass its physical," "meat loaf without basic training," and "the reason war is hell." While Spam solved a crucial supply problem of feeding troops thousands of miles from home, it also became a dominant symbol for the time away from family and loved ones.

In the decades since the war, Spam has often remained an object of comedy, most prominently in a Monty Python's Flying Circus sketch of the 1970s set in a diner where the waitress recites a menu that includes Spam with every item: "Sausage and Spam; Spam, Spam, bacon and Spam; etc." Although the woman trying to order a meal says, "I don't like Spam!" it is impossible to avoid it. From that sketch evolved the use of the name for bombardments of junk e-mail.

Wyman provides recipes for various Spam dishes, noting that the product has never been blamed for a major illness nor been the object of a government recall. She contends that Spam is the ultimate processed food, resembling nothing found in nature.

References

Eggers, Linda, ed. *The Spam Cookbook: Recipes from Main Street.* Atlanta, GA: Longstreet Press, 1998.
Greenberg, Brigitte. "Biography Celebrates History of Spam." Canoe: Canada's Internet Network. August 19, 1999. <http://www.canoe.ca/CNEWSLife9908/19_spam.html/>.
Wyman, Carolyn. *Spam: A Biography.* San Diego, CA: Harcourt Brace/Harvest Books, 1999.

Walter Cummins

The Studebaker Car

Few remember the name today, but the Studebaker literally turned heads in 1946 when it appeared on American streets, the first new car produced after World War II, beating Ford and Chevrolet. The advertising slogan emphasized the fact: "First by far with a postwar car." But what was most striking about these models was not the fact that they won the race to market. It was their appearance—a metal body of sleek curved lines and large glass windows; that is, in comparison to the boxy designs typical of prewar automobiles. Other new cars, like the Ford and the Dodge, were beginning to round off their edges. Yet no car was as radical as the Studebaker Commander coupe, with its rear window wrapping around to the door posts. Compared to the designs of recent years, it looks tame in retrospect. In 1946, however, people were dumbfounded. The common reaction was, "I can't tell whether it's coming or going." With all that glass, the rear looked like the front. Like the Edsel Ford, which came out some eleven years later, the Studebaker Commander was overdesigned, and the public never liked the looks of it.

Ironically, in its issue of September 16, 1945, *Life* magazine featured the company and its new cars, calling them "the epitome of U.S. industrial accomplishment: the careful work of designing automobile bodies and building jigs, the swift, facile assembly of hundreds of tiny engine parts, the noisy slam-bang job of getting cars through the final assembly line." Behind this paean to manufacturing lies a tribute to the breakneck production of military vehicles and airplanes during the war, when American industry demonstrated its rapid ability to retool and refocus to equip an unbeatable military machine. Studebaker contributed by producing trucks, aircraft engines, and the Weasel, a small tracked vehicle. Between 1941 and 1945, the company turned out 200,000 of its US6 trucks, 63,000 engines for the Boeing B-17 Flying Fortress, and 15,000 versions of the all-terrain Weasel, including one that was amphibious. Such production confirmed the nations strength and power. When the fighting ended, passenger cars would be the reward for prevailing.

Other manufacturers, when the tide of battle had turned to inevitable victory, prepared civilian consumers for the rewards ahead, as exemplified by a Cadillac ad of May 1945, just months before VE day. A tank emerges from fiery explosions and clouds of dark smoke, dominating the page, above it—in large print—the word Cadillac and its aristocratic emblem, below the words, "Peacetime Power *with a* Wartime Job!" The future promised possessions in abundance, a magic time of lives fulfilled by the bounty of American industry. Studebaker boasted of a "postwar miracle of riding comfort," drivers clicking off the highway miles while "luxuriously relaxed."

The Studebaker looked far ahead—perhaps too far—in its design, and Americans did not buy enough of them for the company to survive. In the long run, the Studebaker was a short-lived icon. Still, it presaged the future by revealing how design was racing ahead while most of us clung to a past of comfortable familiarity. Perhaps then the return to prewar normality was the calming need of many, at least as far as autos went. Unfortunately for Studebaker, the Commander was ahead of its time. The Studebaker company shut its factory doors in 1966. Today, when small auto manufacturers, oil producers, and Internet firms cannot compete against the giants of their industries, we see that here too Studebaker was ahead of its time.

References

Moloney, James H. *Studebaker Cars*. Osceola, WI: Motorbooks International, 1994.
"Studebaker: Its Assembly Line Is First to Produce a Postwar Auto." *Life*, September 16, 1945: 66–75.
"Studebaker, World War II and Beyond." <http://www.studebaker100.com/stu/Pg4/>.

Walter Cummins

Texaco Service Stations

Texaco and its service stations became a dominant presence in the late 1940s through the company's association with Milton Berle's comedy-variety television hour, *The Texaco Star Theater*. The company began its existence in 1902 as the Texas Company, and the star with the "T" in the middle became its symbol in 1906. By 1928 that logo identified filling stations in every state. With Benton & Bowles handling Texaco's advertising in the 1940s, it was media sponsorship of the Metropolitan Opera on radio and Berle on television that solidified Texaco's prominence among U.S. companies.

Although not the first important television show, Berle's is regarded as the phenomenon that transformed the United States into a television culture. *The Texaco Star Theater* began on June 8, 1948, and by November it had the highest popularity rating ever recorded in that medium. With television ownership still sparse in the late 1940s, neighbors often gathered at a home with a set on Tuesday nights to watch Berle come on stage in one more outlandish costume. Despite the grainy gray tones of the picture, the audience was mesmerized and within a few years succumbed to the imperative to buy their own televisions. The number of sets in American homes grew from 190,000 at the end of 1948 to 12 million in 1951. Berle's show was a major incentive.

Before the star appeared, the show began with a quartet of men dressed in Texaco uniforms who sang of themselves as "The merry men of Texaco" working "from Maine to Mexico." "Tonight," they crooned, "we may be showmen, but tomorrow we'll be servicing your car."

And service was what they sold. Gasoline is essentially a commodity with few real qualities to distinguish brands. In more recent years, the ads and commercials of the petroleum companies have emphasized driving power, engine-cleaning additives, or fast credit card payment. The Texaco men, in contrast, swarmed over a car with cleaning cloths, dedicated to ensuring that the vehicle was as immaculate as their coveralls. By inference, they promised that not only the vehicle but the stations themselves, including the restrooms, would meet a high standard wherever anyone drove in the nation.

The Texaco Star Theater and the Texaco commercials themselves were symptomatic of a time that emphasized friendliness, community, and predictability, the very attributes satirized as colorless conformity in the film *Pleasantville*, a film produced in 1998 about the 1950s. Neighbors congregated to watch the Texaco show, and practically the entire country was its audience, sharing memories and reactions at work, school, and shops the next day. The country participated in this national ritual until the mid-1950s. They expected friendly service when they pulled into a Texaco station to fill their tank—oil checked, windshields washed, whitewalls scrubbed.

References

Berle, Milton. *Milton Berle, an Autobiography*. With Haskel Frankel. New York: Delacorte Press, 1974.
"Explore and Discover—Texaco." <www.texaco.com>.

Walter Cummins

6

Icons of the 1950s

Though the 1950s have been reprised as a time of *Happy Days* and *Grease*, their reality was a little less poodle skirt and bobby sox and more Cold War and McCarthyism. When the decade began, Harry Truman was president, having decisively won the 1948 election over Thomas Dewey (despite newspaper headlines declaring Dewey the winner). The Communists had taken over China in 1949, and by June 1950, the North Koreans, with the help of China and the Soviet Union, had crossed the 38th parallel and invaded South Korea. Truman declared a national emergency, and American troops went to fight in Korea, a conflict from which World War II hero General Douglas MacArthur was recalled by Truman for his conflicting view of how to conduct the war.

Meanwhile, at home, a Red Scare mania took hold, led by Senator Joseph McCarthy of Wisconsin, who held hearings to root out Communists in powerful positions. The Soviet Union was the enemy, and the Cold War was under way. Alger Hiss, a former U.S. State Department official, was convicted of perjury in 1950, and Julius and Ethel Rosenberg were executed in 1953 after being convicted of transmitting atomic secrets to the Soviets. In 1957 the Soviets launched an earth satellite, *Sputnik*, which put them way ahead in what would be called the space race.

The Republican administration of General Dwight D. Eisenhower, president from 1952 through 1960, pursued middle-of-the-road policies that kept the nation steadily growing as people moved to the suburbs, made more money, and turned the 1950s into a boom time in consumerism. Advertising enjoyed boom times too, with television offering unprecedented entry into the family living room. The car companies advertised heavily, their products much in demand as improved highways put Americans on the road in record numbers. Advertising went up 75 percent during the decade, with General Motors leading the way. Ad agencies were born, merged, and prospered. *The Man in the Gray*

Flannel Suit (1955), a novel by Sloan Wilson, and *The Hucksters* (1946), written by Frederic Wakeman, portrayed admen as heroes—or villains— in a punishing, demoralizing rat race, a stereotype that extended to portraits of big business in general in *The Organization Man* (1956), written by William Whyte.

Advertising was taking a new direction with something called motivational research, or MR, which delved into the unconscious realms of consumer motivation, pioneered by Freudian Ernest Dichter. He made his name by informing Chrysler that they were not selling as many convertibles as sedans because the sedan stood for the wife in the male mind while the convertible stood for the mistress. Such explanations led to to new forms of research to discover the hidden springs of consumer motivation. Psychological research had had a vogue in the 1920s with inquiries into consumers' rational behavior, as psychologists like John Watson of Harvard, hired by J. Walter Thompson, and pollster George Gallup at Young & Rubicam researched and surveyed consumer activity. Now that advertising was probing the unconscious, the question of subliminal advertising pitches was raised, and Vance Packard wrote a book about it, *The Hidden Persuaders* (1957). Did those ice cubes in the highball glass contain sexual images seen only by the unconscious? Nobody could prove it.

Advertising capitalized on the domestic reign of women, now returned with a vengeance to the home in the postwar 1950s and presiding over a household of little baby boomers who would change the rest of the century in their quest for the good life. Advertising copy had mostly been written by men until such female copywriters as Shirley Polykoff of Foote, Cone & Belding came along, writing copy that would reach women with better aim. A glance at any women's magazine in the period tells the story: ads for new kitchens, full of the latest appliances, in color; the nursery, outfitted to the nines; and the dressing table, replete with cosmetics, filled the pages. The emphasis for women was on domesticity, motherhood, and femininity. Ozzie and Harriet Nelson reigned on television, portraying the cozy family of the suburban 1950s.

Meanwhile, countercultural forces, such as the Beats and the subversive music of rock and roll, began to disrupt the calm. Elvis Presley made his first record in 1954, appeared on Ed Sullivan's television show, and made many movies. His slicked-back hair à la Brylcreem ("A little dab'll do ya") and his laid-back style, along with that of James Dean in the movie *Rebel Without a Cause* (1955), gave the decade a look and a body language made famous in later reprisals of the decade. Despite the adult outcry and paranoia over what he was doing to "family values," America's younger generation embraced Elvis, put on blue jeans, and marched into the 1960s waving a banner of youth culture that would turn everything, including advertising, upside down.

References

Fox, Stephen. *The Mirror Makers: A History of American Advertising and Its Creators.* New York: William Morrow, 1984.

Sivulka, Juliann. *Soap, Sex, and Cigarettes: A Cultural History of American Advertising.* Belmont, CA: Wadsworth, 1997.

Mary Cross

The Chevrolet Corvette

Few things are more indicative of style trends in America than the design of cars, and in the 1950s, Chevrolet introduced a car that was not only in the forefront of design in the decade, but also came to stand for the decade's aesthetic. The Corvette, the first American-made sports car, was introduced in 1953 in all white with a red interior at a high-end price of $3,490. It was General Motors' answer to the British MG, a two-seater sports car which had been popular with returning GIs at the end of the 1940s. Harley Earl, head of GM's styling division, had charged his design team, "Go all the way and then back off." The result was a sleek, low-lying glass fiber machine with a grill reminiscent of the Ferrari and other European cars. It was, comments Stephen Bayley, author of *Harley Earl and the Dream Machine*, "a car which wore its pretensions on the outside instead of in the crankcase" The Corvette, according to Bayley, "was to the car what *Gone With the Wind* was to weepy movies."

As forward looking as the Corvette was, it was not a huge success on the market. It did not handle well as a sports car, and when Ford came out with the Thunderbird two years later, it outsold the Corvette by 23 to 1. A second engineer, Zora Arkus-Duntov, was brought in to General Motors to improve and refine the Corvette, but it was not until the 1960s that a total redesign and a new name, Sting Ray, brought out the buyers and gave the car the kind of cult status that would, for example, inspire songs like Prince's "Little Red Corvette" in the 1980s. Today, there is an entire museum dedicated to the Corvette, next door to the Corvette factory in Bowling Green, Kentucky. Every classic car show worth its hubcaps has to include at least one well-preserved Corvette.

Chevrolet itself was riding high in the 1950s. In addition to the Corvette, it had two other sporty cars in its stable: the Bel Air, launched in 1951; and the Impala, which came out in 1958 and seemed the apotheosis of the decade's design with its chrome, bullet tail lights, and whitewall tires. It was available as either a coupe or a convertible, perfect for the blossoming American car culture in the post–World War II years. Families and their cars moved to the suburbs and spawned a huge system of car-friendly roadways as well as the drive-in restaurants and movie theaters made famous later in the television show *Happy Days* and movies like *American Graffiti* and *Grease*. Patriotism ran high too, and Chevrolet's 1951 television campaign with Dinah Shore singing "See the U.S.A. in your Chevrolet" reached a receptive audience.

Chevrolet, a division of General Motors, had masterfully advertised its cars with the help of ad agency Campbell-Ewald since 1922. With *The Dinah Shore Chevy Show*, it had a television hit on its hands for the next twelve years, propelling the company to the top of the car market and outpacing its chief rival, Ford. Dinah Shore, like Doris Day, was a girl-next-door type who sang a catchy jingle inviting Americans to drive their Chevrolets through "the greatest land of all." She blew everybody a kiss at the end of the song. The song, written by Leon Carr and Leo Corday, was like a national anthem at a time when Americans' love affair with their cars was blossoming. According to *Advertising Age*, *The Dinah Shore Chevy Show* made Chevrolet an American icon. Though the show ended in 1963, Chevrolet revived the song in 1999 ads, with other American icons like the Statue of Liberty and Marilyn Monroe in the spotlight.

References

Bayley, Stephen. *Harley Earl and the Dream Machine*. New York: Alfred A. Knopf, 1983.
"Corvette History." <http://www.allsands.com/>.

Mary Cross

Clairol Hair Color

Dyeing one's hair was considered the mark of a "fast" woman even in the 1950s when Clairol launched its taboo-busting ad campaign for Miss Clairol on the line, "Does She . . . or Doesn't She?" At the time, people thought that only actresses and prostitutes colored their hair. It was an uphill battle to convince respectable women that using hair color was acceptable. The campaign, which ran for eighteen years straight, used pictures of mothers and daughters rather than glamorous models. By 1960 Clairol had captured more than 50 percent of the market.

Nice girls in the 1950s did not dye their hair, nor would they admit to noticing the double-entendre in Miss Clairol's slogan. The advertising media did, however, and objected at first. *Life* magazine, which ran photos of bikini-clad models and actresses clad in negligees on its covers, thought the slogan was too sexually suggestive and refused to accept the ad until it polled its female employees, who claimed they saw nothing wrong with it. The ad ran in *Life* in 1956, and in 1958 Clairol put it on television.

Shirley Polykoff, a copywriter at Foote, Cone & Belding, wrote the famous slogan that *Advertising Age* later ranked among the top ten of the century. Remembering her future mother-in-law's initial reaction to her own color-treated hair (she was a natural blonde but there was upkeep), Polykoff came up with "Does She . . . or Doesn't She?," followed by the line, "Only her mother knows for sure." This was changed to "Only her hairdresser knows for sure" to avoid offending beauty salons which did most of the coloring at the time. Even in a salon, coloring hair was a messy, expensive, and sometimes all-day process. Given the intense social disapproval of dyed hair, only a reported 7 percent of women in the mid-1950s would admit they colored their grey, changed their color, or bleached their hair blonde. This is a far cry from today, when any color goes, blondes proliferate, and very few women leave their grey hair unretouched. But in the 1950s, the whole idea of coloring one's hair was so suspect that magazines refused to run hair-color ads, and banks were wary of offering financing to companies that made hair color.

The Miss Clairol Hair Color Bath had been introduced in 1950 in a one-step version that would make coloring hair as easy as shampooing it, but even then the product made no headway against social attitudes. It took nearly twenty years and the long-running Foote, Cone & Belding ad campaign to turn the tide. The number of women who admitted to coloring their hair had increased dramatically by the 1970s, a bonus not only for Clairol but also for competitor L'Oreal, which challenged Clairol's dominance with its own "I'm Worth It" campaign in the 1970s.

Polykoff wrote other attention-getting lines for Clairol in the 1960s, including, "Is it true blondes have more fun?" and "If I've only one life, let me live it as a blonde!" As a result of the success of the Miss Clairol campaign, she was promoted to executive vice president of Foote, Cone & Belding and was chosen advertising woman of the year in 1967.

Lawrence Gelb and his wife, Joan, brought the small Clairol company to the United States in 1930 from France after they bought the U.S. marketing rights and formed the Clairol Corporation. The company developed the one-step hair color, Miss Clairol Hair Color Bath, after conducting dye chemical experiments, attending trade shows to hold demonstrations for beauticians, and using Joan as a model in marketing presentations. The success of its eighteen-year advertising campaign led to the development of Loving Care (Polykoff: "Hate that gray? Wash it away"), Lady Clairol, and Nice 'n Easy. From 1985 to 1991, the company revived the original slogan in its print ads and launched a new, more expensive product, Ultress, with *Dynasty* star Linda Evans and, later, model Linda Evangelista as spokeswomen.

Clairol remained the leader in the hair-coloring market until 1998 when L'Oreal overtook it. Clairol is now part of Procter & Gamble, which purchased Clairol in 2001 for $5 billion.

References

Gladwell, Malcolm. "Annals of Advertising: True Colors." *New Yorker*, 22 March 1999:70–81.

Thomas, Robert McG., Jr. "Shirley Polykoff, 90, Ad Writer Whose Query Colored a Nation." *New York Times*, June 8, 1998.

Mary Cross

Colgate Toothpaste

Since most brands of toothpaste are more or less the same, advertising agencies and their copywriters scramble to give their toothpaste a unique characteristic that distinguishes it from all others. For Colgate toothpaste (then called dental cream) in the 1950s, this crystallized around a new copywriting concept called the "unique selling proposition," or USP, dreamed up by adman Rosser Reeves of the Ted Bates Agency, whose idea would become gospel among copywriters and in advertising text-books. As Reeves put it in his own book, *Reality in Advertising* (1961), the USP was a way of cloaking the product in newness and giving the consumer a strong claim on which to focus.

In the case of Colgate, the USP was capsuled in the slogan, "It Cleans Your Breath While It Cleans Your Teeth," written by copywriter Alicia Tobin. The television and print campaign using this slogan in the 1950s took Colgate to first place in the toothpaste market, followed by Pepso-dent and Ipana. The so-called toothpaste wars, with each company vying to outdo the other with a new selling feature, had begun.

Colgate had had other unique selling angles in the past. It was the first toothpaste to be packaged in a tube, in 1896, and by 1911 it had added the flavor of mint. At the beginning of the century, toothpaste was not considered a necessity. People lived with bad breath and bad teeth. William Colgate, a soap, starch, and candle maker in New York City in 1806, founded the Colgate Company but did not live to see it introduce its first toothpaste in 1873, sold at that time in porcelain jars. In the 1900s, the company began handing out free samples of the den-tifrice along with toothbrushes to schoolchildren and their teachers. By the 1940s, toothpaste was considered a necessary part of daily hygiene.

In the 1950s, another new ingredient Colgate called "Gardol" gave the company a new USP and allowed it to talk about preventing tooth decay as well. Print ads asked, "Should a girl let her boy-friend kiss her good night?" (yes, if she can get him to brush with Colgate). Celebrating its 150th anniversary in 1956, Colgate, now Colgate-Palmolive, held a solid market share, but Procter & Gamble's toothpaste, Crest, overtook it by the end of the 1950s with fluoride, another USP-inspired ingredient it called Fluoristan. The Crest "Look, Ma! No cavities!" Television ad campaign engineered by Benton & Bowles in 1958 became a classic.

The ups and downs of the toothpaste war continued. Fast-forward to the 1990s when Colgate came out with Colgate Total in 1997, a toothpaste that claimed to work for twelve hours to combat gingivitis, tartar, cavities, plaque, and bad breath. It won the approval of both the U.S. Food and Drug Administration and the American Dental Association. By 1998 Colgate was once again definitely the market leader in toothpaste.

References

Fox, Stephen. *The Mirror Makers: A History of American Advertising and Its Creators.* New York: William Morrow, 1984.
Reeves, Rosser. *Reality in Advertising.* New York: Alfred A. Knopf, 1961.

Mary Cross

De Beers Diamonds

The idea of a diamond engagement ring is a fairly new one in the annals of romance, and the De Beers Corporation diamond company and its advertising agency can take some credit for making diamonds such popular tokens of affection. Its "A diamond is forever" advertising campaign, beginning in 1948, created by N. W. Ayer & Son with a slogan by copywriter Frances Gerety, revived the diamond market, slumping since the 1930s, and helped make the diamond ring an icon of the rituals of love and marriage. According to *Advertising Age*, by 1951, 80 percent of marriages in the United States began with a diamond ring. The United States now buys 50 percent of the world's diamonds, most of them from De Beers and its mines, and an estimated 70 percent of American women own at least one diamond.

The De Beers story begins with Sir Ernest Oppenheimer who took over Cecil Rhodes's diamond empire in South Africa in 1929 and built the company, then called De Beers Consolidated Mines, Ltd., into a virtual cartel which has managed to dominate the world diamond market ever since. The Ayers advertising campaign was begun when Sir Ernest was having trouble finding markets for his diamonds in the period after the Great Depression. He sent his 29-year-old son, Harry, to New York to meet with Ayer and plan the campaign. The Ayer agency researched the psychological attitudes of Americans about gift giving and romance and came up, initially, with a soft-spoken campaign illustrated with art by Picasso, Dali, and Dufy with such lines as, "Each memory in turn is treasured in the lovely, lighted depths of her engagement diamond." Ayer, trying to change social attitudes about diamonds, also launched a public relations campaign with a weekly news service to the media describing the diamonds of various Hollywood screen stars. They urged political and social celebrities to show off their diamond rings and women's magazines to promote the diamond. Women were encouraged to think of the diamond as a badge, a mark of her man's affection (and the size of his wallet).

When the Soviet Union began flooding world markets and driving down prices with small diamonds in the 1950s, De Beers saved its own diamond prices by inventing the "eternity" ring, a band of twenty-five matched small diamonds, to mark wedding anniversaries. The company promoted the idea of investment and lifelong ownership of diamonds, educating the public about carat size, color, clarity, and cut. Despite the mythologizing, the diamond itself, though classified among the precious stones, is not the rarest of the world's gems and, contrary to popular belief, the resale value of a diamond is often below its wholesale price.

During an early 1990s slump in the diamond market, De Beers launched a worldwide print and television advertising campaign, "Shadows," created with J. Walter Thompson in London and N. W. Ayers in the United States, with local agencies modifying the ads to suit different countries. Male and female models were photographed in shadowy silhouette; the only color was in the shimmering diamond necklaces, bracelets, and rings in the foreground. Classical music supplied the elegant ambience, and the tagline, "A diamond is forever," remained a prominent feature. The campaign revived the diamond business for De Beers and raised the average price of a diamond.

The De Beers Corporation is now under the direction of Nicky Oppenheimer, who ascended to the position upon the death of his father, Harry, in September 2000.

References

Epstein, Edward Jay. *The Rise and Fall of Diamonds: The Shattering of a Brilliant Illusion.* New York: Simon and Schuster, 1982.

Griggs, Robyn. "For De Beers, a Great Slogan Is Forever." *Advertising Age: The Advertising Century.* Special Supplement. Chicago, Crain Communications, 1999: 20.

Kanfer, Stefan. *The Last Empire: South Africa, Diamonds, and De Beers from Cecil Rhodes to the Oppenheimers.* New York: Farrar Straus Giroux, 1993.

Mary Cross

Hathaway Shirts

The Man in the Hathaway Shirt, a series of 1950s ads, featured a picture of a distinguished-looking man wearing an eyepatch and a handsome shirt in the midst of his surroundings—a private library, an art auction, a sailboat—which showed him to be a sophisticated man of the world. The ads made an icon out of the man, almost a 1950s masculine ideal, much as Arrow Shirts had done in the 1920s with ads featuring the handsome blond Arrow shirt man who made women swoon.

Actually, when adman David Ogilvy put an eyepatch on the Hathaway shirt man in a 1951 *New Yorker* ad, Hathaway shirts had already been on the market for nearly 100 years. Ogilvy's man in the Hathaway shirt, however, sold shirts like never before, with sales growing 300 percent and establishing C. F. Hathaway and Company as a leader in men's clothing, outdistancing its decades-long rival, Arrow Shirts.

The eyepatch was a witty way to get attention—Ogilvy claimed he had just picked it up at a drugstore on the way to the photo shoot—but the man in the shirt also had interesting adventures—conducting an orchestra, fencing, sailing, opening champagne, and buying paintings—all situations Ogilvy said he himself would like to experience. The Hathaway man was pictured as an elegant connoisseur in luxurious surroundings; the eyepatch gave him an air of mystery. He was not just a model but a man with an interesting life just like the Hathaway man. He was a White Russian named Baron George Wrangell. The campaign, managed by the Ogilvy, Benson, and Mather agency, also featured sailor Colin Leslie Fox, who had crossed the Atlantic solo, in its 1960s campaign for Hathaway. For a joke, comedian Woody Allen put on the eyepatch and posed for an ad, pretending to be the super-sophisticated Hathaway man. In the 1970s, the Green Domatch agency got the account and featured golfer Jack Nicklaus as the new Hathaway man.

Hathaway shirts, in white cotton with a detachable collar, were made by hand when Charles F. Hathaway started his Waterville, Maine, factory in 1853, which produced two dozen shirts a week at $2.50 each. Hathaway died in 1893, but the business was carried on by his heirs. After World War I, men wanted soft collars, not detachable ones, and the Hathaway company experimented with a variety of collars, including the buttondown. Ellerton Jette took over the company after the Great Depression and built the company up, using new, colorful fabrics ("Never wear a white shirt before sundown," he advised) and adding a small red "H" to the gusset of every shirt.

Until the 1950s, the shirts had never been advertised west of the Hudson River. The Warner Company took over in the 1970s, and the company was sold in 1986 to Warnaco which tried to close the factory. Protests and assistance from the Maine governor and a private investment group reopened the company, and a new line of Hathaway shirts was produced in 1998. The eyepatch campaign, which had run through 1986, was revived in 1998.

References

Morgan, Hal. *Symbols of America*. New York: Penguin Books, 1987.
Ogilvy, David. *Confessions of an Advertising Man*. New York: Atheneum, 1964.
————. *Ogilvy on Advertising*. New York: Crown Publishers, 1983.

Mary Cross

The Jolly Green Giant
(Green Giant Vegetables)

The Jolly Green Giant of canned pea fame stepped off the grocery shelves to become a television star in the 1950s when ad agency Leo Burnett of Chicago launched a campaign to make him better known. The first commercials, which used men painted green and puppet figures with green rubber to depict the giant, had awkward moments. The Green Giant looked like a monster and scared children. With animation, the Green Giant began to look jollier and, pictured in silhouette or partial view, was less threatening (he would be seventy feet tall if he stepped out of his valley). Burnett added the Jolly to his name and, to lighten things up, gave him a hearty laugh, "Ho Ho Ho," along with a song, "Good Things from the Garden." The sixty-second commercial also showed his helpers picking vegetables in the green valley behind him. The Jolly Green Giant became such an icon of American advertising that *Advertising Age* named him one of the top three of the 20th century, after Kellogg's Tony the Tiger (#1) and the Marlboro man (#2).

The phrase "green giant," which had first appeared on the Minnesota Valley Canning Company's packaging in 1925, was used to describe a new variety of unusually large peas, the Prince of Wales, which the company had begun to can. The idea for the giant himself was borrowed from a book of Grimm's fairy tales, according to company lore. Actually, the giant was not green in the beginning. When artist Jack Baker drew his picture holding up a huge peapod in the company's first ads in 1928, the giant was pale and anemic looking, wearing a bearskin. He turned green in 1930 for a campaign launched in the *Ladies' Home Journal*, and he started to appear on cans of yellow corn as well as green peas. In 1950 the company even changed its name to the Green Giant Company.

The Jolly Green Giant has been named one of the top three icons of 20th-century American advertising. Courtesy of Pillsbury.

The name change came on the advice of Leo Burnett, who had been handling the Minnesota Valley Canning Company account since 1935. He also took the giant out of his bearskin and put him in leaves, helping to make the Green Giant gradually less threatening, looking today more like a Disney character than a caveman. The company gave him a television sidekick in 1972 called Little Green Sprout who humanized the giant further. Meanwhile, the Green Giant Company had moved into frozen foods, taking on Birds Eye, its main competitor, and dressing the giant in a leafy toga and a red scarf he wore only on frozen food packages. For his seventy-fifth anniversary in 1999, the giant starred in a national print campaign, created by Burnett, with taglines like, "Give peas a chance."

The Jolly Green Giant now appears on thirty-five products in twenty-six countries. Based in Minneapolis, Minnesota, Green Giant, a brand of the Pillsbury Company, is the largest vegetable brand in the world.

References

Fox, Stephen. *The Mirror Makers: A History of American Advertising and Its Creators.* New York: William Morrow, 1984.

Sivulka, Juliann. *Soap, Sex, and Cigarettes: A Cultural History of American Advertising.* Belmont, CA: Wadsworth, 1998.

"Yearlong Celebration Kicks off 75 Years of the Jolly Green Giant." Pillsbury Company press release, August 10, 1999.

Mary Cross

Levi's 501 Jeans

The blue jeans worn by the Beat poets of the 1950s and aspiring rebels and hippies of the 1960s started out as button-fly 501 jeans for workmen in the late 19th century. A dry goods salesman in San Francisco named Levi Strauss, a German immigrant, and his partner, tailor Jacob Davis, began making riveted pocket "waist overalls" for miners and received a patent for the fastenings in 1873. Strauss used sturdy fabrics like brown cotton duck and thick denim (the word comes from the name of a French fabric, *serge de Nîmes*) that could stand up to the manual labor performed by these men. The word jeans, which came into use later, actually refers to a different, less sturdy fabric, *gene*, made in Genoa and worn by Genovese sailors.

Strauss advertised his pants as "cut full, honestly made." His 1886 trademark, showing two horses in a tug of war with the riveted pants, is one of the oldest in the United States and is still displayed on Levi's 501 jeans (the 501 is the original lot number on the jeans, a garment industry method used to identify pattern and fabric).

In the 1900s, the original riveted 501 jeans were worn strictly by miners, farmers, cowboys, and laborers. Though Levi Strauss died in 1902, his four nephews took over the company and rebuilt it after the San Francisco earthquake in 1906. The company produced plain and printed muslin shirts and denim jackets as well as jeans. Though sold only west of the Mississippi, Levi Strauss clothing established the brand as solid and trustworthy, setting the standard for work clothes.

Little did Strauss or his nephews dream that, as early as the 1930s when the movies gave the cowboy and the American West heroic stature, Levi's jeans would become a status symbol of mythic proportions. No longer just for laborers, blue jeans signaled new messages about self-expression and independence. This was not lost on the company, which capitalized on the trend in its advertising (handled by its longtime agency Foote, Cone & Belding of San Francisco) giving Levi's jeans the cachet of things authentically American. By the 1940s and World War II, even departing GIs were careful to protect their treasured blue jeans, packing them into their overseas duffel bags to keep them from being borrowed by those back home.

In the 1950s, the Levi Strauss Company began to market their products nationally, selling more casually styled denim pants, designed for the

whole family. But jeans were acquiring a different, darker meaning, ~
ing to stand for the social outlaw and the juvenile delinquent. Parents
and teachers punished students who wore jeans to school and were out-
raged at Levi's ads that proclaimed the jeans "Right for School." James
Dean, not John Wayne, was the new American hero in blue jeans. Wearing jeans in the 1950s meant you hung out in the wrong places and had
a bad reputation. By the late 1960s, however, protesting college students
had made jeans de rigeur as a way of proclaiming one's hipness and
opposition to adult society.

Designer and private-label jeans, cashing in on the cachet of jeans,
began to make inroads into Levi's lead in the market by the 1980s. Levi's
launched a blitz of advertising, the "501 Blues" campaign, managed by
Foote, Cone & Belding, to reestablish the brand's cool factor among
young men. In 1995, targeting yet another new generation of potential
jeans wearers, a print and television "501 Reasons" campaign promoted
the button-fly 501 jeans using such irreverent tag lines as, "That's a dangerous place to put a zipper." The campaign never quite got through all
501 reasons (supposedly locked up in a safety deposit box), but Levi's
sales and stature increased, and Foote, Cone & Belding won awards and
was named agency of the year by *Advertising Age* in 1996 for the campaign.

Levi's 501 jeans, originally made for miners, have become powerful,
iconic garments over their 128-year existence, and those 1960s college
students, forty years older and a little thicker in the middle, still wear
them—maybe in a bigger size.

References

Berger, Arthur Asa. *Reading Matter: Multidisciplinary Perspectives on Material Culture.* New Brunswick, NJ: Transaction Publishers, 1992.
Levi Strauss & Company. "The History of Denim." March 6, 2001. <http://
www.levistrauss.com/about/denim.html>.

Mary Cross

The Maidenform Bra

The Maidenform "I Dream" ads were considered daring in the 1950s
when the $20 million print ad campaign presented the nation with pic-
tures of elegant women in beautiful clothes cavorting in exotic and ex-
citing locales—topless in public, except for their bras. Variations of the
headline, "I dreamed I went shopping (or sailing or dancing or skating)
in my Maidenform bra," "I dreamed I was a social butterfly in my Mai-

The "I dreamed . . ." campaign pictured women in fantasy scenarios, wearing their Maidenform bras.

denform bra," "I dreamed I had spring fever in my Maidenform bra," spoke to women's fantasies and ideas of romance even if no 1950s woman would ever consider going out in public in her underwear. The campaign, needless to say, made the brand famous at home and abroad and made the brassiere a staple of women's attire. Nearly every female in America, from the budding pubescent in the training bra to the full-figured matron, felt she had to wear one.

When the "I Dream" campaign began under the aegis of the Norman, Craig & Kummel agency, Maidenform had just introduced the concept of the cup size, further customizing the brassiere. Women were already cramming themselves into girdles and Merry Widow waist-cinchers in the 1950s; now they had to be fitted for a bra and shop for their size. The "I Dream" campaign made it important to look good even under one's clothes. Some said the campaign spoke to women's innate exhibi-tionist tendencies; feminists both applauded and complained; and the media made fun of it. The ads, nonetheless, were beautifully done. Major photographers, including Richard Avedon and Irving Penn, took the pic-tures, and glamorous models were dressed in designer outfits created by Arnold Scaasi and Pierre Cardin, among others.

In the early days of the century, the brassiere, from an old French word meaning armor, was not a standard item in American women's ward-robes. The corset, with a camisole under it, laced women in whalebone to achieve the desired (and dangerous) hourglass figure. World War I and the ensuing flapper flat-chested look, achieved with a wrapped ban-deau, spelled the doom of the corset, but not until rayon and nylon came on the scene in the 1940s did the brassiere really come into its own. It was a feat of engineering made possible by the new fabrics and given a boost by the enduring American obsession with breasts that made low-cut dresses acceptable even in Victorian times and got the sweater girl of World War II painted on the sides of combat planes. Breast-enhancement surgery and implants, common today, testify to the contin-uing fascination and sex appeal of the breast for Americans. Women can now purchase brassieres in almost any shape, color, size, and price, thanks to Maidenform and its chief competitors, Warner's, Bali, Vanity Fair, and Playtex.

The Maiden Form Brassiere Company was started in 1930 when the owners of a custom dress company in New York City, Enid Frocks, re-alized that the bras they were sewing into their dresses were in demand as separate items. One of the owners, Enid Bissett, observing a newly curvaceous look on French women during a trip to Paris, came home and constructed a brassiere she and her partner, Ida Rosenthal, decided to manufacture. Their first advertising slogan, in 1934, announced, "There's a Maiden Form for Every Type of Figure." They advertised on

New York buses and Atlantic City billboards as well as in newspapers, magazines, and on the radio.

Copywriter Mary Fillius is credited with the "I Dream" concept. The campaign never ran on television but it kept going in print for twenty years, appearing in seventy countries and making Maidenform (one word by 1960) the best-known name in the world of brassieres. When women started burning their bras in the feminist days of the 1960s, the Maidenform "I Dream" ads began to seem out of date and were brought to a halt in 1969. The campaign was replaced in 1969 by the Maidenform Woman ("You Never Know Where She'll Turn Up"). The brassiere reached true iconic status, perhaps, when Madonna wore the cone-shaped creation of Jean-Paul Gaultier during one of her concert tours, a one-of-a-kind bra she recently sold at auction.

The Rosenthals' daughter, Beatrice Coleman, and her husband, Joseph, led the company for many years, tripling its sales. The family sold the business in 1997. Oaktree Capital, LLC, now controls the majority of the company's shares.

References

Fontanel, Beatrice. *Support and Seduction: The History of Ccorsets and Bras*, translated by Willard Wood. New York: Harry N. Abrams, 1997.

Spivey, Angela. "Laced, Cinched, and Bound." *Endeavors*, 1999. <www.research.unc.edu/endeavors.htm>.

Mary Cross

Wheaties

Wheaties, a simple cereal of whole-grain low-fat wheat, has had a long connection with the sports world. The first official Wheaties spokesperson was Olympic star Bob Richards, who began endorsing Wheaties in 1958 and continued until 1970. Such sports stars and their endorsements became the signature of Wheaties advertising and packaging beginning in the 1950s, giving the cereal a powerful presence in the market. It was indeed the "Breakfast of Champions," as its slogan said. Endorsements of Wheaties came from many famous athletes, including Babe Ruth and Joe DiMaggio, and the information on athletes and sports events featured on Wheaties boxes made good reading on American breakfast tables. The old boxes have become valuable collectibles.

In a 1950s print ad, Wheaties honored the first black in major league baseball, Jackie Robinson of the Brooklyn Dodgers, as "Champion of the Year." Robinson was quoted in the ad: "A lot of us ball players go for

Boxes of Wheaties featured baseball players and other sports figures in 1950s advertising. Courtesy of the General Mills Archive.

milk, fruit, and Wheaties." It was a sort of "Guess Who's Coming to Breakfast" breakthrough like the Sidney Poitier movie, *Guess Who's Coming to Dinner*, in which the surprise guest is a black man. Wheaties would continue to break racial barriers. Wheaties honored Robinson again in 1997 during Black History Month with the release of a limited-edition Wheaties box and donated $5,000 to the Jackie Robinson Foundation and to the Negro Leagues. For the "You Better Eat Your Wheaties" ad campaign, Wheaties had basketball star Michael Jordan as spokesman for ten years, from 1988 to 1998. Golfer Tiger Woods has succeeded him.

Wheaties first became known in 1924 when the company, Washburn Crosby of Minneapolis, bought a local radio station, giving it the call numbers of its own initials (WCCO), and began broadcasting advertisements for the cereal. In 1928 the company merged with other milling companies to become General Mills. Wheaties is its oldest brand of cereal.

The slogan, "Breakfast of Champions," was adopted in 1933 when advertising executive Knox Reeves of Blackett-Sample-Hummert thought it up for a billboard located at a Minneapolis ballpark. Radio sports broadcasts were popular, and Wheaties was a frequent sponsor (at one point in the 1930s, Ronald Reagan did baseball sportscasting for Wheaties), making the initial connection between sports and a breakfast cereal that would be its advertising trademark. General Mills sponsored the first televised sports program in 1938, a game between the Cincinnati Reds and the Brooklyn Dodgers, with Red Barber doing the commentary. The company also sponsored a radio program, *Jack Armstrong, the All-American Boy*, who played football and basketball. During the 1950s, General Mills tried to corner the market for children with Wheaties, by sponsoring *The Lone Ranger* and *The Mickey Mouse Club* and by promoting new cereals, including Cocoa Puffs, Trix, Frosty Os, and later, Lucky Charms. The sports connection for Wheaties, however, was more powerful.

Along with its rivals in the cereal market, Kellogg's, Post's, and Quaker Oats, General Mills has flooded the grocery shelves with cereal, including Cheerios, a best-seller. Wheaties, still sporting the slogan "The Breakfast of Champions" holds it own as one of the company's strongest brands.

References

Gray, James. *Business Without Boundary: The Story of General Mills*. Minneapolis: University of Minnesota Press, 1954.

Wojahn, Ellen. *Playing by Different Rules*. New York, American Management, 1988.

Mary Cross

Winston Cigarettes

If the first job of any advertisement is to get attention, the ad campaign for Winston cigarettes in the 1950s did it extremely well by deliberately using bad grammar: "Winston tastes good—like a cigarette should." As every English teacher will tell you, "like" is a preposition and must not be used as a conjunction to introduce a full clause. Correctly worded, the slogan should use "as" instead of "like." Along with arousing the grammarians of the country, the slogan made the campaign one of the most famous and profitable for the R. J. Reynolds Tobacco Company. In response to those who objected to the slogan's using the preposition "like" as a conjunction, the company added the tagline, "What do you want? Good grammar or good taste?"

The slogan had been thought up in conjunction with the advertising agency William Esty Company to introduce Reynolds's new filter-tip cigarette, Winston, in March 1954. It was originally run as "Winston tastes real good—like a cigarette should" in a September 1954 ad published in a Pittsburgh newspaper. Later in the year, the word "real" was dropped when the ad ran in *Life* magazine. Within the first nine months of the campaign, billions of packages of Winstons were sold. By 1956 it was the top filter brand, and ten years later, it became the top-selling cigarette in America. Filter cigarettes like Winston and its rival, Marlboro, had been developed initially to appeal to women—who did not like the shredded tobacco taste of nonfilters—and thereby increase sales. Health concerns came later.

By that time, the surgeon general's 1964 report on the link between cigarette smoking and mortality had had an impact. Beginning in 1965, cigarette companies were required to print the words, "Caution: Cigarette smoking may be hazardous to your health," on every package, and all television advertising of cigarettes was banned. Companies began manufacturing filtered, low-tar cigarettes in earnest. Over 100 new brands had been introduced by 1981, and more advertising money—in fewer places—went to sell them.

R. J. Reynolds was the leading cigarette manufacturer from 1910 to 1960 in the United States. When filter cigarettes started to appear on the market, Reynolds kept up and came out with Winston, named after the town where they were made, Winston-Salem, North Carolina. In one early 1960s television commercial, Fred and Barney of the *Flintstones* smoked Winstons, leading to the later charge that the company was targeting minors.

Winston was the third-best selling cigarette by 1961, after unfiltered Pall Malls and Camel; by 1966, it was number one. Marlboro, its chief rival, edged Winston out by the end of the decade with its Marlboro man, becoming the top-selling cigarette in the world. In the 1990s, Winston launched a new campaign and a new slogan, "No Bull," meant to indicate that there were no additives in the cigarette.

References

Griggs, Robyn. "Bad Grammar in Good Taste." *Advertising Century. Advertising Age.* Special Issue. Chicago: Crain Communications, 1999: 34.

Twitchell, James B. *AdCult USA: The Triumph of Advertising in American Culture.* New York: Columbia University Press, 1996.

Mary Cross

Icons of the 1960s

Bangs manes bouffants beehives Beatle caps butter faces brush-on lashes decal eyes puffy sweaters French thrust bras flailing leather blue jeans stretch pants stretch jeans honey dew bottoms eclair shanks elf boots ballerinas Knight slippers, hundreds of them, these flaming little buds, bobbing and screaming, rocketing around inside the Academy of Music Theater underneath that vast old mouldering cherub dome up there—aren't they super-marvelous!
—Tom Wolfe, *The Kandy-Kolored Tangerine-Flake Streamline Baby*

Trying to describe the scene before the start of a performance by a new British rock band called the Rolling Stones, Tom Wolfe can only resort to a list, a catalogue of—well, *stuff*, a run-through of the fast fads and fashions that made the 1960s the flamboyant era they were and speak of a material culture gone riot. Advertising, television, and postwar prosperity had made their mark on consumer culture to the extent that simply reciting the trendy names of their clothing can paint an instant portrait of these rock fans.

After three decades of depression, war, and recovery, the baby boomers, 73 million strong, were coming of age, and they had money to spend. As the United States entered the 1960s, almost half its population was under the age of twenty-five, making the country younger than at any other time in its history. America was on the verge of a "youth culture," and it would be composed of more than just protest marches and hippie communes.

Many affluent young people became part of the counterculture as "hippies," living in communes and experimenting with mind-expanding drugs and free sex. They embraced the music of Bob Dylan and rock groups like the Beatles, the Rolling Stones, Jefferson Airplane, and the Grateful Dead. Slogans like "Flower Power," "Make Love, Not War," and "Never Trust Anyone over Thirty" characterized youth culture as a romantic and religious movement, but in reality it was shaped by the commercial culture it rejected. By 1967 rock music generated all new growth in the record market, earning over $600 million in sales for the corporations that promoted it. Late 1960s concerts held at Woodstock and Altamont underlined the counterculture's sinking into commercialism and violence. No matter how much they questioned authority and refused to trust anyone over thirty, the young had grown up watching television in a consumer culture they still embraced. Richard Nixon's election signaled that adults in the "silent majority" wanted things to return to normal, whatever that was, but the culture wars were just beginning.

Meanwhile, the advertisers whose job it was to beckon customers into the pleasure palaces of material culture were also undergoing a cultural revolution, though it was hardly as radical as some of the currents in the youth culture. Advertisers and their agencies, by their nature, are conservative. Nevertheless, students of American advertising regard the 1960s as the period of its creative revolution. The so-called creative teams were wresting power from the "client service teams," the marketing analysts and account executives, the organization men of the 1950s.

A small, independent agency led the charge. This agency, formed in 1949 in New York, was Doyle Dane Bernbach (DDB), and its creative guru (and the guru of all future agencies that emphasized creativity) was William Bernbach. According to former advertising executive Larry Dobrow, "With Bill Bernbach showing the way, art directors and copywriters teamed up for the first time. All the elements of an ad were integrated into a single, relevant advertising communication. The message that emerged was witty and direct, the form was clean and simple."

DDB's advertisements in the 1960s for American Airlines, Avis Rent-a-Car, Chivas Regal, Polaroid, and especially Volkswagen are legends of the trade. They were witty and sometimes seemed to be spoofing advertising itself. DDB ads had a way of relaxing some of America's most obsessive tensions of the decade, including race. The popular ads for Levy's Jewish rye bread all had the caption "You don't have to be Jewish to love Levy's," and each showed a portrait of a person of a given ethnic background (a black, a Chinese, even a red-headed Irish cop) happily munching on a sandwich made from Levy's.

Bernbach's legend begins with print ads, but television was the medium of the decade. DDB was a pioneer in witty television commercials, including those for Volkswagen; it was also a pioneer in political commercials. One of two spots the agency made for the Democratic National

Committee in 1964 shows a little girl lazily plucking petals from a daisy as she counts them. Then an ominous voice-over begins a countdown from ten to zero, moving closer to the girl's face, apprehensive now, until it evaporates in a nuclear explosion. The message? "Vote for President Johnson on November third. The stakes are too high for you to stay home."

Many advertising agencies, especially the smaller, more creative ones, were hiring more women and minorities. The bigger, more conservative agencies tended to be the exclusive domain of Ivy-League Wasps (Dobrow, 68). DDB itself hired a number of women, including one of the most famous in the business, Mary Wells, who, while working at Jack Tinker Partners, produced a famous television campaign for Alka-Seltzer and eventually started her own agency, Wells, Rich, and Greene, in 1966. She continued to produce Alka-Seltzer commercials and worked on a campaign for Benson and Hedges 100's that humorously focused on the "drawbacks" of smoking this extra-long cigarette: getting it caught in an elevator door, popping a balloon, setting your beard on fire.

While advertising geared up for its own revolution, the bored children of suburbia were creating a counterculture that rejected the values of middle-class life and behavior the ads tried to reflect, even as they enjoyed the fruits of the prosperous land where they lived. The legacy of the 1960s, it seems, was more a rejection of conventional morality than of consumer culture.

References

Dobrow, Larry. *When Advertising Tried Harder: The Sixties, the Golden Age of American Advertising*. New York: Friendly Press, 1984.

Frank, Thomas. Excerpt from *The Conquest of Cool: Business Culture, Counterculture, and the Rise of Hip Consumerism*. Chicago: University of Chicago Press, 1997. June 4, 2001. <http://www.press.uchicago.edu/Misc/Chicago/259919.html>.

Higgins, Denis, ed. and interv. *The Art of Writing Advertising: Conversations with William Bernbach, Leo Burnett, George Gribben, David Ogilvy, Rosser Reeves*. Chicago: NTC Business Books, 1965.

Massey, Sherri Ward. "Advertising." In *The Sixties in America*, edited by Carl Singleton. 3 vols. Pasadena, CA: Salem Press, 1999.

Mewborn, Brant. "Tom Wolfe." *Rolling Stone*. November/December 1987: 214–19.

Parker, Thomas, and Douglas Nelson. *Day by Day: The Sixties*. New York: Facts on File, 1983.

Wolfe, Tom. "The Girl of the Year." In *The Kandy-Kolored Tangerine-Flake Streamline Baby*, 204–20. New York: Farrar, Straus, 1965.

Marilyn Rye and William Zander

Aunt Jemima

In 1968 the image of Aunt Jemima, the iconic black "mammy" on pancake boxes for seventy-nine years (the Southern mammy was actually a nanny, usually a favorite female house slave chosen to look after the children of the master and mistress), underwent a major revision. In Aunt Jemima packaging and advertising, her bandanna became more like a fashionable headband. She slimmed down and, apparently, lost a few years too.

The Quaker Oats Company, which already had thirty-one Aunt Jemima Pancake Kitchen franchises from Disneyland to Yonkers, was awakened to the stereotype it was perpetuating when it proposed a new franchise for the fashionable Brighton suburb of Rochester, New York, in 1963. A formal protest was staged at a planning board meeting by leaders of the National Association for the Advancement of Colored People (NAACP) and the Congress of Racial Equality.

The civil rights movement in the 1960s made advertisers aware that they needed to be more sensitive to the images of African Americans in their ads, and they began using role-model blacks to pitch products to people of all ethnic backgrounds. By the late 1960s, American whites had been reeducated as to the kinds of negative images with which black children had to grow up.

The original image of Aunt Jemima was born in 1889, when Chris L. Rutt and Charles G. Underwood developed the first self-rising pancake-batter mix and began looking for a symbol that would make the product instantly recognizable. They found it at a vaudeville house where a team of blackfaced minstrels was performing a jazzy dance tune called "Old Aunt Jemima." Rutt knew he had the image they had been seeking and determined to steal not only the name but the likeness of the big Southern mammy from the posters advertising the vaudeville act. The pancake mix was a huge success.

As early as the 1920s, however, African Americans began to complain about the image of the black mammy from slavery days, wearing what they called a "head rag" and a big, accommodating grin. Nonetheless, ad agency J. Walter Thompson went to great lengths to provide Aunt Jemima with a biography in which she saves her Southern master by serving pancakes to Union troops. N. C. Wyeth was hired to illustrate the ads.

By the early 1960s, however, the clamor had become so loud that the Aunt Jemima product line (premiums to promote the food line, which came to include more than pancakes) was discontinued as derogatory and denigrating. These products included a rag doll, a syrup pitcher, a cookie jar, and salt and pepper shakers (also featuring "Uncle Mose").

In a major revision in 1989, Aunt Jemima lost her headdress; in fact, she looks more like someone who works in the executive offices of Quaker Oats—or at least a black Betty Crocker. She wears a white collar and pearl earrings, and her hair is neatly coifed (no Afro). All that remains is the big smile.

In 1996 Quaker Oats licensed the Aunt Jemima trademark to Aurora Foods, Inc., which also produces Mrs. Butterworth's, Celeste Pizza, and Mrs. Paul's frozen fish.

References

Kern-Foxworth, Marilyn. *Aunt Jemima, Uncle Ben, and Rastus: Blacks in Advertising, Yesterday, Today, and Tomorrow.* Westport, CT: Greenwood Press, 1994.
———. "From Plantation Kitchen to American Icon: Aunt Jemima." *Public Relations Review* 16 (Fall 1990): 55–67.
Massey, Sherri Ward. "Advertising." In *The Sixties in America*, edited by Carl Singleton. 3 vols. Pasadena, CA: Salem Press, 1999.

William Zander

Avis

By the beginning of the 1960s, the car-rental business was becoming huge in America. The giant was Hertz. "Let Hertz put you in the driver's seat," urged the company's slick television commercials in 1961, which, in a bit of pre-computer wizardry, showed people gliding through the air and into a moving open convertible.

Second to Hertz was Avis. By the end of 1962, the company decided it needed to get more recognition for the Avis name. Its ad budget was increased and Doyle Dane Bernbach (DDB) was hired to spend it wisely.

As with Volkswagen, DDB eschewed slick ads with exaggerated claims. In fact, in an unprecedented move, the agency dared to *advertise* that Avis was in second place in the rent-a-car business. Even more trailblazing was the use of comparative advertising, a commonplace nowadays, where every product claims to be better than its competitor.

The first DDB ad for Avis was full page, black and white, and ran in magazines aimed primarily at businessmen. "Avis is only No. 2 in rent-a-cars," it said. "So why go with us?" The answer: "We try harder." The only illustration appeared in the lower right-hand corner, a man's hand with two fingers extended. Another ad—showing an opened package of Rolaids, of all things—carried the headline: "Are you working like a dog to get to the top? Shake hands with Avis." And the copy began: "When you're not top dog, you try harder. You work more hours. You worry more. You eat much too fast."

This last ad indicates explicitly the campaign's appeal: empathy with the loser. As advertising executive Larry Dobrow points out in his book *When Advertising Tried Harder*, "The ads appealed to every struggling underdog (that's most of us) to strike a financial blow against a smug, swaggering top dog."

In May 1963, Avis president Robert Townsend said of the DDB campaign: "Our first ad appeared January 28. Since then our normal revenue growth rate has doubled. There is no doubt in my mind about the connection between these two facts" ("How to Run Second," 44). The campaign was also the rare example of an ad that helped improve the product. As DDB account executive Lester Blumenthal said at the time, "There is no doubt that the 'we try harder' theme has made everyone at the company do just that" ("How to Run Second," 44).

The claim that Avis tried harder forced old No. 1 to fight back after six years of watching its lead slip away. Hertz hired Carl Ally, Inc., one of the new "creative" agencies, to fight back. The competition can try as hard as it likes, said a Hertz ad in 1968, but Hertz does more; after all, the "biggest *should* do more." Another ad's headline declared, "Hertz has a competitor who says he's only No. 2. That's hard to argue with." Then, with biting sarcasm, the copy lists specific advantages of Hertz in one column and, in the other, "We try harder" as the only lame argument its competitor can muster.

In a way, the Ally campaign prevailed, and Avis remains No. 2. As the 1970s approached, Avis decided to hire Benton & Bowles to do its advertising. This agency paid homage to its predecessor DDB by trumpeting, somewhat inelegantly: "If you think Avis tries harder, you ain't seen nothing yet." But as the 21st century begins, the Ally ads for Hertz are things of the past, but the DDB slogan remains an icon, still seen on the pins Avis agents wear on their red blazers' lapels. And the campaign remains a legend, number ten on *Advertising Age*'s list of the best of the century.

References

"Car-Rental Race Heats Up as New Contenders Push into Lush Field." *Printer's Ink*, October 19, 1962: 13–14.

Clark, Eric. *The Want Makers*. New York: Viking, 1988.

Dobrow, Larry. *When Advertising Tried Harder: The Sixties, the Golden Age of American Advertising*. New York: Friendly Press, 1984.

"How to Run Second and Still Succeed." *Printer's Ink*, May 17, 1963: 44, 46.

William Zander

Hawaiian Punch

Cartoon figures have been part of the pop iconography for centuries. Shortly after the Civil War, when mass production and transportation began to take off, U.S. manufacturers who wanted to market on a national scale began to use such figures to identify their products. These figures evolved into trademarks.

But it was with the development of animation in film and subsequently television that cartoon figures were able to go beyond the familiar logotypes and take on quirks of personality—or some were. A personality trait that became marketable in the 1960s was "edginess," that is, a character (cartoon or otherwise) having a sharp or biting edge rather than the bland virtues venerated in the 1950s. According to Warren Dotz and Jim Morton, in their book *What a Character! 20th Century American Advertising Icons*, "Corporations usually liked their characters to reflect strength, heroism, and honesty. . . . Advertisers started experimenting with ignoble characters and found that people liked them better and—more importantly—remembered them longer." Some of these characters Dotz and Morton call "the nasties" (116–118).

One such character was Punchy, who began representing Hawaiian Punch fruit drink in 1961, going up against competitor Kool-Aid's Kool-Aid man. Created by the Atherton & Privett advertising agency, Punchy appeared as a cartoon character on television for the first time in February 1962. He was a small, big-headed beach bum wearing a rickety straw hat who would approach a big, dumb-looking guy in a Hawaiian shirt (who came to be known as "Oaf" or "Opie") and ask him: "Hey! How about a nice Hawaiian Punch?" Oaf would always say "Sure!," and Punchy would wind up and deck the big fellow with one roundhouse blow. This became one of the longest running gags on television.

Punchy became an instant hit, particularly with young people, after it was aired on the *Tonight Show* in 1963. Jack Paar, the popular host of the time, was so taken aback by the commercial that he asked the control room to run it again.

Hawaiian Punch itself began as an ice-cream topping in 1934 in Fullerton, California. It was concocted from seven fruit juices: pineapple, orange, passion fruit, apple, apricot, papaya, and guava. When customers discovered that the stuff made a tasty drink when mixed with water, Hawaiian Punch as we know it today was born.

At the height of Punchy's 1960s popularity, Hawaiian Punch became the property of R. J. Reynolds. It was later acquired by Procter & Gamble, and in 1999 Cadbury Schweppes, the London-based beverage, confectionary, and food company, bought and still owns Hawaiian Punch.

Procter & Gamble had put Punchy into semiretirement during the 1980s, but he was back in action in the 1990s, with (according to a company Web site) 95 percent awareness among children.

Punchy redux, however, is not as weird-looking as the original. As a Web site that sells Punchy bean bags puts it, "He's sooo CUTE!" On the labels of today's Hawaiian Punch, he's smiling and raising a glass as if in a conciliatory toast, with not a bit of edginess in evidence.

The Hawaiian Punch ad campaign has transcended consumer culture. For example, during the New York Mets' World Series season in 2000, Benny Agbayani, a Hawaiian-born outfielder, was nicknamed the "Hawaiian Punch."

References

Brown, Matthew A. Western Connecticut State University. "A Comparison Between Adult and Children's Advertising on Television." n.d. <http://www.wcsu.ctstateu.edu/~mccarney/acad/brown.html>.

Dotz, Warren, and Jim Morton. *What a Character! 20th Century American Advertising Icons.* San Francisco: Chronicle Books, 1996.

"Hawaiian Punch." *Race Warrior.* July 17, 2000. <http://www.racewarrior.com/alliances/hawaiianpunch.html>.

William Zander

The Marlboro Man (Marlboro Cigarettes)

The powerful appeal of the Marlboro man, one of the most widely recognized advertising images of the twentieth century, confirms the enduring importance of the American frontier as a cultural symbol of freedom and independence. The Marlboro man, a rugged rancher/cowboy, confidently takes pleasure both in the wilderness and in smoking his Marlboro cigarette. He is the American version of the archetypal Western male hero—solitary, strong, indefatigable, and undefeatable. Although the Marlboro man was introduced in the 1950s, he assumed his definitive cowboy image in the 1960s. The Marlboro slogan, "Come to where the pleasure is. Come to Marlboro Country," was introduced during a 1963 advertising campaign, one of the many effective campaigns produced by the Leo Burnett Company in the 1960s.

Marlboro cigarettes, created for an elite market of women and cosmopolitan smokers and introduced by Philip Morris in America in 1924 with a British-sounding name, were originally marketed to a small consumer niche. By the mid-1950s, however, sales of Marlboro cigarettes had dwindled alarmingly. When studies on the negative health effects of cigarettes were released in the 1950s, Philip Morris saw a market niche for Marlboros as filter cigarettes that reduced the hazards of smoking. The company hired the Leo Burnett Company in the mid-1950s to create a radically different advertising image to attract male smokers and make them forget that the cigarette, which had originally targeted women, was introduced with the slogan "Mild as May." To accomplish the makeover, Leo Burnett promoted aggressive masculine imagery in its early campaigns, using strong male figures such as "the tatooed man," race car drivers, and ballplayers. There was even a cowboy, portrayed in a 1957 campaign as plump, middle-aged, and wearing a business suit. In the long run, only the cowboy survived. The early Burnett campaigns also promoted the distinctive red-and-white filter box accompanied by the slogan, "You get a lot to like with a Marlboro: filter, flavor, flip-top box."

Beginning with the 1964 campaign, which introduced smokers to Marlboro Country, the Marlboro man appeared only as a rugged cowboy, an image promoted throughout the 1960s in a series of extremely effective campaigns. The 1967 "Lightening Storm" television spot, which presented images of rugged cowboys with theme music from the film *The Magnificent Seven*, typified the Marlboro man's connection to popular images of the American West. A 1967 magazine advertisement drew on similar imagery. In the foreground, a solitary cowboy sits on his bedroll drinking coffee and smoking his cigarette; the background shows a peaceful scene of grazing horses. These nostalgic images of an idealized American past, like the singing cowboys of the 1940s and the Western television shows of the 1950s and 1960s, from the *Lone Ranger* to *Bonanza*, reflect a desire to reconnect to simpler times.

The 1960s were a turbulent and wrenching decade. Post–World War II Cold War alignments began to break down; the civil rights movement challenged assumptions of white privilege; the second wave of feminism redefined gender roles. The decade, which ended with the withdrawal of American troops from Vietnam, left Americans a legacy of defeat and cynicism about government. Marlboro Country served as a retreat from a complex and changing world. The Marlboro man, an icon of culture as well as of cigarettes, represented the heroic individual who could still make sense of a universe defined by traditional values. Leo Burnett's campaigns centered on the emotional responses of consumers to a powerful icon rather than on a discussion of the product as earlier advertising had done.

In response to the antitobacco lawsuits of the late 1990s, the Marlboro man appeared in Marlboro cigarette ads, but he no longer smoked. Today the ads still invite readers to "Come to Marlboro Country," a magnificent landscape where only rabbits roam. Antismoking groups have used the icon in their campaigns as well. Still, even when absent, the memory of the Marlboro man helps Philip Morris sell 300 billion cigarettes annually.

References

Campaign for Tobacco Free Kids. "Making a *Deadly* Difference. Philip Morris."
     [Advertisement] *New York Times*, January 25, 2000: A23.
Kannor, Bernice. *The 100 Best TV Commercials . . . and Why They Worked*. Random
     House, 1999.
Saunders, Dave. *Twentieth Century Advertising*. London: Carlton Books, 1999.

Marilyn Rye

Mr. Whipple
(Charmin Toilet Tissue)

In *The Art of Writing Advertising*, William Bernbach suggests that good ads are memorable because of their creativity and visual appeal. Benton & Bowles created ads that met these criteria in its 1964 campaign for Charmin bathroom tissue. The campaign introduced the character of a grocer, Mr. George Whipple, played by Dick Wilson, in print and television ads that linked humor, the unforgettable slogan, "Please Don't Squeeze the Charmin," and dramatic vignettes that conveyed the product's outstanding softness as its identifying characteristic. Mr. Whipple's dignified demeanor, his white apron, and glasses suggested a paternal and proper figure that represented values of tradition and order. The humor arose from the discrepancy between the authoritarian Mr. Whipple's commands to customers not to squeeze the Charmin with his own inability to keep his hands off the product when he thought no one was looking. Women customers were always delighted to catch him in the act of violating his own prescriptions and to remind him, "Please don't squeeze the Charmin." In this campaign, viewers saw Mr. Whipple lose his moral and actual authority in ads that made breaking rules and acting out secret desires socially acceptable.

The product's original logo, the "Charmin Lady," introduced the product in 1928, but the image of a baby and the slogan "Charmin Babies Your Skin" replaced it in 1956. Procter & Gamble bought the Charmin Paper Company (originally the Hoberg Paper Company) in 1957. Planning an expansion into the paper goods market, in the late 1950s, Procter & Gamble developed a process to make Charmin even softer. Since the buying public did not distinguish particularly between bathroom tissue brands, Procter & Gamble hired Benton & Bowles to develop an innovative way of convincing large numbers of consumers that their product now was softer. How could they visually convey the sensation of touch?

George Parker, who worked on the campaign, told the *San Francisco Chronicle* that members of the ad team were sitting around a table trying to think of a way to convince customers to "squeeze the Charmin" in the supermarket just like they would squeeze the melons. Each team member grabbed a roll of Charmin from the pile on the table and squeezed it until someone shouted, "Stop squeezing the Charmin." Thus a slogan and campaign were born (Lacter, 1986). In an early 1962 commercial, entitled "Digby," Mr. Whipple was shown calling in Officer Digby to help control women carried away by squeezing the Charmin. Wilson thought the original character he portrayed was too mean, and during the shooting of the commercial he suggested a touch of humor: he would also get caught in the act of squeezing the Charmin. The "Digby" commercial was a hit, and it earned the highest recall score of any test commercial to that point—51 percent. By 1969 Charmin had become the best-selling bathroom tissue, and by 1971, it commanded a market share of 27 percent.

Rarely has an actor become so identified with a character as Wilson was with Whipple after twenty years and 500 commercials. By 1978 Wilson was the third best-known American. Even after his retirement in 1985, people he met addressed him as "Mr. Whipple." In 1995 a Procter & Gamble spokesperson commented about Wilson in the *Detroit News*, "He IS Mr. Whipple, and will always be Mr. Whipple, and we certainly want to make sure that nothing but Charmin goes in his bathroom" (Barisic, 1995). Wilson and Whipple came out of retirement in 1999 to promote Charmin in a new campaign managed by the D'Arcy Agency.

References

Barisic, Sonia. "Lifetime Supply of Charmin Nearly Comes to End of Roll for Mr. Whipple." *Detroit News*, December 30, 1995. <http://detroitnews.com/menu/stories/3082.htm>.

Chervokas, John V. "Confessions of a Creative Chief: 'I Squeezed the Charmin,' " *Advertising Age*, December 25, 1972: F15.

Higgins, Denis, ed. and interv. "William Bernbach." In *The Art of Writing Advertising*, 10–25. Chicago: NTC Business Books, 1965.

"The History of Charmin." 2000. Procter & Gamble. <http://www.charmin.com/history.html/>.

Lacter, Mark. "Those Hated TV Commercials That Won't Die." *San Francisco Chronicle*, May 5, 1986: 30.

"Mr. Whipple—He's Back!" 2000. Procter & Gamble. <http://www.charmin.com/whipple.html/>.

Marilyn Rye

Noxzema

One of the most daring ad campaigns of the 1960s—Noxzema's "Take It Off, Take It All Off—aired its first television commercial for Noxzema shaving cream in 1966. The campaign, which ran from 1966 to 1973, was described as "one of the earliest examples of overtly sexy advertising" in *"Advertising Age*'s 50 Best Commercials" (Fawcett, 2000). It went much farther than previous advertising in using sexual innuendo to market a product, initiating a continuing trend in advertising: the association of a product with the promise of heightened sexual attractiveness. This implied claim was much different than those made by preceding Noxzema advertisements which had presented the testimonials of ordinary people who were satisfied customers. Innovative in the way it expanded previous limits, it became identified as a prototype that marked a milestone in advertising history in its recognition of the emergence of more open attitudes toward sexuality.

In 1914 Dr. George Bunting, a Baltimore pharmacist, invented Dr. Bunting's Sunburn Remedy in a room in his drugstore. This first alternative to greasy medicating creams was popular with customers and renamed Noxzema after a customer commented that it had sure knocked his eczema. In 1921 Bunting's new company opened the first Noxzema Chemical Company factory. The company grew steadily more successful and by 1938 aimed at a national market through radio advertisements, billboards at Atlantic City, and the Noxzema blimp. Its production increased dramatically during World War II when it supplied its cream to soldiers to soothe their feet. The company used television ads in 1955 when it cosponsored Edward R. Murrow's *Person to Person* and in 1956 when it promoted its products on *The Perry Como Show*. These advertisements spurred sales in the very competitive market for skin care products. During the 1950s new products were developed, including Noxzema medicated soap, Nozain Medicated Cream, Nox-Ivy for poison ivy, and shaving cream. In the 1960s the company's focus was its line of Cover Girl cosmetics.

In 1966 the company, now called the Noxell Corporation, decided to introduce its shaving cream in aerosol cans. Noxell wanted a television advertising campaign that would make men sit up and pay attention. This one did. After rejecting an initial proposal to have the ad feature a man shaving while striptease music played, Noxell approved it in a slightly revised form that featured a blond and sexy former Miss Sweden, Gunilla Knutson. In the final version a man shaved using Noxema Shaving Cream and a hand razor. He stripped his face of swathes of shaving cream to the music of "The Stripper," while Knutson held the product and breathily intoned, "Take it off, take it all off." The double entendre was clear and its use was daring for the time. Sales jumped dramatically. The Swedish blond sex symbol, who was suggested perhaps by the Anita Eckberg character who cavorted in a Roman fountain in the film *La Dolce Vita* (1959), the slogan, and the shaving cream were linked in the mind of viewers.

Slightly over a decade earlier, the Kinsey reports about American sex habits (1948 and 1953) revealed the discrepancy that existed between actual and reported sexual behavior in the United States. Not surprisingly, men and women did not usually tell the whole story when it came to their sex lives. Dr. Alfred Kinsey's experiments, however, showed that more was going on sexually than people admitted. In public, however, Americans tended to be prudish and pretended to be shocked at the sexual innuendo contained in the Noxzema ads. But they still went out and bought the shaving cream.

During the 1960s other factors encouraged more frankness about sexual attitudes, including the invention of the birth control pill, the 1965 Supreme Court ruling that the dissemination of birth-control information and devices was legal, and the 1966 publication of Master and Johnson's report on sexual responsiveness. The Noxzema advertisements recognized the presence of "the sexual revolution"—a term in use by 1963—and opted for a boldness that suggested sexual behavior had changed.

References

Baily, Beth. "Sexual Revolution." In *The Sixties: From Memory to History*, edited by David Farger, 235–62. Chapel Hill: University of North Carolina Press, 1994.

Fawcett, Adrienne Ward. "*Advertising Age*'s 50 Best Commercials." 2000. *AdvertisingAge*. <http://adage.com/news_and_features/special_reports/commercials>.

"Feature: History of Noxell." 2001. Procter & Gamble. <http://www.pg.com>.

Garfield, Bob. "Magali's a Beauty, but She's No Noxzema Nordic Goddess." *Advertising Age*, November 27, 1995: 3.

"Noxzema: History 1914–2000." 2001. Procter & Gamble. <http://www.noxema.com/history17/>.

Marilyn Rye

The Pillsbury Doughboy

The Pillsbury Doughboy, the chubby white figure with the chef's hat and giggles, was introduced in 1965 to represent the fresh and easily prepared line of Pillsbury refrigerated dough products. The Doughboy,

The Doughboy, whose real name is "Poppin' Fresh," is a
popular icon for Pillsbury products. Courtesy of Pillsbury.

so named to emphasize the dough, is officially called Poppin' Fresh. He
is a modern-day counterpart of the gingerbread man, one who happily
remains in a warm and cheery kitchen instead of fleeing from it. He has
been the perfect incarnation of Pillsbury dough products since he first
appeared in an advertisement for Pillsbury Crescent Rolls. Like them, he

is made of dough, is lively (i.e., "fresh"), and pops out of the opened container. Since his introduction, he has been closely identified with the products he represents, one of Pillsbury's four main product lines.

Pillsbury, the largest flour company in the world by 1882, introduced convenience baking products in 1945, refrigerated dough in 1950, and refrigerated dough cans that cracked open on the black line in 1952. The company's emphasis on quality baking products and its constant introduction of innovative technology helped secure its preeminent place in the eyes of American homemakers and consumers. When women baked their own bread at home, Pillsbury supplied the flour. After World War II, when women returning from war work to the kitchen turned to convenience foods to lighten their labors, Pillsbury was ready with instant pie crust in a box. The refrigerated dough products introduced next combined the ease of convenience foods with the memories and smells of freshly baked products. Influenced by the emerging feminism of the 1960s, after the 1963 publication of *The Feminine Mystique* by Betty Friedan, and the need to supplement the family income, women sought careers outside the home. However, they struggled to reconcile the demands of a career with those of the more traditional role of woman as homemaker which society still expected them to fulfill. Refrigerated dough products resembled traditional home-baked products but took a fraction of the time to prepare. Poppin' Fresh was presented as the kitchen helper who helped women continue to keep their families satisfied and happy. His cheerful demeanor was supposed to represent the good feelings his products bestowed upon the working woman's family.

Advertising in the 1950s had marketed consumer products for the home as the foundation of a secure and happy family life. By the 1960s, however, companies looked for ways to woo consumers to familiar products through innovative advertising campaigns. In 1965 Pillsbury hired the Leo Burnett Company to create a new marketing campaign for its refrigerated dough products. According to the Doughboy legend, the creative director of the Burnett agency, Rudy Perz, was sitting around a table with other members of the agency. As they were cracking open can after can of the Pillsbury dough, Perz had a sudden inspiration and envisioned the Pillsbury Doughboy.

Recognized by 87 percent of the population three years after his appearance, the Pillsbury Doughboy remains highly popular with consumers. Most Americans instantly recognize him. Thus *New York Times* readers immediately identified his caricature when it accompanied a critique of a recent Pillsbury product and understood the humor behind the misrepresentation of his character. Today the Doughboy has his own Web page to share information about his interests and activities. Doughboy products, from screensavers to cookie jars that giggle when the lids are lifted, appear online in the Doughboy Shop. His icon appears on

Pillsbury refrigerated baked goods and on Pillsbury publications, such as *Come and Eat*, sold at grocery checkout counters. Pillsbury, with headquarters in Minneapolis, Minnesota, is a unit of Diageo PLC.

References

"About Pillsbury: The Pillsbury Doughboy Story." Pillsbury Company. <http://www.pillsbury.com/about/doughboystory.asp/>.
Sheraton, Mimi. "Let the Circle Be Unbroken." *New York Times*, May 15, 2001: Op Ed page.
"The Wonder of Doughboy." *Harpers*, June 1997: 28–29.

Marilyn Rye

Ronald McDonald

"He doesn't sell for McDonald's, he is McDonald's," proclaimed a writer for *Advertising Age* when rating the 1965 advertising campaign using McDonald's icon, the clown Ronald McDonald, as the second best campaign of the century. Ronald McDonald, the red-haired clown in the yellow-and-red costume now promotes McDonald's worldwide in 114 countries and is one of the world's most immediately recognized product logos. Almost 96 percent of American children recognize his face, showing the effectiveness of McDonald Corporation's decision to present Ronald as McDonald's ambassador to children. His friendliness and universality make him appealing to children of all ethnic and national backgrounds, serving McDonald's image well at home and abroad. Conversely, when protests have arisen against McDonald's policies, Ronald's figure has become an object of attack. Competitors like Burger King created their own variations of this character, but none have matched his success.

The history of Ronald McDonald is interesting because, when he was first introduced in an ad by a local franchise, the corporate parent was reluctant to adopt a clown for a national advertising campaign. Yet he proved to be a key element in McDonald's phenomenal growth from a small chain with national aspirations into a multinational corporation. Ray Kroc opened his first McDonald's restaurant in Illinois in 1955. During that decade, President Dwight Eisenhower funded and built America's first interstate highway system, an important contribution to the nation's economic development, as well as a precondition for the fast-food franchises later to develop along major routes of transit. In the 1960s incomes were rising, mostly due to the second family income contributed by women returning to work. With more disposable income and less time to cook, Americans in the 1960s began eating more outside the home, a trend which accelerated during the second half of the century. Kroc's early restaurants focused on low prices to draw customers and did not worry about developing a national image until 1965. Before then individual franchises handled their own advertising.

In 1963 the owners of a Washington, D.C., franchise, John Gibson and Oscar Goldstein, advertised on a local television show starring a clown Bozo who told children to ask their parents to take them to McDonald's. Two years later the sales at their McDonald's had increased so much that other McDonald franchises started using clowns in their own advertisements. Goldstein suggested that the national company adopt the clown character in advertisements. Only Goldstein's high sales figures convinced the reluctant parent company to accept his offer. In 1965 D'Arcy Masius Benton & Bowles Agency of Chicago first used Ronald McDonald in television ads during Macy's Thanksgiving Day Parade in and during the first Super Bowl in January 1966. The sharp increase in January sales indicated the advertising's potential effect.

Ronald McDonald has appeared continuously in McDonald's publicity campaigns, all but one in 1996 directed at children. In 1970 Needham, Harper and Steers created a national campaign promoting the idea of "McDonaldland." In addition to Ronald, ads featured other cartoon characters and franchises built "playlands" with these characters. In 1974 franchises in Philadelphia opened the first Ronald McDonald House to provide housing for families of children receiving extended hospital treatments away from their homes. At present the Ronald McDonald House Charities, McDonald's most important charity, supports more than 150 Ronald McDonald Houses in twelve countries. Today Ronald represents the world's dominant fast-food franchise in the world.

References

Love, John. *McDonald's: Behind the Arches*. New York: Bantam, 1986.
"McDonald's Going After Small Fry." *USA Today*, October 10, 1998: B3.
"Ronald McDonald." *Advertising Age: The Advertising Century*. <http://www. adage.com/>.
"Ronald McDonald in New Role." *Advertising Age: Daily Deadline*. April 25, 1996. <http://www.adage.com/>.

Marilyn Rye

The Volkswagen Beetle

The first Volkswagen to seek an American market in 1949 was met with a yawn. Not a single showroom wanted to become a dealership for

Adolf Hitler's "People's Car" (the English translation of the German word *Volkswagen*), and the American motoring press felt that Detroit could offer anything that Volkswagen could. The German salesman who had brought the showcase Beetle to the new world had to sell it for $800 to pay his hotel bill and buy a ticket home.

Gradually, however, the little car began to catch on as war memories faded. Beetle's success in the 1950s was won without any advertising other than word of mouth, but in 1959, in order to counter an impending threat from Detroit's new compact cars, VW decided to hire an advertising agency.

The agency hired, Doyle Dane Bernbach (DDB), was a small one which had started up about a decade earlier in New York City. It was one of several agencies of that era that had begun to revolt against the plodding, research-oriented approach of the big agencies. Bill Bernbach, DDB's creative director, was to become famous for witty, understated ads that often seemed to satirize the advertising industry itself.

DDB's Volkswagen campaign in the 1960s is, as the saying goes, legendary. In fact, *Advertising Age* has called it the number 1 ad campaign of the century. The theme was "Think Small," a striking contrast to the associations with speed, power, and glamour in most American car ads. DDB made no attempt to make the VW glamorous—quite the contrary. The "Think Small" ad itself (1962) shows a black-and-white photo of a Beetle, tiny against a gray background. The copy stresses the contrast with Detroit and says that, "once you get used to some of our economies," you don't even notice them anymore: "Except when you squeeze into a small parking spot. Or renew your small insurance. Or pay a small repair bill. Or trade in your old VW for a new one."

In fact, as many of the ads stressed, there was no "new one" in the sense of a different model with different parts every year. The photos often showed pictures of older, used models to demonstrate that the Beetle was not just another part of America's throwaway culture. Most parts from a 1956 VW were interchangeable with a 1962 model, making parts easy to find.

When the Beetle first appeared on the American scene, jokes circulated about it, many with negative connotations. Rather than ignore them, DDB's ads capitalized on them. Thus the joke that you had to wind it up to make it go is featured in an ad that shows a Beetle with a wind-up key in its rear and says that it uses so little gas, you might think the joke is true. Another ad announces, "It's ugly, but it gets you there," with a photo of the lunar lander on the moon. The only connection with VW is the logo at the bottom.

Whatever humorous fillips DDB used, the claims made for the car were simple truths. The car got thirty-four miles per gallon of gas. Because the engine was air-cooled, the owner never worried about antifreeze. And it sat in the rear, which provided better traction (as the agency's famous "snow plow" commercial illustrated). A VW was so simple that little could go wrong with it. One ad had the headline "Lemon" under a picture of a Beetle. The copy explained that an inspector at the plant had noticed a blemished chrome strip on the glove compartment, and this particular car was pulled off the line.

VW sales tripled during the 1960s in America, and eventually 15 million Beetles were sold, more than any other make of car in history, including the Model T. Moreover, the Beetle became the quintessential car of the 1960s youth culture.

The swan song for the Beetle in the United States came in 1979, by which time the Rabbit hatchback had been successfully introduced. While Beetles continued to roll out of VW's Mexican plant, they met neither emission nor safety standards in the United States; however, Beetles from bygone days persevere on America's roads to this day.

A "New Beetle" went into production in 1997 (see "New Volkswagen Beetle" entry in Chapter 10). The car looks "Beetlish," but it has no mechanical relationship to the original. As VW's ads put it, "The engine's in the front, but its heart's in the right place." *Motor Trend* magazine, which made the new Beetle its import car of 1999, called it a bargain at a base price of about $16,000 and lauded its 115-horse-power engine: "Unlike those venerable air-cooled 40-horse four-bangers of old, this water-cooled engine is impressively smooth and quiet" (motortrend.com). Beetle owners of the 1960s might recognize the flower holder in the new Beetle but find the rest of its standard equipment a bit over the top. The new Beetle comes with everything from air-conditioning, stereo, and power locks to lighted vanity mirrors and a pollen and odor filter.

References

Abbott, David, and Alfredo Marcantonio. *"Remember Those Great Volkswagen Ads?"* London: European Illustration, 1982.
"Motor Trend '99 Import Car of the Year: Volkswagen New Beetle." *Motor Trend*, February 1999. <http://www.motortrend.com/feb99/icoy/>.
Seume, Keith. *The Beetle*. Ann Arbor, MI: Lowe & B. Hould, 1997.

William Zander

Wisk Laundry Detergent

The "Ring Around the Collar" campaign for Wisk, the first liquid detergent, was launched in 1968 by the venerable Batten, Barten, Durstine and Osborn (BBDO) agency. Lever Bros. (Unilever), the company that manufactured this product, wanted to stress Wisk's ability to remove "stubborn stains."

The commercials and print ads created by BBDO featured a housewife discovering her shameful inadequacy in the form of dirt-and-sweat rings on her husband's shirt collars, even after scrubbing diligently to remove them. This discovery was accompanied, in the commercials, by a taunting singsong voice-over, "Ring around the collar!," repeated several times in the nasty voice and rhythm with which children intone, "NYAH-nyah NYAH-nyah NYAH-nyah." (The voice was that of Bob McFadden, who supplied many voices for cartoons and commercials of the day.) This chant, a kind of slogan, stuck in the mind like a cockleburr.

Bill Machrone, a columnist for *PC Magazine*, once told an advertising executive who worked on the Wisk account that he was so annoyed by this obnoxious ad that he would never buy the product: "With a smug sneer that still rankles, he told me that it was one of the most successful advertising campaigns ever, and that I didn't know what I was talking about." Another writer, Bob Garfield, noted in *Advertising Age* that an advertisement can be memorable precisely because it is irritating.

Indeed that was the case. By the end of the 1970s, Wisk had established a solid niche in the heavy-duty detergent market, challenging Procter & Gamble's powdered Cheer for second place at 9 percent. Lever Bros. was spending about $10 million a year on its tried-and-true "Ring Around the Collar" ads.

Jack Solomon, an English professor at California State University, Northridge, regards the Wisk ads as an appeal to "fear of not belonging, of social rejection, of being different." No one wants to be "guilty" of smelling bad or having a dirty collar. Ads like this, according to Solomon, are "parodies of ancient religious rituals of guilt and atonement."

"Oh, those dirty rings!" the housewife groans in despair. It's as if she and her husband were being stoned by an angry crowd. But there's hope, there's help, there's Wisk cleansing her soul of sin as well as her husband's; the housewife launders his shirts with Wisk, and behold, his collars are clean. Product salvation is only as far as the supermarket. ("Masters of Desire")

In hindsight, one could say that Unilever and BBDO might also have some guilt to atone for. Aside from its irritating qualities, the "Ring Around the Collar" ad firmly places women in the stereotyped gender role from which they were trying to escape. The ad, says Bob Garfield, straining to make a point in a 1998 review, is "a dirty, grimy, male-sweat stain on the fabric of the industry." It may be conventional wisdom in the advertising world that negative ads do not work, but this one for Wisk certainly got the consumer's attention.

References

Garfield, Bob. "Top 100 Advertising Campaigns of the Century." *Advertising Age: The Advertising Century*. Special Supplement. Chicago: Crain Communications, 1999: 18–41. <http://adage.com/search97cgi/s97_cgi/>.

Giges, Nancy. "Wisk, Other Liquids Cleaning Up in Heavy-duty Detergent Market." *Advertising Age*, February 12, 1979: 33–34.

Machrone, Bill. "The Marketers Have Gone Mad." *PC Magazine*, September 9, 1997. <http://www8.zdnet.com/pcmag/insites/machrone/bm970909.htm/>.

Solomon, Jack. "Masters of Desire: The Culture of American Advertising." In *Entry Points*, edited by Elizabeth Alvarado and Barbara Cully, 10–17. New York: Addison Wesley Longman, 1999. <http://www.one-world.org/engl100/solomon.html/>.

William Zander

8

Icons of the 1970s

Trapped between the turbulent 1960s and the Reagan years, the 1970s have often been perceived as a transitional decade, the "undecade," the decade when nothing happened. It is also remembered as a somewhat unsavory period with the scandal of Watergate, the oil embargo, the Iran hostage crisis, and multiple economic woes. It was a decade easily ridiculed for its bad taste, from hot pants to leisure suits to disco. More recently, the decade has been resurrected into a form of nostalgia, evident in fashion designs and television sitcoms like *That 70s Show*.

The decade following the cultural revolution of the 1960s and preceding the Reaganomics of the 1980s is fascinating in its own right. Popular culture, more than ever before, became infused with commercialized objects. In this decade of increased commodification, the 1960s revolution itself became saleable, as fashion reprised hippie and ethnic looks. At the same time, corporate logos proliferated on clothing and other artifacts as never before. Some of the advertising products in the 1970s became iconic, as they seeped into the popular culture and tweaked, ever so slightly, the already complicated national consciousness.

Various books written about the 1970s have tried to analyze this decade and argue for its significance in the evolution of American culture. Many of the initiatives of the 1960s (the women's movement, civil and voting rights, environmental regulations) did not become established until the 1970s. The antiwar movement, specifically protests against the 1970 U.S. invasion of Cambodia, resulted in shooting deaths at Kent State University. Social unrest continued well into the 1970s, exacerbated by a deep recession combined with double-digit inflation. Unemployment and crime were on the rise even as affirmative action programs and social services were being implemented.

The decade that began in 1970, with the first Earth Day celebration, ended in 1979, with the Three Mile Island Nuclear accident. In some ways, it was a decade of disillusion and unease. Political corruption and scandal culminated with the Watergate hearings and the resignation of President Richard Nixon before the impeachment vote was taken in 1974. Despite the pullout of U.S. troops from Vietnam in 1973, international events were overshadowed by domestic economic worries made worse by the 1973 fuel shortage and oil embargo, which resulted in a doubling of oil prices and long gas lines. Consumers faced high inflation and the beginnings of a long recession by the mid-1970s during the presidential term of Jimmy Carter, punctuated by a hostage crisis in the U.S. embassy in Iran. The hostages were released by the time of Ronald Reagan's inauguration in 1981, but the recession lingered, as unemployment coupled with high interest rates ate into consumer budgets.

The 1970s were full of such complications. Called by some the "decade of the woman," there is no doubt that the women's movement grew into a major political and social force in the 1970s. *Ms.* magazine was launched in 1972, and the U.S. Supreme Court's *Roe v. Wade* verdict supporting abortion was issued in 1973. The National Organization of Women and other groups drew attention to the continued exploitation of women. While equality for women improved, however, many media images continued to project a woman defined primarily by the cosmetics and fashion industries.

As the recession worsened and inflation, along with gas prices, soared, car prices skyrocketed. Safety regulations and the recall of millions of cars besieged the auto industry. Efficient Japanese models flooded the market, while Detroit tried frantically to create smaller cars. By 1975, however, the energy crisis seemed to be over, and luxury cars once again beckoned the American consumer.

In 1970 IBM introduced the floppy disk, and in 1976 the Apple computer was born. The advent of computer technology meant, in part, that marketing strategies were greatly improved. As the economy slowed down, the need for finding new consumers arose. This was achieved through computer bases, telemarketing, and narrowcasting. The marketplace was now more centralized, in part due to the growth of retail franchises and the shopping mall.

Advertising was considered serious business in the 1970s. Television networks dominated the share of viewers, making television commercials particularly effective. Award-winning campaigns resulted in catchy jingles like Alka-Seltzer's "Plop Plop Fizz Fizz, Oh What a Relief It Is" and Coca-Cola's "I'd Like to Teach the World to Sing." In the early 1970s, the standard length for television ads shifted from sixty to thirty seconds, and by 1977, gross television advertising revenues reached $7.5 billion, or 20 percent of all U.S. advertising, according to *Advertising Age*.

Advertising also faced some challenges in this decade. The congressional ban on radio and television cigarette advertising took effect in 1970, stripping the broadcast business of about $220 million in advertising. Also, as a result of continued petitions circulated by groups like Action for Children's Television (ACT) the networks finally agreed in 1972 to reduce commercial time for children during their weekend programming and to prohibit "tie-ins" linking programming and commercials. The extensive television coverage of the Senate Watergate hearings in 1973 meant fewer commercials and cost millions in lost ad revenues and airtime.

References

"Advertising Age's History of TV Advertising." <http://adage.com/news_ and_features/special-reports/tv/1970s.html/>.

Carroll, Peter. *It Seemed Like Nothing Happened: America in the 1970s*. New York: Holt, Rinehart and Winston, 1982.

Edelstein, Andrew J., and Kevin McDonough. *The Seventies: From Hot Pants to Hot Tubs*. New York: Dutton, 1990.

Frum, David. *How We Got Here: The 70's—The Decade that Brought You Modern Life—For Better or Worse*. New York: Basic Books, 2000.

Miller, Stephen Paul. *The Seventies Now: Culture as Surveillance*. Durham, NC: Duke University Press, 1999.

Waldrep, Shelton, ed. *The Seventies: The Age of Glitter in Popular Culture*. New York: Routledge, 1999.

Elise Salem

Alka-Seltzer Tablets

Alka-Seltzer's animated puppet, Speedy created at Wade Advertising Agency in the 1950s, quickly became one of the most recognizable characters on television. Originally known as Spanky, his name was changed to Speedy to fit with Alka-Seltzer's promotional theme of "Speedy relief." The six-inch model of a cheerful boy with a tablet as a hat appeared in over 200 commercials from 1954 to 1964. Buoyantly offering relief for indigestion or a hangover, Speedy easily transformed the squeamish subject of discomfort into domestic humor.

Alka-Seltzer continued to link its products with a funny narrative, including the famous "Spicy Meatball" ads of the late 1960s, in which a middle-aged man suffers from indigestion after sampling his mother's spaghetti: *"That's* a spicy meatball." By the early 1970s, Alka-Seltzer commercials had won major awards, including the Clios, ensuring brand recognition and excellent sales. In 1972, however, more stringent regulations by the Food and Drug Administration cast some suspicion on the category of nonprescription drugs, including Alka-Seltzer products. Instead of altering its humorous ads, however, Alka-Seltzer decided to stick with the upbeat formula that had served them so well in the past. While most competitors used serious testimonials with statistics and medical charts, Alka-Seltzer launched its most successful humorous ad campaign to date.

In the early 1970s, Alka-Seltzer shifted its ad account from Wade to Wells, Rich, Greene, who, in 1972, developed the award-winning "I Can't Believe I Ate the Whole Thing" commercial. In the mid-1970s, the agency came up with the most memorable of the Alka-Seltzer campaigns, with the catchy phrase, "Plop, plop, fizz, fizz, Oh what a relief it is!" Composed by Tom Dawes and Twin Star Music, the jingle proved infectious, and the ads were immediate hits.

A series of different commercials with the famous jingle included one in which Alka-Seltzer tablets were dropped in glasses, and the effervescent quality of the product was reinforced by the famous jingle. Another one in 1978 featured Sammy Davis, Jr., singing a jazzy version of "Plop, Plop" before a big band. Davis's star quality lent credence to a product (and jingle) that had become a cultural icon. The ad even achieved fame in the United Kingdom where, in 1976, the agency of Jack Tinker and Partners altered the slogan to read, "Plink, Plink, Fizz, Fizz." Clearly, the indigestion tablet had achieved the status of big, and international, entertainment. The obvious irony proved ludicrous and humorous.

The "Plop, Plop, Fizz, Fizz" slogan is still one of the most recognizable ad phrases, even to a generation who did not experience the earlier commercials. In a 1994 episode of *The Simpsons*, for example, Homer chants his own words to the tune of the Alka-Seltzer ad.

Alka-Seltzer is a brand of the Bayer Corporation.

References

Alka-Seltzer Home Page. <http://www.alka-seltzer.com>.
"Best Television Spot of the Millennium: Alka Seltzer's Magadini's Meatballs." <http://www.hrts-iba.org/tvgoldenreel.html/>.
Dotz, Warren, and Jim Morton. *What a Character! 20th Century American Advertising Icons*. San Francisco: Chronicle Books, 1996.
"Memorable TV Commericals of the Seventies." <http://www.geocities.com/SunsetStrip/8678/commrcls.html/>.

Elise Salem

Bounty Paper Towels

Many household products are fundamentally generic, commodities seemingly indistinguishable by their function and appearance—toothpaste, detergents, garbage bags, paper towels. Marketing specialists devote their talents to creating distinctions, often where none of substance is apparent. They create catchy names, colorful packaging, or memorable slogans, seizing on any subtle differences they can find. A paper towel, for example, that absorbs wet spots faster than its competitors might enjoy a marketplace advantage if advertisers can convince buyers that better absorbency matters.

This tactic succeeded for Procter & Gamble's Bounty paper towels, which in the 1970s became "the quicker picker-upper," a semi–tongue twister that stuck with audiences. Millions of television viewers became convinced that a sheet of paper's ability to soak up spilled liquid should play a major role in a buying decision. Bounty commercials gave vivid visual demonstrations.

Central to the success of the 1970–1975 campaign was actress Nancy Walker, who played Rosie, the tough-talking diner counter waitress. In each of four ads filmed during that period, Rosie found herself burdened with a clumsy customer who spilled coffee or tipped over a class of cola. Rosie quickly reassured the embarrassed patron not to worry. She would tear a sheet of Bounty from the roll at hand and blot up the accident in a split second. Then she would give a comparative demonstration of Bounty versus an unnamed flimsy competitor which left splotches on the counter and fell apart. The customers were clearly impressed.

Walker herself, after a long career on Broadway, had become a recognizable personality to television viewers from her role as Rhoda Morgenstern's mother on *The Mary Tyler Moore Show*. Her diner setting, eventually named Rosie's, became famous because of the commercials. Originally built in 1945 and called the Silver Dollar Diner, it was located on the Route 46 circle in Little Falls, New Jersey. In 1990 Jerry Berta, a ceramic artist, had the diner sawed in half, strapped to a flatbed truck, and moved 700 miles west to Rockford, Michigan. Ten years later, Berta put Rosie's up for sale at $790,000 so that he could focus on his career as an artist, including making ceramic miniatures of Rosie's. By then, the diner had become the namesake of a nationwide franchise, and Berta is featured on The Original Rosie's Diner Web site.

Bounty remains a successful product without advertising as memorable as the Rosie campaign. For many consumers, the motto has stuck, and Bounty remains quicker than the other paper towels on supermarket shelves.

References

"For $790,000, Rosie's Can Be a 'Picker-Upper.' " *Record Online*. August 31, 2000.
    <http://www.bergen.com/morenews/rosie31200008314.htm/>.
The Original Rosie's Diner. <http://www.rosiesdiner.com/>.

Walter Cummins

The Breck Girl
(Breck Shampoo)

The iconic blondes, brunettes, and redheads portrayed in the Breck Girl advertising campaign present a virtual history of hair styles from the 1940s to the 1970s, their shimmering locks testimony to the benefits of using Breck shampoo. Most of the women in the ads were teenagers or younger, and during the 1970s, Breck Girls included some very-soon-to-be-famous young women. A childish Brooke Shields appeared in a 1974 ad with her doll and the headline, "Breck at Christmas." Jaclyn Smith, Kim Basinger, and Cheryl Tiegs were other Breck Girls of the 1970s. The campaign, which ran from 1944 to 1978, helped make Breck one of the country's best-selling shampoos, with the slogan, "Beautiful Hair Begins with Breck."

The company, John H. Breck, Inc., had begun in 1910 as a laboratory producing tonics and creams. In 1929 John Breck's pharmacist son, Edward, introduced Breck shampoo and other hair products. American Cyanamid acquired Breck and Company in 1963, and it eventually became part of one of Cyanamid's subsidiaries, Shulton, Inc. The Breck Girls campaign was initially thought up by Edward Breck and an artist, Charles Sheldon, in 1944, and the thirty-four-year campaign became well known for its portraits of young women and their beautiful hair, drawn by various artists. Ads in the 1960s and 1970s not only discussed the benefits of using Breck, but offered information about the women themselves, describing their lifestyles and hobbies. Many of the real-life models were chosen for their achievements as well as their hair, and the ads described their activities, Breck product choices, and hair care routines.

The glamorous campaign made icons out of the Breck Girls, who now have their own exhibit in the Smithsonian Institution, based on materials donated by the Dial Corporation which bought the brand in 1991 and discontinued it in 2000. A new owner, the Himmel Group of New York, purchased Breck in June 2001 and plans to bring back the Breck Girl, whose strong image, it says, is the brand's competitive edge in the hair care market. New Breck products are expected to arrive on the shelves in 2002.

References

Banta, Martha. *Imaging American Women: Idea and Ideals in Cultural History.* New York: Columbia University Press, 1987.
Grossman, Andrea M. "Breck Is Back." *Women's Wear Daily,* 21 July 2001.

Mary Cross

Burger King

Trailing behind McDonald's in the relatively new fast-food industry, Burger King launched a $3 million ad campaign in 1974 that sought to distinguish it from its competitor. "Have It Your Way" succeeded in promoting Burger King as a fast-food store that offered something unique: not only would the food be quick, but special orders could be the norm.

Created by Batten, Barton, Durstine and Osborn (BBDO), the campaign was credited for boosting sales by 29 percent in 1975. The "Have It Your Way" concept appealed to consumers who were not always satisfied with standard fare. The brilliant jingle that accompanied the television spots, written by Dennis Berger, featured Jenny's Daughters (three sisters from the Bronx):

> Hold the pickles
> Hold the lettuce
> Special orders won't upset us
> All we ask is that you let us
> Serve it your way
> Have it your way at Burger King

Still considered one of the most successful customer-building campaigns in advertising history, "Have It Your Way" became a recognized slogan across America. The idea of allowing customers to create their own product appealed to consumers' desire for individual treatment in an increasingly impersonal world.

The campaign began in full swing with radio, television, print, and billboard advertising. The special treatment provided at Burger King was intended to be a direct hit at McDonald's, whose service and production methods did not cater to individual needs. The first ads featured a family pleased that their special orders did not result in extra waiting time. A second wave of ads, totaling $6 million, continued to focus on Burger King's individualized service. One of the spots, "Slow Motion," humorously exaggerated the slow service at other supposedly fast-food restaurants. In 1975 the third wave of ads was aimed primarily at children, featured Nicholas who despised pickles on his hamburgers.

Since the 1970s, Burger King has not had a stellar advertising track record. Many campaigns in the 1980s simply flopped, especially the one built around an anonymous nerd called "Herb." Following the nostalgia trend, Burger King, in the late 1990s, repeated its "Have It Your Way" theme using flashbacks of 1970s characters, but it received mixed reviews from a majority of consumers.

The Burger King slogan emphasized that special orders—"hold the pickles, hold the lettuce"—were no problem. ™ and © 2001 Burger King Brands, Inc.

Home of the Whopper, Burger King is identified by its "Have It Your Way" food customization. The phrase has become a cultural icon, easily tossed about in conversation as an admission of recognized individuality.

References

"The Background of Burger King Corporation." <http://burgerking.com/company/background.htm/>.

"Burger King Flashbacks Leave Consumers Torn." <http://www.ovationmar.com/whatsnew/enews12_28_98.htm/>.

"Custom Is King." <http://www.dwcdesignet.com/DWC/July'99/takenote.html/>.

McCarthy, Michael. "Burger King Follows Urge to Jilt Turner." <http://www.usatoday.com/money/index/ad318.htm/>.

McMahan, Harry W. "McMahan Picks 100 Top TV Commercials of 1974." *Advertising Age*, January 27, 1975: 43+.

Elise Salem

Datsun

When Japanese automobiles first arrived in the United States in the late 1960s, they targeted the low end of the market. The small, tinny vehicles seemed oddities, square-shaped and dwarfed beside the large, powerful domestic products. Some of the earliest models neglected to take into account U.S. driving conditions, like the salted roads of Northern winters. Their bodies quickly rusted, and metal literally flapped against the tires. But these missteps, unlike those of such European manufacturers as Fiat and Renault, were temporary.

The 1970s saw the flourishing of Japanese cars in the American market. Without a doubt, the main impetus for auto buyers was the oil crisis of the decade that led to severe gasoline shortages and rapid price rises. The 1973 OPEC oil embargo and resulting hours of waiting in lines at the pumps for limited amounts of fuel gave a quick boost to the appeal of efficient, high-mileage, four-cylinder engines. Datsun vaulted into the lead when its Sunny model finished first in the 1973 Environmental Protection Agency's fuel economy tests (nissan-lobal.com).

In the 21st century, Datsun may be a forgotten make for most people, one abandoned by its parent company, Nissan, in the early 1980s in a quest for a uniform worldwide corporate identity. Yet Datsun was a dominant nameplate in the 1970s, especially with its terse and effective slogan, "Datsun Saves." The immediate implication, of course, was that of saving fuel and money, both in initial cost and upkeep. It also echoed a more timeless promise, "Jesus Saves," an excessive claim for a car, but one that resonated with consumers.

In addition to high mileage, Japanese cars offered another advantage over domestic models. The manufacturers learned quickly from their quality control mistakes. By the 1970s, engineering skill and assembly line efficiencies soon brought Datsun, Toyota, and Honda reputations as superior products, the epitome of mass-produced auto quality. Ford Pinto, Chevrolet Chevettes, and Dodge Horizons were no match for Toyota Coronas, Honda Civics, and Datsun 510s. By 1974 imports—primarily Japanese—had risen from less than 1 percent in the late 1950s to 20 percent of U.S. car sales. Many American drivers, more concerned with gas prices and availability, embraced vehicles produced by a country that had been a hated World War II enemy not long before.

Beyond economy and efficiency, Datsun quickly developed a reputation for adventurous driving, with its 240Z sports car. Known affectionately by the shorthand name of Z, these two-seaters beat Toyota and Honda in appealing to a market niche and adding to the prestige of the brand. The first Zs cost $3,500. In 1997 Nissan sought to enhance its reputation though a nostalgic resurrection of past glories by buying up some existing 1970–2 Zs and restoring them in a program called "Vintage Zs." Engines and transmissions were rebuilt or replaced, interiors reinstalled, cooling systems enlarged, carriages undercoated. The renewed Zs were to sell for $25,000, and although production was limited to about 200 cars, initial demand was many times that number.

Other vintage cars have been reproduced over the years, but always by small independent operators, usually emulating a design rather than restoring an original. The rebuilt Zs were the first effort made by an original manufacturer to capitalize on the past. More than repairing a vehicle, Nissan was seeking to repair a major marketing mistake when it abandoned the Datsun brand. For a number of years, customers remained confused by the name change.

Doron Levin, writing for the Knight-Ridder newspapers in 1996, underlined Nissan's mistake: "Nissan Motor Corp. enjoys a decent reputation for its vehicles among those who have any reason to know. But after more than a decade of trying, Nissan has failed to generate much resonance as a brand." Levin notes that Nissan is not alone in the strategic error of abandoning a successful brand or slogan:

There's a certain mystery to brands, slogans and names. No one really knows why some catch on and others don't. A bright spark at Westinghouse once decided that the time had arrived to get rid of the slogan, 'You can be sure if it's Westinghouse.' Westinghouse brought out a series of new slogans, all dismal failures. Several years later, consumers still remembered the slogan; the company, to its credit, brought it back.

Nissan did not bring back the Datsun name in 1997, but it attempted to recapture the cachet of the past with an advertising campaign developed by the TBWA/Chiat Day agency. Called "Dream Garage," a two-minute commercial displays a grouping of Datsun classics, including the Z and 510. An actor plays the role of Mr. K, recalling Yutaka Katayama, the man who founded Nissan Motor's U.S. subsidiary in 1960. But one industry analyst, Ken Gross, found that buyers were confused by the association of past Datsun cars with the latest Nissan products.

Throughout the 1990s, Nissan suffered severe economic losses despite positive evaluations of its cars. By the end of that decade, control of the company went to a French automaker, Renault, which—ironically—had failed in the U.S. market decades before. By 2001 the new company was making a profit.

References

Gross, Ken. "Marching Resolutely Backward." *Automobile Industries* 176, no. 10 (1996): 16.

Levin, Doron. "Alas Poor Nissan, We Hardly Know Ye." *News-Times Automotive*, August 23, 1996. <http://www.newstimes.com/archive96/aug2396/aua. htm/>.

Mateja, Jim. "Nissan Restoring Past with 1970s Datsun Z." *News-Times Automotive*, May 27, 1997. <http://www.newstimes.com/archive97/may2797/-

auf.htm/   http://www.nissan-lobal.com/GCC/Japan/History/history/
main-e.html/>.

Oldham, Scott. "A Century of Cars." <http://www.popularmechanics.com/
popmech/auto3/0001AUTKM.html/>.

Walter Cummins

Dr Pepper

Dr Pepper (the period after the Dr was dropped in the 1950s) is America's oldest major soft drink. It predates all colas (although it looks like one) and has a unique flavor that is sometimes described as spicy. It was developed in 1885 by an employee of Morrison's Drug Store in Waco, Texas. Though today Dr Pepper is the best-selling non-cola soft drink in the United States, the beverage was largely a regional brand sold primarily in the South and Midwest for much of its early history.

In the latter half of the 20th century, Dr Pepper began to expand its reach, becoming more of a national brand. In 1971 the company launched its first full-scale national advertising campaign. Early ads for Dr Pepper, which were often humorous and sometimes irreverent, attempted to establish the soft drink as an unusual beverage for the unique individual with unique tastes. The familiar Dr Pepper clock, showing just 10, 2 and 4 o'clock on the dial, was meant to show people when they should have the pick-me-up of a Dr Pepper. One 1971 commercial featured a young couple on a porch swing. "How do you know I'll like it?" the young woman asks suggestively. After some urging from her boyfriend she does try it—it being Dr Pepper of course—and declares, "I love it!" Also in the 1970s Dr Pepper advertising featured the slogan "the most original soft drink ever in the whole wide world," a revision of a 1960s slogan which labeled Dr Pepper the "most misunderstood" of all soda beverages. In both campaigns the emphasis was on promoting the soft drink as a niche beverage for the independent thinker who wanted something different from the big colas: Coke and Pepsi.

All that changed, however, in 1977 with the introduction of one of the most memorable ad campaigns of the 1970s. Developed by advertising agency Young & Rubicam, the "Be a Pepper" spots relied on a catchy jingle and the high-energy antics of actor David Naughton. Naughton danced through the streets singing, "I'm a Pepper" and inviting everyone around him to "be a Pepper too." As the commercial progressed, the crowds fall in behind Naughton, dancing along with him. These are the newly inaugurated Dr Pepper drinkers, following the soft drink's own pied piper to a kind of beverage bliss.

The emphasis in Dr Pepper advertising had clearly shifted. Dr Pepper,

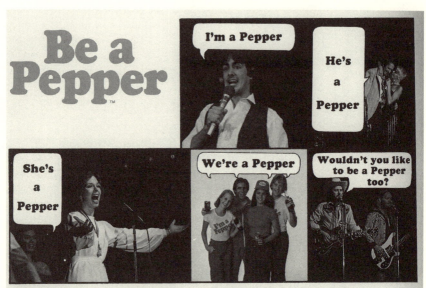

What's a Pepper?

A Pepper is a person who *loves* DR PEPPER.

So a Pepper can be anyone. And any age.

Because being a Pepper is really more a state of mind than a counting of years.

The only thing about a Pepper that's sure is their absolute craving for originality.

Even what they drink must be unique.

Peppers aren't weird, strange or oddball.

They're positive, self-confident, bold and willing to try something new.

Peppers are proud. And Peppers are popular.

So wouldn't you like to be a Pepper too?

The first full-scale national advertising campaign for Dr Pepper was launched in the 1970s. © 2001 Dr Pepper/SevenUp, Inc.

as the gathering crowd dancing through the streets behind Naughton showed, was a soft drink for the masses. Some six years earlier, a Coca-Cola ad featured a multicultural, multiethnic selection of singing young people suggesting that world peace and unity could be achieved if we could just "buy the world a Coke" (see "Coca-Cola" entry in Chapter 6). Dr Pepper also suggested that song and a soft drink could bring people together, though on the whole the Dr Pepper people seemed to take themselves a little less seriously. Indeed the "Be a Pepper" commercials were almost pure fun. The catchy jingle and energetic visuals were straightforward.

"Be a Pepper" was, by most accounts, one of the most recognizable advertising campaigns of the 1970s. Consumer surveys consistently ranked the commercial as one of the most memorable on the air. The jingle was ideal for getting stuck in a person's head. The success of the campaign from a purely business standpoint is, however, more difficult to judge. Sales of Dr Pepper increased throughout the 1970s and were robust for 1977 but grew more slowly thereafter.

In the early 1980s the "Be a Pepper" campaign was abandoned. Dr Pepper, unable to break the stronghold Coca Cola and Pepsi had on the bulk of the market, reverted to their former strategy of emphasizing Dr Pepper's unique appeal. Focusing on differentiating itself from the cola giants, Dr Pepper encouraged people to "hold out for the out of the ordinary."

Nevertheless, "Be a Pepper" maintains a place in the American consciousness. The slogan is often parodied, and consumer products, such as hats, T-shirts, and key chains declaring, "I'm a pepper," are still sold through various outlets. Dr Pepper became part of Cadbury-Schweppes in 1985 and merged in 1986 with 7Up.

References

Alsop, Ronald. "Dr Pepper Is Bubbling Again after Its 'Be a Pepper' Setback." *Wall Street Journal*, September 26, 1985.

Dr Pepper Museum home page. <http://www.drpeppermuseum.org/>.

Official Dr Pepper home page. <http://www.drpepper.com/>.

Rodengen, Jeffrey, and Karen Nitkin. *The Legend of Dr Pepper/7-Up*. Fort Lauderdale, FL: Write Stuff Syndicate, 1995.

Jessica Hausmann

Jell-O

Comedian Bill Cosby's pitch for Jell-O, starting in 1974 and continuing today, is the longest-standing celebrity endorsement in advertising, making the more than 100-year-old gelatin dessert an iconic brand recognized by 99 percent of Americans in 1998 ("The Cool History of Jello"). Jell-O was patented for plain gelatin by Peter Cooper in 1845, who never used the patent. Fifty-two years later, in 1897, cough medicine maker Pearl Wait and his wife, May, of Leroy, New York, obtained the patent, added fruit flavoring to the gelatin, and named it Jell-O. They sold the business two years later for $450 to the founder of the Genesee Pure Food Company, Orator Francis Woodward, who made a fortune from it.

Jell-O, produced today by Kraft Foods, has had many other celebrity endorsements in its history, including Jack Benny, Roy Rogers, and Bob Hope, as well as the stars of such television shows as *Green Acres* and *Gomer Pyle*. Cosby, the brand's sole spokesman since 1974, has been a hit with Jell-O's traditional target market, children from two to fourteen, as well as with their parents. His combination of low-key humor and straight talk has appealed to the baby boomers who were becoming parents but were also nostalgic for the comfort foods of their childhood. Cosby had credibility; consumers of all ages trusted him because he talked plainly without the usual ad hype. When he said Jell-O was fat free but tasted too good to be fat free, there was no argument. Cosby's easygoing, funny persona helped Young & Rubicam's campaign for Jell-O introduce new brands to kids and their parents from instant puddings to blue gelatin and yogurt.

Jell-O advertised its wares in the 1920s with illustrations by such artists as Maxfield Parrish and Norman Rockwell. In the 1930s, it sponsored a *Wizard of Oz* radio show, offering author Frank L. Baum's children's books as product tie-ins with Jell-O recipes on the back cover.

Jell-O is simple to make, requiring only a cup of boiling water, one cup of cold water, and some time in the refrigerator, and the Jell-O Company supplied consumers with plenty of recipes to give the brand more coverage on the family table. It introduced lime Jell-O and opened up the world of the gelled salad with recipes in the 1930s. Women were let in on the secret shortcut to fast Jell-O: use ice cubes instead of cold water. The introduction of tapioca in 1948 and instant puddings in 1950 put Jell-O into pies, and the first sugar-free versions of Jell-O were introduced in 1984. Now it is available in snack cups, ready made for school lunches. In the 1990s, Jell-O launched another product tie-in, linking itself with the video release of the movie *Jurassic Park* and its dinosaurs, and broke the taboo against blue food with a successful introduction of Berry Blue Jell-O. Bill Cosby's playing the piano and singing about it helped promote it. Jell-O's Sparkling White Grape flavor, "The Champagne of Jell-O" was introduced for the brand's 100th anniversary in 1997. Kraft Foods runs a Jell-O restaurant and a Jell-O museum, and it has revived Jell-O's original 1902 slogan, "America's Most Famous Dessert," claiming

Jell-O is in three out of four American homes and sells more than a million boxes of its 120 products a year.

Jell-O history was the subject of a Smithsonian Institution academic conference in 1991, featuring topics like "The Semiotics of Jell-O."

References

Baue, William D. "Bill Cosby Jell-O Campaign." *Encyclopedia of Major Marketing Campaigns.* Ed. Thomas Riggs. Detroit: Gale Group, 2000: 916–20.
"The Cool History of Jell-O." Kraft Foods. <http://www.kraftfoods.com/jell-o/>.

Mary Cross

Life Cereal

Quaker Oats Company introduced Life Cereal in 1961 as a good-tasting, nutritious cereal which "would help kids grow strong." For ten years, the cereal did moderately well, but in 1972 a hugely popular commercial for Life was aired, which significantly increased sales and, in the process, created a new American icon.

Presweetened cereals had come under attack in the 1970s by the American Dental Association and Action for Children's Television. The sale of sugared cereals was in decline, and the cereal companies sought to develop healthier, less sugary cereals. Kellogg's and General Mills both came out with new products, but Quaker Oats led the industry with Life Cereal, a whole-grain oat brand. The accompanying advertising campaign was able to convince both parents and kids that a nutritious cereal could also taste good.

In 1972 Doyle Dane Bernbach created an ad for Life Cereal which proved to be one of the most popular of all time. The premise for the ad was simple: little Mikey, the boy who hated all foods, surprises his brothers by actually devouring the new cereal. The chubby-faced, freckled Mikey, played by three-year-old John Gilchrist, became one of the most recognized faces on television. In the original commercial (which aired from 1972 to 1984), Mikey's older brothers (played by Gilchrist's actual siblings), are suspicious of a new, nutritious cereal being served by their mom. Knowing that their younger brother is finicky about food and would certainly reject the new cereal, they call him—"Hey, Mikey"—and place a bowl of cereal in front of him. To their surprise he digs in. "He likes it," the brothers exclaim in disbelief. "Hey, Mikey" would soon enter into the national lexicon.

A recent research study revealed that 70 percent of adults could identify the Life Cereal ad from just the description of the commercial, although it had not been shown regularly on television for over fifteen years. In 1999 *TV Guide* ranked "Mikey" commercial among the top fifty commercials of all time.

Indeed, the nostalgia for the original ad encouraged Quaker Oats Company to resurrect it in the 1990s. In 1997 the company launched the "Be the Next Mikey" contest, with the winner's picture gracing the next generation of Life cereal boxes. Over 35,000 children entered the competition, and four-year-old Marli Hughes of Florida was announced the winner in 1998.

The life of John Gilchrist, the actor who played little Mikey, has been followed by the media. In the 1980s it was rumored that Gilchrist had died when his stomach exploded after eating Pop Rocks, a popular fizzing candy, with soda. Gilchrist went on to work in advertising and has appeared in more than 250 commercials.

From January to June 2000, the Mikey ad campaign was relaunched with an all-adult cast. Everything about the original commercial was the same, except the actors playing Mikey and his breakfast mates. The handsome new twentysomething Mikey, Jimmy Starace, sits reading his morning newspaper alongside a man and woman. All of them act like kids. In July, Life Cereal began reairing the original Mikey commercial as well.

References

"*Advertising Age*'s 50 Best Commercials." <http://www.adage.com/news_and_features/special_reports/commercials/years.1970.html/>.

Nashawaty, Chris. "Coming Back to Life." *Entertainment Weekly*, April 19, 1996: 22.

"Quaker Oats Life Cereal—Through the Years." <http://www.lifecereal.com/about/mainthrough.html/>.

Elise Salem

Miller Lite Beer

Prior to the Miller Brewing Company's campaign in the 1970s for a light beer, the beer industry had failed to generate much enthusiasm for a low-calorie brew. Initially marketed in the 1960s as a "female-oriented" diet beer, Miller Lite was too narrowly marketed, and consumers did not like the taste. And yet there was an increasing interest in carbohydrate reduction and a health-conscious lifestyle. Miller was able to capitalize on the public's needs and a void in the market.

McCann-Erickson, then Miller's advertising agency, decided to target a specific group, young male sports fans, for their campaign. Not coincidentally, Miller also bought up ad time during big sporting events, boosting the lucrative marriage between beer and sports. The television advertising campaign used ex-jocks who turned the unpopular female diet beer into a manly drink. Lite Beer from Miller soon soared to the top of the market.

The first series of commercials (fourteen, total) used the tag line, "Everything you always wanted in a beer . . . and less." Most of the ads featured a popular sports star, like the New York Jets running back Matt Snell, who explained the benefits of reduced carbohydrates, and then recited the tag line. This "All Stars" campaign involved a group of ex-athletes who became famous all over again. Eventually, McCann-Erikson shortened the tag line to the award-winning "Tastes Great, Less Filling" slogan. The first of these ads pitted basketball star Tommy Heinsohn against NBA referee Mendy Rudolph. In a bar they argued over whether Lite Beer from Miller was superior because of its flavor ("Tastes Great") or its low calories and hence "Less Filling" quality. This tag line would prove to be one of the most memorable in advertising history.

In 1973 Lite Beer from Miller was test-marketed with favorable results, and it began to dominate the market. By 1977, it was second only to Anheuser-Busch. The success of Miller and its new beer was attributable to the dynamic advertising campaign that targeted young male sports fans and captured their interest with great tag lines and simple humor.

Sales of Lite Beer from Miller had nearly doubled by 1977. The humorous commercials, along with the increasingly popular beer, improved the sales of all other Miller beers as well. Not surprisingly, the success of Miller Lite generated new products and advertisements from its competitors. Anheuser-Busch brought out its Natural Light beer in 1977 and its even more successful Bud Light in 1982. Lite Beer from Miller, however, continued to dominate the market until 1993, when Bud Light took over after another great series of ads, the "Spuds MacKenzie" campaign of the late 1980s, featuring a bull terrier with one black eye, "the original party animal."

In the past decade, Miller sales have not been so promising, and the brewing company has tried to introduce new brands, changing its advertising, revamping its packaging, and even lowering prices. There is discussion under way about whether to bring back an updated version of the Miller Lite All-Stars campaign that dominated beer commercials in the 1970s and 1980s. In 1999 the Leo Burnett Company of Chicago, Miller Lite's previous ad agency, was replaced by Fallon McElligott from the New York region. The idea was to shift the focus back to Miller Lite, which still accounted for 40 percent of Miller's total sales.

Your first Lite Beer does a nice thing for your second.

It leaves room for it.

True. Lite Beer is actually less filling than our regular beer.

It has one-third less calories.

And Lite Beer tastes great. That's very important.

After all, there's not much sense in leaving room for a second beer unless you've enjoyed the first.

Lite® Beer from Miller.
Everything you always wanted in a beer. And less.

© 1976 The Miller Brewing Co., Milwaukee, Wis.

A dynamic advertising campaign that targeted young male sports fans made Miller Lite a success. Courtesy of Miller Brewing Company.

References

Beatty, Sally. "Miller's Attempt to Woo Cool Drinkers with Offbeat Ads Flops." 1999 Indian Express Newspapers. <http://expressindia.com/fe/daily/19990513/fle13078p.html/>.

Gallun, Alby. "Miller Brewing Regroups amid Declining Sales." 1999 American City Business Journals, Inc. <http://milwaukee.bcentral.com/milwaukee/stories/1999/02/08/story2.html/>.

Garfield, Bob. "Dick's Lower Profile Gives Lift to Lite Ads." *Advertising Age*, June 29, 1997.

Johnson, William O. "Sports and Suds: The Beer Business and the Sports World Have Brewed Up a Potent Partnership." *Sports Illustrated*, August 8, 1988: 68.

Lazarus, George. "The Lite Years: How Miller's Move Started It All." *Adweek's Marketing Week*. August 15, 1988:9.

Miller Brewing Company Web site: <http://www.millerbrewing.com/>.

Van Munching, Philip. *Beer Blast: The Inside Story of the Brewing Industry's Bizarre Battle for Your Money*. New York: Times Books, 1997.

Elise Salem

Virginia Slims Cigarettes

In 1968 Philip Morris introduced Virginia Slims, a new, slimmer cigarette for women (only 23 mm in circumference, a "full" 2 mm thinner than regular cigarettes). The advertising campaign designed by the Leo Burnett Company of Chicago (initially both in print and on television) targeted the fast-growing market of women smokers. These ads became especially popular in the 1970s after Slims sponsored a new women-only tennis tournament in Houston in 1970. The ad campaign (featured only in print media after the 1971 decision to ban cigarette advertising from broadcast media) modified the slogan to read, "You've come a long way, baby." The ads struck a chord, and the Slims slogan became a national catch phrase in the 1970s and into the 1980s.

Although the modern women's movement had begun in the 1960s, its impact was not felt until the next decade. The National Organization for Women (NOW) was founded in 1966 under the leadership of Betty Friedan, whose 1963 book *The Feminine Mystique* assaulted the advertising industry for encouraging the oppression of women through demeaning stereotypes. In 1970 congressional hearings held on discrimination against women highlighted the negative portrayal of women in the media. In the early 1970s, NOW and other women's groups began systematically to boycott and condemn ads that glorified the depiction of woman as housekeeper and sexual object. More women entered the workforce and gained purchasing power, and the advertising industry itself became more representative of women. The 1970s signaled an important time of change for women.

One of the most successful responses to the women's movement within the advertising industry was the woman-centered marketing strategy of Virginia Slims. Its humorous condemnation of the oppressive old days (depicted in sepia and white like an old photograph) featured the exploitation and social exclusion of women trying to sneak a smoke. The contrasting color photo showed a supremely self-confident, independent, and successful modern woman standing with a cigarette in her hand. "You've come a long way, baby" is offered as a confirmation of her liberation. The boldness and ingenuity of these print ads spoke for a new generation of employed and hence empowered women. The humor, relatively rare in ad campaigns of "the serious seventies," favorably caught people's attention, but some still found the ad demeaning because of its insistence on thinness and beauty for a model of liberation (supermodel Cheryl Tiegs) and for its patronizing use of "baby" in the slogan. Indeed, the addition of the word "baby" at the end of the slogan was a subject of debate within the ad agency. Some found the term offensive, but when the tagline was tested without the word it fell flat.

When *Ms.* magazine, which began publication in 1972, ran an ad for Virginia Slims, it provoked such a negative reaction in the readership that the magazine refused to carry the ad again. Clearly, finding ads that would mirror the women's movement was easier said than done. Although cosmetics, fragrance, and hair products all suffered flat or declining sales during the 1970s, this did not mean that cultural notions of beauty and femininity were not still linked with the advertising industry and its promising products. The example of Virginia Slims demonstrates the complexity of cultural icons as they impinge upon issues of gender and identity. (A competing product in the 1970s was Eve cigarettes, marketed as the cigarette of choice for the mid-1970s socially independent but still fashionable new woman. The ad's slogan was, "There's a little Eve in every woman.")

To further complicate the message of the women's liberation cigarette was the growing realization that lung cancer among women was growing astronomically. The very successful advertising campaign of Virginia Slims, targeted specifically to women, certainly played a part in these alarming statistics. The popular print ads with the same tag line continued into the 1990s and, despite a challenge in the 1980s by Brown & Williamson with its Capri brand, Virginia Slims remained the leading women's cigarette. By the mid-1980s, the $500,000 Virginia Slims Tennis Championships, held at New York's Madison Square Garden every November, continued to keep the cigarette in full public view. But women's and antismoking groups protested these events with placards that read,

"Yes, Virginia, there is lung cancer." Philip Morris began to withdraw the Virginia Slims name from some tennis tournaments, substituting its non-tobacco brand name "Kraft" instead.

References

Bretl, D. J., and J. Cantor. "The Portrayal of Men and Women in U.S. Television Commercials: A Recent Content Analysis and Trends over Fifteen Years." *Sex Roles* 18 (1988): 595–609.

Craig, Steve. "Madison Avenue versus *The Feminine Mystique*: How the Advertising Industry Responded to the Onset of the Modern Women's Movement." <http://www.rtvf.unt.edu/people/craig/madave.htm/>.

Dann, Sammy R., ed. *Advertising and Popular Culture: Studies in Variety and Versatility*. Bowling Green, OH: Bowling Green State University Popular Press, 1992.

Simly, John. "Virginia Slims." In *Encyclopedia of Consumer Brands*, edited by Janice Jorgensen, vol. 1, 622–24. Detroit: St. James, 1994.

Wernick, Andrew. *Promotional Culture: Advertising, Ideology and Symbolic Expression*. London: Sage Publications, 1991.

Elise Salem

Icons of the 1980s

If the 1970s was a decade of discontent, remembered best for a weak economy, the Vietnam War, and a president's resignation, the 1980s was a time when the United States rediscovered itself. America was the world's great democracy, with a strong military presence throughout the world and a seemingly thriving economy at home. The individual who best exemplified America's emergence from the shame of defeat and corruption was a former movie star elected president in 1980 who promised, "It's morning in America." Ronald Reagan was the "great communicator" who brought his media savvy with him to the White House and presided over a booming era of advertising and conspicuous consumption.

The 1970s ended with the taking of sixty-three American hostages in Iran, bringing to a climax the sense of frustration and powerlessness that began with the Vietnam War. On Reagan's Inauguration Day, January 20, 1981, the hostages were freed. Reagan's good fortune with the hostage situation signaled a decade of sweeping historic achievements both here and abroad. For Reagan there were the good guys and the bad guys. The Soviet Union wore the black hat; America wore the white one. Drawing on the imagery of one of the most successful films in American cinema history, *Star Wars* (1976), President Reagan labeled the Soviets "the Evil Empire." Yet by the time Reagan completed his second term in 1989, the Soviet Union had been dissolved, and by the end of 1990, East and West Germany had been reunified. All of this pointed toward the victory of democracy, capitalism, and America over totalitarianism, communism, and the Soviet Union. The Cold War was over.

American heroes of the 1980s were, for the most part, those who found a way to succeed by merging, liquidating, buying, and selling. It was an era of deregulation and big business. "Greed is good," Gordon Gekko, a character in the movie *Wall Street* (1987), told us in 1987. Acquiring wealth increasingly became the focus of achievement not only on the financial scene but among ordinary citizens as well. "He who dies with the most toys wins," a sardonic comment on the decade, heralded the "Me" decade and the population of yuppies (young urban professionals) who came to symbolize it, even as a new population of the homeless clogged city streets.

The 1980s made conspicuous consumption acceptable. Designer labels sprouted on the outside of handbags and blue jeans. Once considered a vulgar display, labels were now flaunted as status for the wearer. A revival of the preppie look, that pink-and-green WASP-y style of the 1950s, was also under way, only this time around it was a tongue-and-cheek, ironic take. Back came the buttondown collars, the penny loafers, the khaki pants, horn-rimmed glasses, and the alligator polo shirts. Lisa Birnbach's *The Preppie Handbook* (1980), a humorous look at it all, made sure everyone got the joke.

Politicians, meanwhile, were calling for a return to the "family values" of the 1950s, drawing nostalgic pictures of two-parent families in which mothers and fathers played clearly distinct roles and raised happy children. Nonetheless, the 1980s saw an unprecedented rise in the divorce rate.

In October 1987 the stock market crashed, falling more than 500 points on one Black Monday. The party was over for a while. Many ad agencies, like Saatchi & Saatchi ("Where's the Beef?"), had been on a spending spree, buying up other agencies. The fallout from agency megamergers in the 1980s and a recessionary economy in the early 1990s spawned small boutique ad agencies and new creativity.

The dizzying array of consumer goods in the 1980s had kept agencies busy, with technology leading the way. Cassette tapes and compact discs (CDs) replaced records, and the Sony Walkman was ready to market. The personal computer wars, for which agencies produced some groundbreaking ads, were on between Apple and IBM. Cable television offered Americans many more choices than network television, which started to lose advertising. And MTV (music television) appeared, with a style of jump-cut filming that advertising hijacked for its own fast-cut television commercials.

America's image in the world had exposed its cracks in the mid-1980s: the Challenger spacecraft exploded in 1986, the stock market collapsed in 1987, the Iran Contra scandal involving arms sales to a country holding Americans hostage came to light, and AIDS made headlines and inroads on sexual freedom. In spite of the problems, it was still the American Century. The story of America in the 1980s, triumphing over adversity, was like a Hollywood epic, led by a president who had been a movie star.

References

Birnbach, Lisa. *The Preppy Handbook*. New York: Workman, 1980.
Garfield, Bob. "Top 100 Advertising Campaigns of the Century." AdAge.com.
Holt, Sid. *The Rolling Stone Interviews: The 1980s*. New York: St. Martin's Press, 1989.
Tor, James D., ed. *The 1980s*. San Diego: Greenhaven Press, 2000.

Geoffrey Weinman and Sylvia Skaggs-McTague

Absolut Vodka

What do Queen Latifah, Salman Rushdie, Spike Lee, Susan Sontag, Philip Glass, and Trey Parker and Matt Stone (of *South Park* fame) have in common? They have all posed for Absolut Vodka ads. In fact, each of these personalities—and personality is the operative word here—appears in the July 2000 issue of *Vanity Fair* magazine's twenty-four-page spread, along with other notables, celebrating the famous vodka's "20 years in America." In an age and a country where beer was the favorite accompaniment to leisure activity, particularly among men, and wine was growing in popularity as a sign of sophistication among the yuppie population, the advertising world was floored by the success of the ad campaigns for an essentially tasteless and colorless liquor.

That campaign began in 1979 with the introduction of what has since become an icon: the Absolut bottle. The Swedish Absolut company, about to celebrate the 100th anniversary of the vodka's origin (1879), wanted to introduce it to America and consulted with the N. W. Ayer advertising agency in New York City. Together, they decided to package the vodka in a clear glass bottle, with blue lettering for 80 proof vodka and red lettering for 100 proof. Ayer did not keep the account, which went to the TBWA advertising agency. While working on the account one day at TBWA, Geoff Hayes sketched a halo over the bottle as a symbol of purity, which he labeled Absolut Purity (later changed to Absolut Perfection). Then he drew a bottle with wings, labeling it Absolut Heaven. He showed his idea to Graham Turner who also worked on the account, and the two of them came up with a dozen different ideas for Absolut ads.

Thus was born "Absolut Art," the American advertising campaign that would launch over 1,200 ads and give more than 350 artists a chance to depict the Absolut bottle in various artistic ways. The first Absolut Art ad, which appeared in 1985, was done by Andy Warhol of Campbell Soup fame, who had asked to make a painting for Absolut. He received $65,000 for his Absolute Warhol, and both he and the Absolut bottle received tremendous media attention because of the ad. Next, in 1987, was Kenny Scharf, known for his grafitti-like drawings in the New York City subways. In the 1980s, artists such as Stephen Sprouse, Ed Ruscha, and Julie Wachtel followed in Warhol's and Scharf's footsteps, creating their own Absolut statements. Indeed, Absolut has become an industry attracting not only painters and sculptors but also fashion designers such as Nicole Miller, Versace, and Richard Tyler, as well as numerous literary and film celebrities.

Over the next two decades, under the executive leadership of Michel Roux, Seagrams, the parent corporation, has spent hundreds of millions of dollars transforming Absolut Vodka into a work of art—whether it is high culture or low is still being debated. *Advertising Age* has ranked the bottle's presentation through advertising as seventh among the top 100 advertising campaigns of the 20th century. As Bob Garfield put it in the Special Supplement issue of *Advertising Age*, "Absolut Vodka achieved what Stolichnaya could never do: establish a burgeoning marketplace for premium vodkas. It is a neat trick for a product that is by law and by its very nature a flavorless commodity" (26).

1996 saw the publication of the *Absolut Book: The Absolut Vodka Advertising Story* by Richard W. Lewis, the advertising genius in charge of the Absolut account with TBWA Chiat/Day since 1987. In this work, Lewis discusses the lengths to which the creative teams involved in designing the Absolut ads would go to keep Absolut Vodka in the minds and on the lips of people throughout the world. He describes, for example, the use of wheat to attract pigeons to the Piazza San Marco to form the shape of an Absolut Vodka bottle. The result: "Absolut Venice," a portrait of the piazza and its pigeons in the shadows of the setting sun. Special ads and promotions have also been created, such as Absolut Centerfold for *Playboy*, Absolut Spring (with seeds), Absolut First Class (with stamps), and Absolut X-ray (on real x-ray plastic). There were Father's Day ties featuring Absolut as well as Christmas magazine ads that played "Jingle Bells."

In the past twenty years, Absolut Vodka ads and displays have become collector's items. A search for Absolut on the Web reveals how extensive this phenomenon has become. Sites include an advertising archive; a "millennium market" with new ads, old ads, and a trading corner; an Absolut Collectors Society; and the Absolut Connection, which claims to "find all the information you would ever want or need to know about Absolut Vodka ad collecting. Includes history, facts, and drink recipes."

In 1994 Carl Horton, vice president for marketing at Seagrams Spirits and Wine Group, launched Internet marketing of Absolut and increased the company's sponsorship of artists, fashion designers, and local events. Absolut is no longer just a drink. It is a cultural force, and the 1980s proved the perfect time in our history to launch this product in America:

no protests, a seemingly sound economy, the emergence of the yuppie culture, and a nod to charitable and social work that might get the aspirant in the society pages of the *New York Times* or the fashion pages of *Women's Wear Daily*. Absolut was absolutely on target.

References

"Absolut." <http:www.Absolut.com/>.

Brown, C. "Absolutely Ingenious." *Forbes*, April 15, 1991: 128.

Garfield, Bob. "Top 100 Advertising Campaigns of the Century." *Advertising Age: The Advertising Century*. Special Supplement. Chicago: Crain Communications, 1999:18–41.

Hamilton, Carl. *Absolut: Biography of a Bottle*. New York: Texere, 2000.

Hayes, Geoff. "The Absolut Model." *Adweek—Western Edition*, August 1, 1994: 27.

Lewis, Richard W. *Absolut Book: The Absolut Vodka Advertising Story*. Boston: Journey Editions, 1996.

McGlinn, E. "Absolut Marketing." *Forbes*, December 11, 1989: 282.

Geoffrey Weinman

Apple Computers

When George Orwell wrote the novel *1984* in 1949, he projected a future in which technology, in the hands of the powerfully corrupt, would threaten our individuality, our freedoms, and our creativity. The phrase, "Big Brother is watching you," which came from this famous work, is still being used today to suggest the lack of freedom existing in dictatorships around the world. It also is used, however, to describe the increasing threats to personal security and privacy in an age in which computer technology has invaded personal space, coming into people's homes, and sharing information about their personal lives, buying habits, financial status, and sexual preferences and lifestyles.

Drawing on Orwell's vision, Apple Computer launched a one-time only commercial for its new Macintosh 128K which ran during the third quarter of the 1984 Super Bowl. This sixty-second piece, created at a cost of $400,000 and broadcast at a cost of another $500,000, pictured a frightening world dominated by an oppressive, mind-numbing IBM-like mentality (IBM was Apple's chief competitor; see the "IBM Personal Computer" entry in this chapter). Onto this scene of cold sterility enters our hero, single-handedly smashing the giant screen that brings Big Brother into our lives and allows him to watch over and control us. The Mac represents the new future, this ad tells us—a future in which individuality and creativity take the place of sameness and programmed controls.

The ad, directed by Ridley Scott, best known for such futuristic films as *Blade Runner* (1982) and *Alien* (1979), caused quite a stir. Indeed, though the commercial had received little advance publicity, there were those insiders who tuned into the Super Bowl specifically to see it. It was the most expensive ad ever created for a one-shot showing, and it became, because of its production values and avant-garde aura, an event—and an icon—in itself. Not surprisingly, it won every major advertising award for that year. *Advertising Age* ranked it twelfth in the top 100 advertising campaigns of the century. As recently as 1996, Packard-Bell and Sun Microsystems were referencing this ad in their own campaigns for the computer market.

Aside from the drama and hoopla attending this event, the Mac itself had practical advantages over its competition at the time. It was the first affordable computer to include a graphical user interface and the first with a floppy drive that took 3.5-inch disks. At $2,495, it was beginning to bring the computer into the range of the personal shopper, although it was still too expensive for most consumers.

Apple's biggest appeal has been to the elementary and secondary education market as well as to those focusing on graphics. In recent years, it has seen its competition, not only IBM, which transformed itself into a modern, "with it," user-friendly organization, but the numerous clones and less expensive models on the market, subsume much of its audience.

Whether Apple continues to be a major player into the 21st century or not, its "1984" ad redefined the computer market. It told people not to be afraid, that computers were not only for those hidden behind the walls of huge corporations but for the little man or woman. The computer was going to be user-friendly and affordable: compact, fun, non-threatening. Chiat/Day and the creative team that put this ad together understood the psychological and mythic fears of the audience to which it was speaking. Even those young people who had never heard of Orwell could understand what that ad was telling them. The computer was going to be an integral part of their lives.

References

Apple Computer. *Inside Macintosh.* Reading, MA: Addison-Wesley, 1994.

Linzmayer, Owen W. *Apple Confidential: The Real Story of Apple Computers, Inc.* San Francisco: No Starch Press, 1999.

Malone, Michael S. *Infinite Loop: How the World's Most Insanely Great Computer Company Went Insane.* New York: Currency/Doubleday, 1999.

Geoffrey Weinman

AT&T

"Reach out, reach out and touch someone! / Reach out, call up, and just say Hi!" This catchy jingle, first introduced to the American public on July 27, 1979, has become part of our pop culture vocabulary over the past twenty-plus years. Created for AT&T by the N. W. Ayers advertising agency and its creative group, the series of ads employing this phrase played on television and radio until 1983, replacing "Long Distance Is the Next Best Thing to Being There," which ran for most of the 1970s.

Few advertising campaigns have received the attention devoted to "Reach Out and Touch Someone," thanks largely to Michael J. Arlen's series of articles on advertising which ran in the *New Yorker* in 1979 and which he published as a book, *Thirty Seconds*, in 1980. The Arlen piece on AT&T describes, often tongue in cheek, the making of the first "Reach Out" television commercial, called "Tap Dancing" (titled after the little girl in the commercial who tap danced as her grandparents across the country listened to the sound of her tap shoes) as an example of what goes into the making of a thirty-second spot.

AT&T, the long distance arm of the Bell System, was looking to increase the volume of long-distance calls with these ads. In this age of cell phones and the Internet, it is hard for us to realize that long-distance phone calling was viewed, even into the 1980s, as an act reserved for special occasions. Often those occasions were negative: reports of illness or even death. AT&T wanted its advertising agency, Ayer, to change that perception and to make the act of long-distance phoning an emotionally rewarding one—and one used to share all kinds of good news, to express warm feelings, to keep in touch. The message was clear: "Reach out and *touch* someone"—with your voice, your caring, your love, your desire to share.

The audience for these ads was identified as relatively young (25–49), upwardly mobile, and predominately female, but the first ad tried its best, within that precious thirty seconds, to reach as broad an American audience as possible. With the tune playing at various points in the background and foreground, the piece featured a female jockey talking on the phone after a victory, a young man calling from his Army barracks, a rodeo cowboy, two women—one black, the other white—communicating while performing yoga standing on their heads, a hockey player (minus his front teeth) talking to his son in hockey uniform (minus his front teeth), and, of course, the little girl tap dancing as her grandparents share in this experience.

Long-distance calling brought families and friends together for the purpose of sharing the joys of life. How could anyone resist? And with Phoebe Snow, José Feliciano, Ray Charles, Tammy Wynette, Roberta Flack, and other superstars of the 1980s giving voice to this message in television spots, hardly anyone could.

Having had a healthy run until 1983, the "Reach Out" campaign lay dormant until 1987 when it was revived by the now-divested AT&T organization for three more years. That it would have been discontinued in 1983, in spite of its great success, is understandable given what AT&T and the Bell System were going through at the time. In January 1982, the federal order for divestiture was finalized. And both AT&T and "Ma Bell" knew there was no choice but to break up or be broken. The divestiture of the Bell System proved traumatic for the thousands of employees who had devoted their professional lives to what they viewed as an American institution. No wonder, then, that the notion of "reaching out" seemed ironic at a time when the pieces of a once-unified series of operations were being pulled apart.

In 1987 the "Reach Out" campaign was restored and updated and, though discontinued once again in 1990, the song and its message live into the 21st century. The phrase, however, is no longer associated exclusively with AT&T. It has been co-opted numerous times by writers discussing such diverse matters as phone rage, sexual harassment, and the use of the Internet. Like "Where's the Beef?," another 1980s phrase that helped establish Wendy's as a fast-food icon, it has taken on a life of its own.

References

Arlen, Michael J. *Thirty Seconds*. New York: Farrar, Straus and Giroux, 1980.

Gamet, R. W. *The Telephone Enterprise: The Evolution of the Bell System's Horizontal Structure*. Baltimore: Johns Hopkins University Press, 1985.

Todd, K. P. Jr., comp. *A Capsule History of the Bell System*. New York: AT&T, 1979.

Geoffrey Weinman

Ben & Jerry's

Friends since childhood, Ben Cohen and Jerry Greenfield, both thirty-nine in 1978, got together to see if they could sell ice cream. They rented a former gas station that year in Burlington, Vermont, and began to experiment with ice cream flavors. At Ben and Jerry's Homemade, Vermonters found rich, unusual ice cream flavors. Ben & Jerry's first ice cream cartons displayed the unpretentious decoration of two average-looking guys. As business grew, it became clear to Ben and Jerry that they could turn into yet another example of the commercial success of the 1980s. The two men distinguished their company by forging a social mission, pledging that business could be responsible for social concerns. Theirs was "Ice Cream for the People." They produced a television commercial, "Cheap," in the early 1980s, a low-budget effort in which Ben and Jerry themselves were shown poking their heads through their pictures on the ice cream carton.

The wild flavors of Ben and Jerry's quickly grew popular. The flavors featured rich ice cream blended with chunks of candy or cookies. Meanwhile, the psychedelic colors of their packaging and parlors celebrated 1970s pop-culture. Ice cream lovers, young and older, were drawn to their colors and the idea of "all natural" milk and cream. The ice cream titles were fun. Among the most popular flavors were Cherry Garcia, named for Jerry Garcia of the Grateful Dead, and Chunkey Monkey, banana ice cream dotted with huge chunks of chocolate chips. As the story went, Greenfield added flavor until Cohen felt he had arrived at the full taste.

In the midst of Ronald Reagan's trickle-down economics, Ben and Jerry's shaped a new business ethos. The company's social mission seemed unusual in its popular version and striking in its complexity. The ice cream cartons announce that Ben and Jerry's donates a portion of its proceeds to peace organizations. The company contributed 7.5 percent of the pretax profits to national peace organizations, and other company profits went to charities. Moreover, according to company rule, neither founder can make more than five times the salary of the lowest paid employee. Cohen and Greenfield also contribute generously to the lives of their employees, offering extra benefits like inexpensive day care and free health club membership—to counterbalance the effects of daily free ice cream. They continue to take strong stances against health hazards, such as bovine growth hormones, ignored by other companies.

Marketing for the company initially was mostly word of mouth. The quirks of the owners got them plenty of press for themselves and their ice cream. Basically anti-advertising, Ben and Jerry's did promotions rather than buy time on television or in print media, using bumper stickers, festivals, free cone days, and other gimmicks. Their work and donations for social causes also earned them many press clippings.

Despite having changed during the 1980s from a twelve-flavor ice cream shop to a $58 million business, Ben and Jerry's still conjured an image of casual freedom. This was their basic marketing philosophy. They appealed to Americans as a couple of average guys. Cohen and Greenfield once drove cross-country in a mobile home, giving out free ice cream. Though the company cultivated a grassroots image, by 1989 Ben and Jerry's had become the nation's second largest premium ice cream distributor.

Ben and Jerry's personal approach appealed to a public who sensed that a booming economy and growing conservative reforms threatened individuality. Its brightly colored packages and parlors recalled a 1970s spirit of questioning authority, and its social mission invited the hope that commercial success could still support civic responsibility.

In 2000 Unilever, makers of Breyer's and Good Humor products, acquired Ben & Jerry's Homemade of South Burlington, Vermont, for $326 million, placating the owners and overriding customer protests by creating an additional $5 million venture capital fund for companies in low-income areas. Unilever plans to open European markets for Ben & Jerry's.

References

Adler, Jerry, and Carol Friday. "Calories of the Rain Forest." *Newsweek*, December 3, 1990: 61. <http://www.benjerry.com/>.
Hubbard, Kim. "For New Age Ice Cream Moguls Ben and Jerry, Making 'Cherry Garcia' and 'Chunkey Monkey' Is a Labor of Love." *People*, October 9, 1990: 73–75.
Tagliabue, John. "In a Global Fight, Sprinkles Are Extra." *New York Times*, August 19, 2001: BU6.

Sylvia Skaggs-McTague

California Raisins

When Marvin Gaye recorded "I Heard It Through the Grapevine" in the 1960s, he could never have guessed that more than twenty years later the song would be resurrected as the soundtrack for one of the most successful ad campaigns of the 1980s. The song was used to promote raisins, California raisins to be exact, a product that would not seem to lend itself to a multimillion dollar television campaign. What could be duller than a wrinkled piece of dried fruit? Foote, Cone & Belding, the advertising agency hired by the California Raisin Board to produce this series of commercials, faced a serious challenge.

Their response: the use of Will Vinton's new process Claymation (an animated format with clay figures, like those used in the movie *Toy Story*), to showcase a group of hip dancing and singing raisins. Though animation is usually viewed by the advertising industry (and adults) as less credible than live action, the raisins proved an exception. As David Martin described it in his *Romancing the Brand: The Power of Advertising and How to Use It*, "It hit the baby boomers squarely on the nostalgia button, and picked up millions of younger fans as well. The finger-snappin', toe-tappin' Claymation raisins danced all the way to the cash register for the California Raisin Board." Raisin sales jumped 9 percent over the previous year during the months the commercials aired.

The ads were the favorite of television viewers in 1987, topping Bud Light, Pepsi, Miller Lite, and McDonald's. They also demonstrated it is not always how much you spend that determines viewer recognition or acceptance. Television spending for that year for the raisin ads was $5.4 million as compared with a whopping $344.1 million for McDonald's.

The song and the Claymation raisins remained popular, though the ad campaign was been put to rest some years ago. Unfortunately for the raisin-growing industry, sales of raisins have declined in recent years, with no new campaign to match the dancing raisins. In fact, the California Raisin Advisory Board disbanded in 1994 after forty-five years as a result of conflicts between large and small packagers and a decline in raisin revenues. It was five years before the industry could put together a new marketing board.

The new board's first decision was to bring back the dancing raisins. According to the *Sacramento Business Journal*, "Industry leaders and growers hope the return of the animated characters will revive interest in the fruit. Last time around, they practically sparked a revival of Marvin Gaye albums as they pranced around to 'I Heard It Through the Grapevine.' " The return of the dancing raisins, however, did little to spur raisin sales.

Still, the dancing raisins have emerged as icons adopted and adapted to serve ends other than the one for which the commercials originally were created. Among the projects in which the raisins participated were 1990 public service spots encouraging young people to use the library, read, and follow good nutritional habits. Like "Where's the Beef?" and "Reach Out and Touch Someone," "I Heard It Through the Grapevine" has become an advertising classic.

References

Barrier, M. "The Clay's the Thing." *Nation's Business*, December 1988: 57.

"California Raisins Star in TV Spot for Libraries and Literacy." *Emerging Librarian*, 18, no. 21 (November/December 1990): 75.

"Comeback for Raisins: Ads Are Dusted Off as Raisin Sales Dry Up." *Sacramento Business Journal*, November 11, 1999: 4.

Martin, David N. *Romancing the Brand: The Power of Advertising and How to Use It*. New York: American Management Association, 1989.

Geoffrey Weinman

Calvin Klein Jeans

The designer jeans craze of the 1980s was a bizarre phenomenon that followed the first appearance of designer jeans in 1979. Jeans shifted from being casual wear that indicated relaxation to being casual wear that touted sex appeal. Companies like Levi's and Lee, which sold the rugged look, were quickly less visible than those like Calvin Klein and Bonjour, which sold sexiness.

Designer jeans were expensive, and people knew it. Perhaps paying more helped build the rage of this trend. The labels were a status symbol. They were also a sign of conspicuous consumption. Blue jeans, once referred to as "jeans," were now referred to by their labels. Confidently, Americans thought little of displaying the cost of their clothes through the label.

Calvin Klein was at the forefront of this shift, the first designer of Seventh Avenue to sew his name to the back pocket of a pair of jeans. All the other jeans companies followed suit. The pocket labels were all about brand awareness. In most magazine and television ads, the camera zeroed in on a model's tightly fitting jeans, featuring a label readable on the back pocket.

Calvin Klein's jeans became icons of advertising's turn in the 1980s to open sex appeal. His Brooke Shields television ad in 1980, shot by Richard Avedon, was the first of many taboo-breaking Klein ads. It showed the fifteen-year-old Shields, girl-like and innocent with long straight hair and clear eyes, wearing a pair of Calvin Klein jeans. Turning slowly around toward the camera, she asked boldly, "Know what comes between me and my Calvins? Nothing." People only vaguely knew Shields before the ads. She had starred in *Blue Lagoon*, a teen film known for its nude scene. But the ads made Shields a well-known name. People had seldom seen anything so explicit on primetime commercials. There was something mildly perverse, or at least suggestive, about such a young girl talking that way. But, as Calvin Klein himself said, "Jeans are about sex."

When the jeans market hit a slump later in the decade, Klein shifted to advertisements featuring Kate Moss, who became a symbol of the thin look that critics would say encouraged anorexia nervosa. By the 1990s, Klein's male models garbed in suggestive underwear and photographed by Bruce Weber were a common sight on billboards in New York and other cities. As Klein judged that Americans were ready for more and more suggestive or sexual advertising, he made sure that he and his clothing line were in full view with a series of provocative ads, not only for jeans but for Obsession, his new fragrance, where television ads showed men and women in a hazy background doing things one couldn't quite make out.

Aiming at a new generation of teenagers in the early 1990s, Klein, whose ads were all done in-house by his own agency, CRK Advertising, launched a campaign on television and on the sides of New York buses showing very young models posed in jeans and suggestive poses in what looked like a seedy recreation room. Once again, Klein used a famous fashion photographer, Steven Meisel, to shoot the campaign. The resulting outcry over "kiddie porn" was huge. Even President Bill Clinton and his wife, Hillary, protested. After it was determined by the U.S. Justice Department that no minors were being used as models in the ads, Klein, having gotten all he wanted out of the publicity (there is no such thing as bad publicity, as the saying goes), withdrew the campaign less than two months later. Calvin Klein had pushed the boundaries again, riveting America's focus on his name and brand, and making his jeans iconic symbols of sexuality.

References

Elliott, Stuart. "Will Calvin Klein's Retreat Redraw the Lines of Taste?" *New York Times*, August 29, 1995: D1+.

Kaplan, James. "What Makes Calvin Run?" *New York*, September 18, 1995: 46–57, 101.

Sylvia Skaggs-McTague

IBM Personal Computers

When International Business Machines (IBM) introduced its first portable personal computer in 1983, it was called the Crackerjack, an old slang term long familiar to American consumers as the brand name of a candied popcorn. IBM's first desktop personal computer in 1981 was called the Acorn. Such rustic, familiar names helped people relate to the brand-new technology coming down the pike, and IBM was trying hard to catch up to Apple, then the leader in the home computer revolution.

IBM closed the gap with an advertising campaign in the mid-1980s using a character out of the silent movies, Charlie Chaplin's "Little Tramp," a bumbling, lovable character with whom consumers could identify in the baffling world of computer technology. Academic computer gurus advised, "High tech, high touch," and the Little Tramp with his amusing antics humanized the seemingly cold, hard computer, making it look easy to use. He never spoke, but the facial expressions and body language Chaplin had made memorable in silent film dramatized the confusion and amazement inspired by computers. The character was played by a stage actor, Billy Scudder, with voice-overs and headlines proclaiming things like, "Hold on to your hat," one of the Little Tramp's favorite gestures. Put together by the Lord Geller advertising agency, the print and television campaign had enough impact to put IBM ahead in the PC wars, where ordinary consumers and small businesses were the target audience. Apple and IBM took turns at the top of this market over and over in the 1980s. Apple's advertising (see the "Apple Computers" entry in this chapter) was highly creative, and when IBM discontinued its Little Tramp campaign in 1985, it began to lose market share.

Big Blue, as IBM came to be known, had been around since 1911 as a business-to-business company, Computing-Tabulating-Recording Co., which produced small business machines. The early mainframe computers built by IBM filled a room, and only the corporate world could afford to own one. Even the personal computers Apple Computer began to introduce in the late 1970s were too expensive for most people. Apple's Macintosh, created to be a cheaper, more accessible PC, still cost $2,500 when it was introduced in 1984. Though IBM was slow to get into the PC market, its first model in August 1981 with Intel inside helped IBM capture more than a third of the PC market by 1983, and established IBM computer programs as a standard that Apple's Macintosh tried to counteract with an easier-to-understand program of icons.

By the beginning of the 1990s, sales of IBM's PCs had fallen, with competitors Apple, Compaq, and Dell capturing more of the market. The Little Tramp, so successful in the 1980s, was brought back in 1991 for an encore in IBM television and print ads, but the campaign did not have the same impact on sales the second time around. IBM hired Ogilvy & Mather in 1993 and ran several other major ad campaigns. By 1995 IBM had recouped some of its losses, capturing more than 10 percent of the PC market.

References

"Computer History." IBM Corporation. <http://www.ibm.com/>.
"A History of IBM Firsts." <www.storage.ibm.com>.

Mary Cross

Motel 6

Until the mid-1980s, Motel 6 was just one indistinguishable member of sixty economy motel groups, but, in 1985, when Tom Bodett agreed to do his Motel 6 radio commercials, Motel 6 built its reputation. In the space of one year, during which people listened to Bodett chatting in casual tones on their car radios, occupancy rates at Motel 6 rose six points to 72.7 percent, and more people felt they knew Motel 6 as a place to stay.

When the Motel 6's Dallas agent called him, Bodett had already begun forging his reputation as a writer who spoke simply and directly in print and on National Public Radio. One article he wrote, for instance, suggested that men should wash their socks by hand rather than risk the washing machine's tendency to separate socks. That same directness made the commercials for Motel 6 popular; they seemed to be spoken by a simple man who spoke of the interests of the average person. Accompanied by fiddle and guitar, Bodett's voice sounded like that of a neighbor or a friend one might be reassured to see before a good night's sleep. Bodett reassured people that they all basically wanted the same things: "You know, in some ways, a Motel 6 reminds me of one of those big fancy hotels. They've got beds, we've got beds. They've got sinks and showers, by golly we've got 'em too." And each commercial ended in the slogan of Motel 6: "We'll leave the light on for you."

By the mid-1980s, budget motels were the fastest growing part of the hotel business. Their reputation changed: motels, once seen as half-reputable places to stop on the road, were soon viewed as places where smart, price-conscious travelers stayed the night. At a no-frills motel, one could expect to find the basic amenities. Each offered a reasonably sized, dimly lit bedroom, furnished with a bed, dresser, and night table; a small, but clean bathroom, laid with thin, white towels; a sparsely furnished check-in lobby, staffed at all hours; and a coffee pot, refilled day and night. Budget motels drew businessmen and truckers who wanted a cheap overnight place to stop. They drew young couples and families who were pleased to get away from home and did not expect luxury. They drew college students who sought an overnight adventure. People used the motels as a home base to tour cities or wander in the mountains. In 1985 it cost just $17.95 to spend the night in a Motel 6 (Rudolph, 1985).

In the mid-1980s, gigantic billboards were still legal in every state, and the advertisements for these motels literally loomed above the highway, urging people to stop there for the night. Soon certain logos grew familiar, and the Motel 6 red symbol of a large 6 on a circular yellow background was just such a sign. Other motels drew people in through their slogans. The Red Roof Inns lured travelers from the highway with a promise to "sleep cheap!"

But the Motel 6 slogan captured the essence of what travelers of the 1980s wanted to hear—that they would be left alone, not pampered or peered at as they rushed from the motel into their busy lives. At the same time, they heard that, in the anonymous world of travel, someone would have their needs in mind; someone would be looking out for them—someone, in short, would leave the light on.

References

Gross, Ken. "Alaska's Tom Bodett Is the Folksy Voice of Motel 6, but for Him There's No Place like Homer." *People Weekly*, August 1, 1988: 60–62.
Marcial, Gene G. "Why Motel 6 Is Waking Up." *Business Week*, September 25, 1989: 206.
Raffel, Dawn. "We'll Leave the Light on for Ya" *Redbook*, November 1989: 60.
Rudolph, Barbara. "Cheaper Havens on the U.S. Road." *Time*, July 15, 1985: 49.
Toy, Stewart. "Motel 6: Wooing the Frugal Business Crowd." *Business Week*, July 14, 1986: 76–77.

Sylvia Skaggs-McTague

Victoria's Secret

Victoria's Secret emerged as a commercial success in the 1980s by advertising unabashed sexuality, discovering a market that is still vital today. With dark pink carpets and walls, each store was dimly lit, with classical music playing quietly in the background, as if to encourage fantasy. Bras and panties of all colors and styles hung everywhere: women and men could choose from simple cotton to stylish lace and from those that cover to those that reveal. Amid the rainbow of underwear were a few racks of slinkier apparel, deep-colored slips, garters, and negligees. When a customer arrived at her choice, a smiling attendant wrapped each purchase in pink tissue paper and laid it in a small bag decorated with the Victoria's Secret logo.

As the rebellious spirit of the 1970s shifted toward the conformity of the 1980s, Victoria's Secret had an advantage over miscellaneous lingerie shops that played to prurient interests. Victoria's Secret stores validated the urge to feel sexy and helped make lingerie sales more acceptable, less sleazy, and less racy. They helped build the expectation that whatever a woman wears, the outfit does not expose the secret self under her clothing. The "secret" captured by the stores might be that consumers wanted a place to find their sensuality validated in mainstream shopping culture. As young, attractive saleswomen approach shoppers, their boldness is cloaked in a cool philosophy of sexuality as a part of life.

Entrepreneur Roy Raymond opened the first Victoria's Secret in San Francisco in 1977. Raymond envisioned a place where men as well as women could shop for lingerie in comfort, removed from the seediness associated with such stores as Frederick's of Hollywood. It began as a family-run business. Raymond's wife greeted customers from behind the counter, and his parents did the bookkeeping and inventory. According to Raymond, the title originated from the store's decor, which featured dark wood and rose tints in a Victorian sitting-room style. In 1982 The Limited, under Leslie Wexner, offered to buy out the five stores. Under Wexner, the stores underwent a tremendous growth, multiplying so that it seemed as if few malls were long without a Victoria's Secret store.

The marketers for Victoria's Secret understood that women strive to create their self-images. Victoria's Secret, the stores and the catalogue, targets upper-income women from eighteen to sixty. A shopper at these stores must be willing to spend some money on herself, for bargain sales are rare at Victoria's Secret. Prices are nevertheless moderate, unlike those of the more expensive lingerie shops that preceded it. Victoria's Secret's hugely successful catalogue, which carries its own line of clothing including jeans, sweaters, and sleeping apparel, features models who are dressed (or half-dressed) in everything from blue jeans to business suits. Victoria's Secret has not used print or television advertising extensively, relying on its catalogue and reputation to market its goods. To launch its Miracle Bra, however, and to counteract competitor Wonderbra's advertising blitz, the company ran a $3 million television campaign in 1994.

The stores capitalize on women's urge to feel sexy, and they do not deny men's participation. The annual Victoria's Secret Web site fashion show, presented online and on a real runway, is a sellout among men, like the *Sports Illustrated* swimsuit issue.

References

Chakravarty, Subrata N. "Secret Success." *Forbes*, May 9, 1983: 79.

Kantrowitz, Barbara. "Victoriana Rules Again." *Newsweek*, January 16, 1989: 60–61.

Kazanjian, Dodie. "Victoria's Secret Is Out—and Thousands of Women Are Responding to the Blandishments of Both Catalog and Stores." *Vogue*, April 1992: 218+.

Schwartz, Mimi. "A Day in the Life of a Victoria's Secret." *Mademoiselle*, April 1990: 238–39+.

Woodman, Sue. "Victoria Reigns . . . Again." *Working Woman*, September 1991: 77.

Sylvia Skaggs-McTague

Wendy's

In January 1984, Wendy's launched a series of four television commercials, featuring a little old lady named Clara Peller and her two sidekicks who, after examining the contents between the buns of those other hamburgers (from big chains McDonald's and Burger King), demanded, "Where's the Beef?" This feisty trio with their grey hair, glasses, and lace collars were seated at the counter of a fast-food restaurant where a sign behind them announced, "Home of the Big Bun." Examining their food, the three search for the hamburger inside the big buns. "It's a very big bun," one observes, as the second agrees, looking inside it at a tiny hamburger the size of a pickle slice. Clara Peller will have none of it: "Where's the Beef?" she demands. This television commercial so appealed to the American public that the ads, created by Dancer Fitzgerald Sampler, registered the highest consumer awareness in the advertising industry's history up to that time and were voted by the industry the most popular commercials in America for 1984, according to *Advertising Age*'s monthly poll. Walter Mondale, Jimmy Carter's candidate for vice president in the 1984 election, used the "Where's the Beef?" slogan in his campaign.

Previous television commercials had featured the founder of Wendy's, Dave Thomas, whose folksy style set the tone for the company. He had started Wendy's (named after one of his daughters) in 1969, having learned the fast-food business by managing a Kentucky Fried Chicken franchise. Wendy's caught on with the public and expanded its operation over the years by introducing new approaches to the fast-food market. In late 1970, for example, Thomas came up with the concept of the "pickup window," which allowed customers, for the first time, to drive up, order, and drive away with their food in record time. Other innovations included a salad bar and, in 1983, Wendy's became the first fast-food franchise to offer baked potatoes nationwide.

The company was equally creative in its advertising. Until 1977 Wendy's had confined its advertising to local television and radio spots, but in that year they began the first of a series of successful and often innovative ad campaigns with related slogans. These included "Hot 'n Juicy," "Wendy's Has the Taste," "Ain't No Reason (to go any place else)," "Wendy's Kind of People," "The Russian Fashion Show," and "Old Fashioned Guy." None had the impact, both immediate and lasting, of their 1984 "Where's the Beef?" campaign, however.

Wendy's was the third largest hamburger chain in the United States when the campaign began. But, though the commercial and its slogan remained high in consumer awareness well into the 1990s, Wendy's went through a period of declining sales until 1989 when, once again, Dave Thomas began doing the television commercials. His credibility quotient actually gave Wendy's an advertising awareness even higher than that of the "Where's the Beef?" campaign. Nonetheless, the phrase, "Where's the Beef?," remains part of the American vocabulary, used whenever people feel they are not getting what they deserve, that the promise fails to live up to the delivery.

Dave Thomas's death in January 2002 brought tributes from millions of his fans worldwide.

References

Thomas, R. David. *Dave's Way: A New Approach to Old-Fashioned Success.* New York: G. P. Putnam's Sons, 1991.
"The Wendy's Story." <www.wendys.com>.

Geoffrey Weinman

Icons of the 1990s

The 1990s began, ominously, with a war and a recession. George H. W. Bush was in the White House when Iraq's invasion of Kuwait resulted in the Persian Gulf War in 1991. The mind-set of excess and consumption so prevalent in the 1980s was replaced when the economy took a dive, and words like "re-engineering," "downsizing," and "rightsizing" suddenly became part of the American vocabulary. By the end of the decade, however, the stock market was reaching unprecedented heights and the economy was back up and on a roll. More Americans than ever before owned stocks, and they felt rich, at least on paper. Advertising geared up to sell them more of what they had always wanted, now that they could afford it. Even though more people had more money, it was considered gauche to flaunt it 1980s-style. Instead, a minimalist approach in fashion and in consumption style masked the private luxury underneath, like cashmere wallpaper or made-to-order underwear.

Part of this consumption style was the rugged-looking sports utility vehicle (SUV), classified as a truck and capable of tough off-road action, although it seldom went off it on the way to the supermarket. SUVs were a major status symbol, and every car company in America put out a model, filled with cup holders, video monitors, CD players, and comfortable seating. Advancements in technology produced luxuries of instant communication as the cellular phone became ubiquitous and the personal computer and Microsoft became standard equipment at home and office. Online access to the Internet and World Wide Web opened up the world to e-commerce, e-mail communication, and online advertising.

In 1995 advertisers spent more than $50 million on Internet advertising; by 1998, that number had increased to the billions. Advertising on the Web took two primary forms: corporate home pages and banner ads.

The corporate home pages offered information about the company and its products, and many sold products directly from the site. Banner ads are paid placements in another site's space with a link to the advertiser. So far, despite the money invested in it, Internet advertising has yet to make much return, and ad agencies are at work to improve its reach. Meanwhile, consumers found shopping online directly from the source easy and convenient, day or night.

Advertisers were well aware in the 1990s that they were now playing to a media-savvy audience, and much of the advertising in the 1990s was done with a wink and a nod in the consumer's direction. Advertising began to make fun of itself, deconstructing its ads and exposing its claims to ridicule. The Energizer Bunny is perhaps the best example of the kind of self-parody advertising indulged in, breaking into fake ads and making fun of the hard sell. In the postmodern mode, ads borrowed from each other, reached back for nostalgic songs and slogans to lure baby boomers, and used plenty of humor, as in the "Got Milk?" campaign, along with irony to mirror jaded consumers' attitudes. In addition, advertising began to notice some well-off consumers—gays and senior citizens—it had largely ignored in the past.

Advertising also made much of integrated marketing communications (IMC), an advertising term meaning the unifying of all parts of a promotional campaign, to send a consistent, persuasive message to target audiences. The aim is synergy; for example, the 1998 campaign for the iMac. Key elements of the campaign included television spots; outdoor, magazine, and radio advertising; and Web site promotions, all with a very similar look and feel. The Volkswagen campaign described in this chapter also made use of IMC in promoting the release of the new Beetle. Advertising seeped farther into media content with the infomercial, program-length commercials that arose when the Federal Trade Commission did away with commercial time limits in 1984. Product placement, that is, lobbying to get moviemakers and television producers to use products with the labels visible in their shows, was on the rise in the 1990s as well. For example, in the 1994 film *Forrest Gump*, the star, Tom Hanks, appeared in Nike running shoes and a Nike T-shirt. The popular television program *Seinfeld* was well known for its inclusion of products such as Junior Mints, Pez Candy, and Kenny Rogers Chicken.

The decade of the 1990s, with its blitz of advertising, created a generation of consumers grown cynical with sales pitches. Advertising responded by taking an entirely new direction, turning to Budweiser Frogs, the Taco Bell Chihuahua, and Energizer Bunnies to entertain them instead.

References

The Authentic History Center: Primary Sources from Popular Culture (independently owned and operated by Michael S. Barnes, Byron Center High School, Byron Center, MI). Available on-line at <http://www.authentichistory.com/1990s.html>.

"1990s Flashback." Programmed and hosted by ecFactory. <http://www.1990sflashback.com/>.

O'Guinn, Thomas C., Chris T. Allen, and Richard J. Semenik. *Advertising*. 2d ed. Cincinnati, OH: South-Western College Publishing, 2000.

Sivulka, Juliann. *Soap, Sex, & Cigarettes: A Cultural History of American Advertising*. Belmont, CA: Wadsworth, 1998.

Wells, William, John Burnett, and Sandra. Morarity. *Advertising: Principles & Practice*. 5th ed. Upper Saddle River, NJ: Prentice Hall, 2000.

Jennifer Lehr

The Budweiser Frogs

Can frogs sell beer? Yes, some would argue, quite effectively. D'Arcy, Masius, Benton & Bowles, Anheuser-Busch's ad agency for seventy-nine years, was credited for developing the idea of beer-loving frogs. Anheuser-Busch, the largest brewery in the world, was concerned that fewer people between the ages of twenty-one and twenty-seven were drinking beer, the time when most beer drinkers form brand loyalty. Indeed, the number of beer drinkers in that age group dropped between 1990 and 1998. In 1994 Anheuser-Busch, as a result of a loss of confidence in D'Arcy, Masius, Benton & Bowles over a conflict of interest, fired the agency. Doyle Dane Bernbach Needham (part of DDB Worldwide) was retained to take the frogs idea and tailor the campaign for this critical audience.

The original three frogs made their debut during the Super Bowl in 1995. The commercial featured a desolate swamp and three animatronic bullfrogs which slowly began to croak, "Bud," "Weis," and "Er," individually. A hanging neon Budweiser sign flickered in the background. Supported by an estimated half-billion dollar marketing budget, the Budweiser bullfrog campaign spread like wildfire from television to radio, print ads, billboards, and clothing.

Response from the first commercial was so great that DDB continued with a second, "Frogs II." In this spot, the frogs croak "Bud–weis–er" by the side of the road. As a large delivery truck with the Budweiser logo drives by, one frog quickly extends his tongue and attaches himself to the back, as the other frogs watch, unfazed.

"Frogs III" introduced the campaign's first female frog during ABC's

Croaking "Bud-weis-er" and sitting in a swamp, the Budweiser frogs (along with Louie the Lizard, shown on the right) were stars of television, radio, print, and outdoor advertising in the 1990s. Copyright © 2001 by Anheuser-Busch, Inc. used with permission of Anheuser-Busch, Inc. All rights reserved.

Monday Night Football. She and a male frog exchange croaks "Bud" and "Weis" until the male frog finds the female and ends the commercial with a satisfied "Er." A fourth Frogs spot aired during the 1996 Super Bowl, placing the frogs in a snowstorm as they attempted to croak "Bud–Weis–Er" with frozen tongues.

In 1997 Anheuser-Busch invested more than $40 million in a new campaign with Goodby, Silverstein & Partners of San Francisco to continue targeting the Budweiser market with animals. The campaign starred two lizards with Brooklyn accents who were jealous that Budweiser chose to make stars of the frogs instead of them. "I can't believe they went with the frogs," one said. "Our audition was flawless."

The lizards, especially the energetic Louie, were convinced they would be celebrities if they could only get rid of the frogs. The humor echoed the frog campaign, and the lizards had several spots during NBA games and Super Bowls. During the 1998 Super Bowl, several spots featured their attempts to get rid of the frogs. In one spot, Louie hired a ferret hit man; in another he tried to perfect a Texas accent when he discovers that one frog was a Texan. The comical campaign received the Grand Clio for radio in 2000.

The entire campaign was immensely popular and became internationally recognized. In May 2000 Anheuser-Busch received the Grand Clio Hall of Fame Award, one of the ad industry's most prestigious. *Advertising Age* said the campaign tripled their targets' brand recognition and captivated viewers with a fresh image of modern humor and entertainment, instead of using hard-sell tactics. Anheuser-Busch could now appeal to a larger spectrum of people—including women. Unlike other brewers' campaigns utilizing what many people regarded as a "suds and sex" strategy, Anheuser-Busch's frogs campaign was not exploitative. The frog campaign allowed Anheuser-Busch to make a strong connection with its male audience, without offending women.

Not everyone was satisfied by the success of the frogs, however. Activists, such as Mothers Against Drunk Driving (MADD), made claims that the animation-like frogs targeted children to boost sales. Anheuser-Busch denied that their campaign was aimed at underage drinkers. Ultimately the frogs were removed from the campaign, but Anheuser-Busch continues to refute claims made by activist groups, saying that they simply wanted to keep the campaign fresh. The lizards campaign replaced the frogs.

No doubt the lizards were popular, but with fewer beer drinkers, and with many new beer brands flooding the market during the 1990s, it is difficult to determine how effective the lizard campaign was. Regardless, it was still recognized as one of the most popular campaigns of the decade. In fact, the lizards continue to have a strong presence on the Budweiser Internet site. The frog campaign, as well as the lizard campaign, made the Budweiser brand highly recognizable, earning the amphibians the right to be considered advertising icons of the 1990s.

References

"Campaign Clout: Budweiser's New Menagerie Hops to the Top of the Ad Charts." *Advertising Age*, March 18, 1998.
"Frankie & Louie." Budweiser: King of Beers home page. <http://www.budweiser.com/life/lizards/index.html/>.

Jennifer Lehr

The Energizer Bunny (Energizer Batteries)

He keeps going, and going, and going . . . right through the 1990s and beyond. The remarkable staying power of this advertising icon is evidenced by a campaign that began in 1989, carried through the duration of the 1990s, and continues today.

Energizer invented the first commercially viable alkaline battery in 1949 and marketed it until the 1980s under the Eveready Alkaline name. In 1980 Eveready, owned by Union Carbide Corporation, created the Energizer brand to distinguish this battery from standard Eveready products. The second half of the 1980s was also a prime time for corporate takeovers, which led to the sale of Eveready and Energizer to Ralston Purina in 1986 for $1.4 billion. But since selling batteries was not the same as selling dog food, Ralston Purina struggled at first, and its battery market share began to slip. In 1989 Ralston Purina realized that they would need to take action: they would need to take on Duracell.

The first Energizer Bunny commercial, created by Doyle Dane Bernbach (DDB) Needham, aired in October 1988 and employed a direct attack on Duracell's advertising theme. The commercial used a crowd of marching toy bunnies similar to those used in a Duracell spot. The small toy bunnies were soon interrupted, however, by the larger Energizer Bunny with a voice-over claiming that the only reason Duracell was able to claim itself the best battery was because Energizer had never "been invited to the party." Although this first commercial was viewed as only the first phase of what would need to be a long-term plan for Energizer, it was a solid first step toward improving market share.

Although the ad successfully directed consumers to question the performance of Duracell, Energizer wanted to do more than that. They wanted to convince consumers that no battery on the market was better than Energizer. They invited their incumbent agency and Chiat/Day/Mojo of Venice, California, to determine ways to build on this foundation. Chiat's approach was to relaunch the initial spot, but at the end of the spot the Bunny would actually break out of the commercial and into TV land. Once in TV land, the Bunny would interrupt other advertising for a variety of fictitious products. Each spot ended with the phrase, "Still going . . . nothing outlasts Energizer. It keeps going and going and going . . ."

This leg of the campaign, which began in 1989 and ran for three years, covered more than thirty-five different fictitious products. These ads appealed to a vast array of consumers because as soon as they were drawn in by the spoof of the product category, the Bunny would break in at a critical moment and poke fun at these worn advertising scenarios. When Energizer ran out of product categories to parody, they shifted to having the Bunny pursued by a variety of villains. Needless to say, the villains always ran out of steam before the Bunny did.

Since 1989, 112 television commercials have generated more than 124 billion consumer impressions linking Energizer to battery performance that will keep you "going and going." In the process, Energizer and the

Energizer Bunny have become cultural icons representing perseverance, determination, and everlasting power.

Though many of the Energizer spots were quick to parody others, Eveready has been much less inclined to think that imitation is the sincerest form of flattery. This was revealed in 1991 when Eveready sought an injunction against the Coor's Brewing Company in an effort to stop the airing of a television commercial which featured actor Leslie Nielsen in a pink bunny suit, looking very much like the Energizer Bunny. Of course, Coor's was not alone. The Energizer Bunny is often compared to celebrities and noteworthy events, including former President Bill Clinton, Sean Connery, Mick Jagger, Bob Hope, Dick Clark, and the 2000 presidential election. The Energizer Bunny has been invited to appear at class reunions, birthday parties, and even church services.

In 1996 Energizer's agency (which by this time had merged with TBWA to become TBWA Chiat Day) shot a new series of commercials that coincided with the release of the film *Twister*, one of that summer's blockbuster movies. The plot of the film follows a team of nerdy scientists who chase tornadoes. The Energizer campaign also features a team of nerdy scientists chasing the Bunny. Each of the spots, shot by commercial director Phil Morrison, has the look and feel of a documentary. Although the seven-commercial series did not seem to impact sales and market share for Energizer, the campaign kept the Bunny in the limelight a bit longer.

Today the Bunny is actively helping market a new brand of high-performance battery: the Energizer e^2 with titanium technology. Viewers see the Bunny pulsing in and out of the silver e^2 battery, with an announcer asking, "Do you have the Bunny inside?" Like all Energizer advertising, the campaign works on literal and emotional levels, asking if you have the power of Energizer batteries in your device and the spirit of the Bunny in you.

Clearly, this is an icon with staying power, which is what Energizer (which spun off from Ralston Purina in 2000) is counting on—that "Nothing outlasts the Energizer. It keeps going and going and going."

References

Enrico, Dottie. "Eveready Energizer Bunny." *The Advertising Century, Advertising Age*. Special Issue (Spring 1999).

Liesse, Julie. "How the Bunny Charged Eveready." *Advertising Age*, April 8, 1991.

Teinowitz, Ira. "Coors in a (Rabbit) Stew over Parody." *Advertising Age*, April 29, 1991.

Jennifer Lehr

"Got Milk?"

Two slogans, "Got Milk?" and "Where's Your Milk Mustache?," which began as separate catch lines for the same product, joined at the close of the 1990s to form a single, hard-hitting advertising campaign that not only became an icon of popular culture for the 1990s, but also boosted lagging milk sales which had been declining since the late 1970s. Although Americans knew milk was good for them, by the early 1990s Americans had become more health conscious and were avoiding milk as a way of avoiding the extra grams of fat in milk. Americans were also bypassing milk for more "adult" beverages such as soft drinks like Pepsi and Coke, sports drinks like Gatorade, and the newly emerging iced tea, Snapple. Branded beverages also had the clout of multimillion dollar advertising campaigns behind them which gave milk, a commodity rather than a brand, an even greater challenge to overcome.

The original "Got Milk?" campaign, created by the San Francisco–based Goodby, Silverstein & Partners for the California Milk Processor Board and launched in 1994, included both print ads and televised commercials that focused more on the foods that accompany milk, rather than on the milk itself. In the past, advertisements that featured milk as the central product were only minimally effective. This campaign emphasized the point that certain foods simply are not the same without milk, so consumers needed to have some on hand. The campaign preyed on people's fear of deprivation and their cravings for comfort foods. In a Christmas spot, Santa enters a home, consumes a brownie, finds no milk, and takes his presents away. In another commercial, a new father agonizes over a bowl of dry cereal, deciding whether to take the milk from his baby's bottle. The campaign, which started in California, went national in 1995, at nearly the same time that another key milk campaign was getting under way.

In January 1995, the National Fluid Milk Promotion Board (NFMPB) debuted a $52 million print advertising campaign with a photo of supermodel Naomi Campbell sporting what would soon become the infamous milk mustache on her upper lip, as though she had just drunk a glass of the milk (the milk mustache that we see in the photographs is a special combination of whole milk, heavy cream, and iced cream that is painted on each celebrity).

The campaign, developed by Bozell Worldwide, Inc. (now a unit of True North Communications), originally sought to reach women between the ages of twenty-five and forty-four, but eventually expanded to include teens and men as well. This expanded target market was reached by using a broad range of celebrities in the print ads. More than

In addition to the backstroke and the butterfly, I can perform a world-class chug-a-lug. With milk. It has protein for my muscles, plus essential vitamins and minerals like calcium and potassium. All of which help me get the one mineral every Olympian craves. Gold.

MILK

Where's *your* mustache?™

Wearing a milk mustache, celebrities like swim champion Amy Van Dyken posed for print ads and made it seem cool to drink milk. Courtesy of Bozell Worldwide, Inc.

100 models, actors, actresses, athletes, and musicians have appeared in the clever print ads, each of which closes with four short lines of copy that reflect the personality of the celebrity. In fact, some celebrities have called to request an appearance in a milk-mustache ad. To keep the ads

fresh, Bozell often uses celebrities of the moment. For example, a milk mustache appearing on the winning quarterback the day after the Super Bowl is almost a standard now.

In 1998 the "Got Milk" and "Milk Mustache" campaigns merged. The milk mustache still appears in each print ad, and the four lines of catchy copy are also there, but the tag line has been changed from "Where's Your Milk Mustache?" to "Got Milk?" As a sign that the milk mustache has secured its position as an icon of popular culture, Jay Schulberg released *The Milk Mustache Book* in 1998, a compilation of full-size reproductions of the print advertisements. It would seem that milk is finally cool.

References

Beatty, Sally Goll. "Celebrity Milk Mustache." *Wall Street Journal*, May 20, 1996. <http://www.milk.com/value/innovator-spring99.html/>.
Lauro, Patricia Winters. "What Do Drinking Milk and 'Survivor' Have in Common?" *New York Times*, August 22, 2000.
Schulberg, Jay, Bernie Hogya, and Sal Taibi. *The Milk Mustache Book: A Behind the Scenes Look at America's Favorite Advertising Campaign*. New York: Ballantine, 1998.

Jennifer Lehr

Joe Camel

Ray-Ban sunglasses, leather flight jacket, cigarette, dromedary—these are the four main ingredients that made up the "Smooth Character" that the R. J. Reynolds Tobacco Company (RJR) hoped would help them capture a new and different share of the cigarette-smoking market. The emergence of a slick, well-dressed cartoon camel in 1989 led to new-found popularity for a brand that had been around since 1915. He was a 1990s phenomenon.

RJR hoped that the product's new image would attract the prime target of young people between eighteen and twenty-four and convince them that Camel was no longer just for older men. Plastered on billboards, magazines, and free T-shirts, this cartoon camel portrayed an image of 1990s cool and confidence, playing pool as he stylishly puffed on Camel cigarettes. Joe Camel quickly became a successful advertising icon, perhaps too successful.

Throughout the campaign—created by longtime RJR agency Mezzina/ Brown of New York—a great deal of energy was spent on character development, and differing print ads and billboards featured a broad range of "Joe" conceptualizations including Heroic Joe, Joe the Beast,

Historical Joe, Fantasy Joe, Celebrity Joe, and Prankster Joe. Joe Camel also spurred a promotional campaign called "Camel Cash" in the early 1990s. During the campaign, specially marked packs of Camels contained a C-note of Camel Cash, redeemable for a broad range of items including shirts, hats, and jackets. Many of the items bore Joe Camel's image or the Camel logo. The first round of the Camel Cash promo was so successful that, in 1993, RJR offered buyers a second catalog with items such as watches, lighters, shower curtains, and cups for hot and cold drinks, all bearing Joe's face (there was a rumor that Joe Camel's nose was supposed to resemble male genitalia—the public by now was alert to subliminal advertising; see the introduction to Chapter 6 for fuller explanation). In the short term, the campaign was a huge success. In 1993 and 1995, Camel's market share rose almost half a percentage point, a major gain in the highly competitive tobacco industry.

Anti-tobacco activists began to suspect that Camel's sudden increase in sales was because the Joe Camel image attracted teen smokers, and "Say No to Joe" became the popular battle cry of anti-underage smoking activists throughout the 1990s. In 1991 articles published in the *Journal of the American Medical Association* (JAMA) accused RJR of using the suave character to target underage smokers. Many of the articles reported high recognition of the Joe Camel character by children and teens, but the articles contained no solid data supporting a relationship between Joe Camel advertising and an increase in underage smoking. In fact, later rebuttals questioned the legitimacy and techniques of the JAMA articles. But by this time the Federal Trade Commission (FTC) had stepped in, filing an administrative complaint against R. J. Reynolds alleging that Joe Camel's marketing practices violated federal fair trade laws and targeted minors.

Joe Camel made his official exit on July 10, 1997. After nine years as the company's primary marketing symbol, Joe Camel was phased out of RJR's point-of-purchase advertising. Print ads and billboards would soon follow. The move to pull Joe Camel came just weeks after R. J. Reynolds and other tobacco companies agreed to a $368.5 billion settlement with a coalition of states seeking to recover the costs of treating tobacco-related illnesses.

Whether Joe Camel was directly responsible for an increase in underage smoking is debatable. R. J. Reynolds Tobacco Company claims that Joe Camel was retired simply because they chose to refresh the brand's image to correspond with changing consumer interest. Many observers argue, however, that the litigation and pressure from the FTC simply drove him out of town. Today there is no trace of the once popular dromedary. Not even the RJR Web site offers any mention of him. But he is certainly unforgettable. And collectors everywhere clamor for bits and pieces of Joe paraphernalia and Camel Cash items. Even nonsmokers can recall the debonair character in great detail. He is unmistakably an icon of the 1990s.

References

Calfee, John. "The Historical Significance of Joe Camel." *Journal of Public Policy and Marketing* 19; no. 2 (Fall 2000): 168–82.
Cohen, Joel. "Playing to Win: Marketing and Public Policy at Odds over Joe Camel." *Journal of Public Policy and Marketing* 19; no. 2 (Fall 2000): 155–67.
"R. J. Reynolds to Drop Joe Camel." *Facts on File: World News Digest*, August 21, 1997. <http://www.facts.com/wnd/camel.htm/>.

Jennifer Lehr

M&Ms

The M&Ms characters, "Red" and "Yellow," were first introduced in 1972, but it was not until fifteen years later that they would take on the personalities that made them the advertising spokespeople for the world-renowned candy. 1987 was a pivotal year because it marked the return of the red M&M and the emergence of Red, the M&M candy spokes-person. Both Red (a plain M&M) and Yellow (a peanut M&M) took on their current shape with the help of Batten, Barten, Durstine and Osborn (BBDO) Worldwide of New York. The advertising campaign that fol-lowed has catapulted these two personable guys—Red is the brainy, snide one; Yellow is the slow, ditzy one—into advertising stardom.

Several aspects of their campaign through the 1990s led these two puppet-like characters to take on iconic status. First, in 1995, a huge marketing event asked Americans to vote for a new color to appear in the traditional color mix. The choices included blue, pink, purple, or no change. Blue won by a landslide. Subsequent commercial spots would make use of Blue, an almond M&M. 1996 was another banner year as the campaign that made use of Red and Yellow was voted to the number one position (out of more than sixty campaigns) by *USA Today*. 1997 was marked by the introduction of Green, the first female M&Ms character. These commercials centered on Green's world tour promoting her au-tobiography, "I Melt for No One."

In 1998 the M&Ms characters proclaimed themselves the official "spokescandies" of the new millennium. Since MM in Roman means 2000, the company was able to take advantage of the unique connection for well over a year. Interestingly enough, M&Ms made it through the second half of the health-conscious 1990s in part because diet-conscious consumers had been leaning toward bite-sized candies that allow them to control calorie and sugar intake. It almost seems as though M&Ms were created with the 1990s in mind.

According to company legend, it was on a trip to Spain in 1941 that Forrest Mars, Sr. (the son of Frank C. Mars, creator of Mars' Milky Way bar, Snickers, and Three Musketeers) came up with the idea for his sugarcoated chocolate candies. During his trip, Mars came across soldiers who were eating chocolate pellets encased in a hard, sugary coating designed to keep them from melting. Mars became obsessed with the idea and, upon returning to his own kitchen, he developed and tested the recipe for his M&Ms chocolate candies. Other versions of the story suggest that the sugarcoated candies were a joint enterprise between Forrest Mars and an associate, Bruce Murrie—the M and M of M&Ms.

Regardless of the true story, the design was patented on March 3, 1941. M&Ms were a big hit with American GIs during World War II because they were packaged in cardboard tubes making them a convenient snack that held up in any climate. As M&Ms became more widely available to the public, they became more popular, and in 1948, the packaging changed from the cardboard tube to the standard brown plastic bag that is still used today.

In 1954 M&Ms added the peanut version to their brand, and in this same year the famous slogan, "Melts in Your Mouth, Not in Your Hand" made its television debut. In 1960 the peanut version added three new colors to the mix: red, green, and yellow. Orange joined the color lineup in 1976 and in that same year, red was pulled from the color mix because of the controversy surrounding red dye #4. Although M&Ms claims that this particular dye was never used in their products, they still pulled the color to avoid potential consumer confusion.

In 1964 Forrest Mars took over his father's candy company and brought M&Ms (which up until that time were being produced by Food Products Manufacturing) into the family business. Forrest, with the help of his siblings, built Mars into one of the world's biggest food companies, housing Milky Way and Snickers candy bars, Combos and Twix snacks, and pet food brands Kal Kan and Pedigree.

Although M&M/Mars is rather hesitant to reveal market share information, according to *Confectioner*'s 1991 ranking of the chocolate elite, M&Ms ranked the highest at $1 billion in annual manufacturers' sales. By preserving the simplicity of M&Ms and the M&Ms characters, M&M/Mars "has made an endearing and enduring symbol of America's sweet tooth."

References

Brenner, Joel Glenn. "Melts in Your Mouth, Not in Your Hand." *Washington Post*, January 7, 1991: 3.

Christenson, David. "This Collection Is All Smiles." *Old Times Newspaper*. <http://www.theoldtimes.com/past/0301_1.html/>.

"Confectionary Elite." *Confectioner*, March/April 1992.

Cornfeld, Betty, and Owen Edwards. *Quintessence: The Quality of Having It*. New York: Crown Publishers, 1983.

"M&M's Industrial Candy & Magic." <http://www.m-ms.com/factory/history/hist.html/>.

Jennifer Lehr

Microsoft Windows Operating System

By the early 1990s, Microsoft Windows could be found on over 30 million computers worldwide and was considered the standard operating system (OS) for personal computers. A branding campaign, which began in 1994, followed by the release of Windows 95 (in 1995, of course), allowed Americans to see just how interconnected Microsoft and American culture had become.

Developed in 1975 by William H. (Bill) Gates and Paul G. Allen, Microsoft was not incorporated until 1981. The company had successfully released several products including BASIC, COBOL, and FORTRAN, but in November 1983 Microsoft introduced their most successful product to date, Microsoft Windows. This product radically changed the way in which Americans (and the world) used computers by offering a user interface that was easy to navigate and enhanced with graphics, removing some of the fear that was once associated with learning to use certain computer applications.

Although the company had typically undertaken advertising campaigns that featured products and services, in 1994, Microsoft announced plans to develop a corporate branding campaign. After a highly publicized and extensive search for the right agency, Microsoft settled on Wieden & Kennedy of Portland, Oregon.

The key component of the campaign was the somewhat ambiguous tag line: "Where do you want to go today?" The line was first introduced in a 1994 television spot entitled "Anthem" and supported by magazine, newspaper, and outdoor advertising. Eight-page inserts appeared in such magazines as *Newsweek, People*, and *Rolling Stone*. The initial phase of the campaign ran through July 1995, when Microsoft began gearing up for another major event, the release of Windows 95.

August 24, 1995, marked the kickoff of the million-dollar advertising campaign aimed at promoting Windows 95, the newest version of the Windows platform. Wieden & Kennedy, already on hand for the branding campaign, created the television and consumer print ads while Anderson & Lembke of San Francisco took over the trade advertising. The television spots attempted to create excitement by showing Windows 95 users in action accompanied by the Rolling Stones song "Start Me Up" playing in the background. The start button to launch Windows 95, one of the main selling points, was featured prominently in print ads that appeared in the United States. The "Start Me Up" campaign ran until June 30, 1996, and although many were turned off by the huge marketing blitz, it accomplished its goal of sparking consumer interest in Windows 95.

Microsoft faced legal trouble late in 1997 when the Department of Justice filed suit charging Microsoft with violating a 1994 consent decree by allowing computer makers a license to use Windows 95 only if they installed and featured Microsoft's Internet Explorer on the computers they made. Since this injunction did not apply to Windows 98, which was scheduled for shipment in May 1998, this suit would fall by the wayside. On May 18, 1998, the federal government and twenty states sued Microsoft in one of the most significant antitrust cases of the last twenty-five years, accusing the company of illegally engaging in predatory practices in order to protect its monopoly in personal computer operating systems. The case came to trial in October 1998, and on November 5, 1999, the dreaded ruling would come to pass: Microsoft was a monopoly and would be required by law to split into two companies. The ruling was overturned on appeal in 2001. Public opinion of the software giant throughout the trial and accompanying media frenzy remained favorable. In fact, a 2000 Gallup poll revealed that the public has held a consistently favorable opinion of the company and its founder, Bill Gates, since 1998. As a point of comparison, Gates's favorability rating was higher than the ratings of the two leading candidates for president in 2000, George W. Bush and Al Gore.

References

Gallup News Service. "Justice Departments vs. Microsoft: The Public's Opinion." Poll analysis, June 7, 2000. <http://www.gallup.com/poll/releases/pr000607c.asp/>.
"Timeline of Events in the Microsoft Anti-Trust Case." November 5, 1999. <http://seattletimes.nwsource.com/news/business/html98/timeline_19991105.html/>.

Jennifer Lehr

The New Volkswagen Beetle

As noted in Chapter 7, Volkswagen's original Beetle, referred to affectionately as the Bug, was a counterculture status symbol of the 1960s.

The new Beetle, which made its way onto the scene in March 1998, shared only two things with the original model: the name and a spare approach to advertising. Surprisingly, the ad campaign for the new Beetle generated as much anticipation as the revamped auto itself.

Arnold Communications of Boston, the advertising agency that handled the 1990s version, took the unusual step of focusing the advertising campaign on the attitudes of Beetle drivers, rather than on the car itself and the good reviews that the car was receiving for safety and efficiency. There was also the matter of straddling the generational hurdle since Volkswagen wanted to reach a broader target market this time around.

Ads for the new Beetle were simple and clever. Both the print and television ads used short, powerful copy and uncluttered product photography with no spokespeople. "If you sold your soul in the 80's, here's your chance to buy it back," says one ad. "The engine's in front, but its heart is in the same place," says another. "Less flower. More power," says a third. Others include, "A work of art with side air bags and a bud vase," "Suddenly the world's glass is half full again," and "So, anything interesting happen in the last 19 years?" The nostalgic echoes of the original award-winning campaign were meant to trigger baby boomers' memories of the Beetle of their youth.

But Volkswagen did not rely solely on fond memories to sell their new cars. One commercial, aimed at younger drivers, featured a Beetle spinning at a furious pace. The copy read, "Reverse engineered from UFOs." The new ads also poked fun at some of the shortfalls of the 1960s cars. For example, the copy of one ad read, "Comes with wonderful new features. Like heat." Another headline read, "Digitally remastered," touching on the combination of nostalgia and new technology of the new VW.

The commercials' soundtracks—no voice-overs were used—used music from semi-obscure bands such as Stereolab, Fluke, and Spiritualized. The goal was to sound hip enough for college kids without alienating their parents. In fact, consumer research showed that people from sixteen to ninety have fond memories of the original Beetle, which was last sold in the United States in 1981. The outdoor advertising also made use of simple photography and included city-specific lines such as these two for New York City billboards, "Cabbies will smile before cutting you off" and "Just what New York needs, a car that stops traffic."

Although the car and its spare approach to advertising have already crossed the century mark, it is unlikely that the car's atypical shape and witty tag lines will help Volkswagen surpass the 400,000 cars a year mark they once reached. But one thing is certain, the new Beetle has become as much a symbol of life in the 1990s as the original Beetle was an icon of the 1960s. It has captured the fancy of Americans looking for more fun in the sixty-hour workweek so typical of life in the 1990s. Or, to borrow another of their clever tag lines, "Hug it? Drive it? Hug it? Drive it?"

References

Molis, Jim. "Volkswagen Beetle Bridges a Generation Gap." *Atlanta Business Chronicle*, September 25, 1998. <http://atlanta.bcentral.com/atlanta/stories/1998/09/28/focus7.html/>.

Span, Paula. "Return of the Beetle: Volkswagen Puts New Ad Campaign in Gear." *Washington Post*, March 13, 1998. <http://bl/rapdinet.com/raleigh/vw/html/press.html/>.

"Volkswagen Debuts One of the Most Anticipated Marketing Campaigns of the Year with Its New Beetle Ads." Company press release, March 12, 1998. <http://www.hvwc.net/zeitung/newsvwtext3.html/>.

Wollenberg, Skip. "Volkswagen Relies on Beetle's Distinctive Shape, Fond Memories in New Ads." *Detroit News*, March 14, 1998. <http://detnews.com/1998/autos/9803/14/03140018.htm/>.

Jennifer Lehr

Nike

Nike's "Just Do It" campaign, initially planned for just one month, was so successful it ran for ten years throughout the 1990s, making Nike a potent brand and the Nike "swoosh" an iconic advertising logo. By 1996 the company maintained an impressive share of the American market, and "Just Do It" had become a popular idiom.

In 1986 Nike began working with advertising agency Wieden & Kennedy, which released the "Just Do It" campaign in 1988. The tone and style of the "Just Do It" advertisements and commercials varied greatly, but the common thread was the emphasis placed on athletic performance. Many of the ads showed everyday men and women exercising in Nike shoes; however, the bulk of the ads featured superstar athletes. The advertisements were very popular, and in addition to the massive gains that Nike made in sales and market share, both Nike and Wieden & Kennedy received several awards for the spots as well, including several Clio awards and an Emmy for Outstanding Commercial in 1999.

In the 1990s, Nike began to focus more attention on the sports and fitness categories dominated by women. The focus of this effort sought to position sports as being empowering to women, a clear sign that Nike's advertising strategy was very much in line with the cultural shift taking place in the United States at this time. Nike's images of female athletes, coupled with the heavy exposure afforded to the women of the

1992 and 1996 Olympic Games, ensured that female sports and athletes had found a home in American culture.

The Nike story began in 1964. After a trip to Japan that convinced him there was a future to be had in selling Japanese athletic shoes, a man named Philip Knight, now in charge at Nike, teamed up with Bill Bowerman, his former track coach at the University of Oregon, to form Blue Ribbon Sports. Knight handled business matters, and Bowerman worked on shoe design and development. In 1971 Blue Ribbon Sports began to manufacture and sell shoes under their own brand, Nike, named after the Greek goddess of victory. Also in 1971, Carolyn Davidson, an undergraduate student at Portland State University, designed the Nike swoosh logo for which she was paid the sum of $35.

In 1972 Nike stopped selling Japanese shoes after a dispute over distribution rights and began actively marketing and promoting their own brand. Throughout the 1970s and 1980s, Nike continued to strive for increased brand recognition by signing top U.S. athletes to wear Nike products. Despite this crafty positioning, there was increased pressure from top competitor Reebok in the early 1980s and, consequently, Nike profits began to slip. It was the signing of basketball superstar Michael Jordan to a campaign that would be anchored by a namesake product, the Air Jordan, that would begin to turn things around.

The mid-1990s brought some bad press for Nike, as well as others in the athletic footwear industry, in the form of accusations that the company was underpaying employees in Third World countries. Nike, the industry leader, took the brunt of the bad press, which often glossed over several key issues. First, virtually every company in the industry makes their products in these countries. Second, Nike pays companies, not workers, and always at locally competitive rates. Third, the costs incurred when making a pair of sneakers are many, and by the time labor, materials, shipping, overhead, training, benefits, and warehousing are factored in, Nike's profit margin is right in line with most U.S. manufacturers.

Although Nike is no longer seeing the rapid growth of the early 1990s, it continues to dominate the athletic footwear, apparel, and equipment markets, with annual sales that exceed its top three competitors—Reebok, Adidas, and Converse—combined. Nike also continues to use the "Just Do It" slogan in many print ads to continued praise. In 1998 Nike launched a new "I Can" campaign ("I can be the next Michael Jordan"), targeting younger consumers.

References

Wieden, Dan. "A Sense of Cool: Nike's Theory of Advertising." *Harvard Business Review*, July-August 1992: 97.

Yang, Dori Jones. "How Nike Blasted Off." *Business Week*, April 6, 1992: 10.

Jennifer Lehr

The Taco Bell Chihuahua

Although Taco Bell and Foote, Cone & Belding (part of Chicago-based True North Communications) mounted the successful "Run for the Border" campaign in 1994, it was the appearance of a Chihuahua named Dinky in 1997 (created by TBWA/Chiat Day) that created the highest level of product and brand awareness Taco Bell had over known.

Taco Bell Corporation, a division of Tricon Global Restaurants, Inc. (which also includes KFC and Pizza Hut), has long been the only Mexican style fast-food restaurant in the United States, but by 1995, Taco Bell found itself suffering from declining revenues. In 1996 Taco Bell began to seek the help of the advertising industry and creative powerhouse TBWA/Chiat Day of Venice, California.

The miniscule Chihuahua with the permanent smirk and evocative voice first barked, "Yo quiero Taco Bell" (I want Taco Bell), in the summer of 1997 during an ad that ran only in the Northeastern United States. The dog was immediately a hit. Recognizing that consumers wanted more of the dog, Taco Bell quickly shifted the emphasis to the Chihuahua who goes to great lengths to get his paws on the restaurant's fast-food Mexican fare. After each commercial adventure, the spot ends with the dog mouthing the catch phrase, "Yo quiero Taco Bell," as the subtitled English translation flashes on the screen. According to the company's own Web site (www.tacobell.com), the Chihuahua's character is supposed to be perceived as a nineteen-year old man in a dog's body.

Televised spots featuring the tiny canine were ranked among the top fifty campaigns by *Adweek* magazine and among the top ten for 1997 by *Entertainment Weekly*. As a result of the campaign, Taco Bell enjoyed an increase in same-store sales for 1997 and 1998.

The Chihuahua's image was soon plastered on billboards across America; posters and cardboard cutouts with Dinky's picture appeared in Taco Bell restaurants; and Taco Bell even put an 800-number into place for consumers to order Dinky T-shirts. In 1998 Dinky returned to promote Taco Bell's Gorditas, a new menu item.

The campaign has endured some rough spots. Early on, some Hispanic groups complained that the dog and his accent were poking fun at Hispanic heritage. Gabriel Cezares, then president of the League of United Latin American Citizens, said the chihuahua was insulting. Cezares urged Hispanics to write letters and boycott Taco Bell, but the popularity of the dog continued to grow.

Dinky managed to stay in the public eye through the end of the decade, but in a surprising move in mid-2000, Taco Bell decided to dismiss TBWA/Chiat Day after three successful years and reassigned the account to Foote, Cone & Belding (FCB) Worldwide. Declining sales were blamed, but the move still came as a surprise (as did the dismissal of then Taco Bell president Peter Waller). This may mean the end of Dinky because many advertising analysts speculate that FCB will shift away from using the dog. Despite the fact that this particular icon was somewhat short-lived, there is little question that the popular dog made his mark (figuratively, that is) during his fifteen minutes of fame.

References

Johnson, Greg. "Taco Bell Chihuahua Is an Advertising Triumph." *Lexington-Herald-Leader*, March 22, 1999. <http://www.kentuckyconnect.com/heraldleader/news/032299/business/bizmon_docs/22TacoBell.htm/>.
"Taco Bell Consumers Say "Yo Quiero More Chihuahua!" Press release. Irvine, CA, December 29, 1997. <http://www.tacobell.com.>.

Jennifer Lehr

Yahoo!

Yahoo! was the first on-line Internet navigator to the World Wide Web and has been one of the most successful. During an ongoing dot com downturn since the stock market bottomed out in the spring of 2000 and venture capital evaporated, Yahoo! is one of the few left standing and still making a profit, much reduced though that may be from the heady days of the technology stock boom. Although a claim to iconicity may be premature, Yahoo!'s dominance in the market, its 200 million-plus visitors a month, its catchy tag line, "Do You Yahoo!?," and even its ability to turn a profit in the midst of so much dot com carnage make it at the very least a significant symbol of the Internet boom that blew through the 1990s and swept up everything in its path. As a site for advertising, Yahoo! has also managed to defy the conventional wisdom that Internet ads do not produce much revenue.

Yahoo! started out in 1994 as the private hobby of a pair of doctoral candidates in electrical engineering at Stanford University. David Filo and Jerry Yang, frustrated at trying to keep track of all their favorite sites on the Internet, created their own central site they called Jerry's Guide to the World Wide Web. After arranging their site lists into categories and subcategories, they realized they had something other Internet users might need, a single place to find Web sites. They gave it a name: Yet Another Hierarchical Officious Oracle, or Yahoo! (actually, the inventors claim they also liked the dictionary definition of a *yahoo* as someone rude, unsophisticated, and uncouth—the word comes from the crude Yahoos Jonathan Swift satirized in *Gulliver's Travels*). Their new site had its first one-million-hit day (a hit, in Internet talk, is a visitor to the site) in the fall of 1994. Filo and Yang incorporated the site and went out looking for venture capital in Silicon Valley.

Sequoia Capital, investors in Apple Computer, Atari, Oracle, and Cisco Systems, funded Yahoo! in April 1995 with nearly $2 million. Yahoo! began taking advertising in August 1995 and, a year later, with forty-nine employees, went public in an initial public offering (IPO) that tripled the opening stock price by the end of the day. The company did so well that it was added to Standard & Poor's 500 Index of companies in December 1999.

Yahoo! has put together a package for advertisers called fusion marketing—"beyond banners, clicks and conversions," the usual Internet ad forms—that gives merchants a mix of media, e-commerce, direct marketing, broadcast, and communication to reach customers. With a substantial 79 percent month-to-month retention rate of visitors, Yahoo! can give advertisers an assured audience of consumers, many of them in the coveted age range of from eighteen to thirty-four. On average, Yahoo! carries more than 3,000 ads in a three-month period.

Being successful at Internet advertising has generally eluded advertising agencies and merchants, primarily because a Web site has so many other distractions for the consumer. The visitor to a Web site is not leisurely paging through a magazine or newspaper but is actively looking for information or entertainment. Banner ads, the floating strips across the top, middle, or bottom of the page, have to deliver a message fast or get ignored; links leading to advertising off the page are subject to the whim of the visitor. Most Internet advertising seems to shout with bright colors, movement, and special effects. It has to, just to get attention. Internet advertising is currently the subject of much debate and analysis in the advertising industry, as it seeks strategies to succeed in yet another new media.

In the souring market and slowdown of advertising in 2001, Yahoo! laid off 12 percent of its workers. Trying to branch out beyond dependence on advertising revenue, the company is developing premium services like Corporate Yahoo! (for internal communication), Yahoo! Broadcast (audio and video streaming) and Yahoo! Small Business (domains, Web sites, servers). It also offers a line of Web site services and corporate products. In April 2001, Yahoo! surprised the industry by announcing it would not list pornography sites, a cash cow for other browsers.

The headquarters of Yahoo! are located in Sunnyvale, California, with other offices in twenty-four countries.

References

Kaplan, David A. *The Silicon Boys and Their Valley of Dreams.* New York: William Morrow, 1999.
"Yahoo History." <http:www.yahoo.com/>.

Mary Cross

Selected Bibliography

Allen, Frederick Lewis. *Only Yesterday: An Informal History of the Nineteen-Twenties.* 1931. Reprint, New York: Harper and Brothers, 1957.

Arlen, Michael J. *Thirty Seconds.* New York: Farrar, Straus and Giroux, 1980.

Atwan, Robert, Donald McQuade, and John W. Wright. *Edsels, Luckies & Frigidaires: Advertising the American Way.* New York: Dell Books, 1979.

Bayley, Stephen. *Harley Earl and the Dream Machine.* New York: Alfred A. Knopf, 1983.

Berger, Arthur Asa. *Reading Matter: Multidisiciplinary Perspectives on Material Culture.* New Brunswick, NJ: Transaction Publishers, 1992.

Brenner, Joel Glenn. *The Emperors of Chocolate: Inside the Secret World of Hershey and Mars.* New York: Random House, 1999.

Burton, Jean. *Lydia Pinkham Is Her Name.* New York: Farrar, Straus, 1949.

Cahn, William. *Out of the Cracker Barrel: The Nabisco Story, from Animal Crackers to Zuzus.* New York: Simon and Schuster, 1969.

Clark, Eric. *The Want Makers.* New York: Viking, 1988.

Collins, Douglas. *America's Favorite Food: The Story of Campbell Soup Company.* New York: Harry N. Abrams, 1994.

———. *The Story of Kodak.* New York: Harry N. Abrams, 1990.

Cowan, Ruth Schwartz. *More Work for Mother: The Ironies of Household Technology from the Open Hearth to the Microwave.* New York: Basic Books, 1983.

Dobrow, Larry. *When Advertising Tried Harder: The Sixties, the Golden Age of American Advertising.* New York: Friendly Press, 1984.

Doody, Alton F., and Ron Bingaman. *Reinventing the Wheels.* Cambridge, MA: Ballinger, 1988.

Dotz, Warren, and Jim Morton. *What a Character! 20th Century Advertising Icons.* San Francisco: Chronicle Books, 1996.

Douglas, Susan. *Inventing American Broadcasting 1899–1922.* Baltimore, MD: Johns Hopkins University Press, 1987.

Edelstein, Andrew J., and Kevin McDonough. *The Seventies: From Hot Pants to Hot Tubs.* New York: Dutton, 1990.

Epstein, Edward Jay. *The Rise and Fall of Diamonds: The Shattering of a Brilliant Illusion*. New York: Simon and Schuster, 1982.

Evans, Harold. *The American Century*. New York: Knopf, 1998.

Ewen, Stuart. *Captains of Consciousness: Advertising and the Social Roots of the Consumer Culture*. New York: McGraw-Hill, 1976.

Fishwick, Marshall, and Ray B. Browne. *Icons of Popular Culture*. Bowling Green, OH: Bowling Green University Popular Press, 1970.

Fontanel, Beatrice. *Support and Seduction: The History of Corsets and Bras*, translated by Willard Wood. New York: Harry N. Abrams, 1997.

Fox, Stephen. *The Mirror Makers: A History of American Advertising and Its Creators*. New York: William Morrow, 1984.

Frank, Thomas. *The Conquest of Cool: Business Culture, Counterculture, and the Rise of Hip Consumerism*. Chicago: University of Chicago Press, 1997.

Goodrum, Charles, and Helen Dalrymple. *Advertising in America: The First 200 Years*. New York: Harry N. Abrams, 1990.

Gray, James. *Business Without Boundary: The Story of General Mills*. Minneapolis, MN: University of Minneapolis Press, 1954.

Green, Harvey. *The Uncertainty of Everyday Life 1915–1945*. New York: HarperCollins, 1992.

Hamilton, Carl. *Absolut: Biography of a Bottle*. New York: Texere, 2000.

Hamilton, Neil A., et al. *Atlas of the Baby Boom Generation*. Detroit: Macmillan Reference U.S.A., 2000.

Handley, Susannah. *Nylon: The Story of a Fashion Revolution*. Baltimore, MD: Johns Hopkins University Press, 2000.

Higgins, Denis, ed. and interv. *The Art of Writing Advertising: Conversations with William Bernbach, Leo Burnett, George Gribben, David Ogilvy, Rosser Reeves*. Chicago: NTC Business Books, 1965.

Horowitz, Daniel. *Betty Friedan and the Making of the Feminine Mystique: The American Left, the Cold War, and Modern Feminism*. Amherst: University of Massachusetts Press, 1998.

Jennings, Peter, and Todd Brewster. *The Century*. New York: Doubleday, 1998.

Kammen. Michael. *American Culture, American Tastes: Social Change and the 20th Century*. New York: Alfred A. Knopf, 1999.

Kannor, Bernice. *The 100 Best TV Commercials . . . and Why They Worked*. New York: Random House, 1999.

Kaplan, David A. *The Silicon Boys and Their Valley of Dreams*. New York: William Morrow, 1999.

Kern-Foxworth, Marilyn. *Aunt Jemima, Uncle Ben, and Rastus: Blacks in Advertising, Yesterday, Today, and Tomorrow*. Westport CT: Greenwood Press, 1994.

Ketchum, Alton. *Uncle Sam: The Man and the Legend*. New York: Hill & Wang, 1959.

Lears, T. J. Jackson. *Fables of Abundance: A Cultural History of Advertising in America*. New York: Basic Books, 1994.

Levenstein, Harvey A. *Revolution at the Table: The Transformation of the American Diet*. New York: Oxford University Press, 1988.

Lief, Alfred. *"It Floats": The Story of Procter & Gamble*. New York: Rinehart, 1958.

Love, John. *McDonald's: Behind the Arches*. New York: Bantam, 1986.

Marchand, Roland. *Advertising the American Dream: Making Way for Modernity 1920–1940*. Berkeley: University of California Press, 1985.

Margolin, Victor, Ira Brichta, and Vivian Brichta. *The Promise and the Product: 200 Years of American Advertising Posters*. New York: Macmillan, 1979.

Marquette, Arthur F. *Brands, Trademarks, and Good Will: The Story of the Quaker Oats Company*. New York: McGraw-Hill, 1967.

Martin, David N. *Romancing the Brand: The Power of Advertising and How to Use It*. New York: American Management Association, 1989.

Morgan, Hal. *Symbols of America*. New York: Viking Penguin, 1986.

Norris, James D. *Advertising and the Transformation of American Society, 1865–1920*. Westport, CT: Greenwood Press, 1990.

Ogilvy, David. *Confessions of an Advertising Man*. New York: Atheneum, 1964.

———. *Ogilvy on Advertising*. New York: Crown Publishers, 1983.

Oliver, Thomas. *The Real Coke. The Real Story*. New York: Random House, 1986.

Olney, Martha. *Buy Now, Pay Later: Advertising, Credit and Consumer Durables in the 1920s*. Chapel Hill: University of North Carolina Press, 1991.

Peacock, Nancy. *Dave Thomas*. Philadelphia: Chelsea House Publishers, 2000.

Pendergrast, Mark. *Uncommon Grounds*. New York: Basic Books, 1999.

Peterson, Theodore. *Magazines in the Twentieth Century*. 2d ed. Urbana: University of Illinois Press, 1972.

Riggs, Thomas, ed. *Encyclopedia of Major Marketing Campaigns*. Detroit: Gale Group, 2000.

Rodengen, Jeffrey, and Karen Nitkin. *The Legend of Dr Pepper/7-Up*. Fort Lauderdale, FL: Write Stuff Syndicate, 1995.

Room, Adrian. *NTC's Dictionary of Trade Name Origins*. Rev. ed. Lincolnwood, IL: NTC Business Press, 1991.

Rowsome, Frank, Jr. *They Laughed When I Sat Down: An Informal History of Advertising in Words and Pictures*. New York: McGraw-Hill, 1959.

———. *The Verse by the Side of the Road: The Story of the Burma-Shave Signs and Jingles*. Brattleboro, VT: Stephen Greene Press, 1965.

Saunders, Dave. *Twentieth Century Advertising*. London: Carleton Books, 1999.

Schudson, Michael. *Advertising, the Uneasy Persuasion: Its Dubious Impact on American Society*. New York: Basic Books, 1984.

Schulberg, Jay, Bernie Hogya, and Sal Taibi. *The Milk Mustache Book: A Behind the Scenes Look at America's Favorite Advertising Campaign*. New York: Ballantine, 1998.

Selinger, Iris Cohen, ed. *The Advertising Century*. *Advertising Age* Special Issue. Chicago: Crain Communications, 1999.

Sivulka, Juliann. *Soap, Sex, and Cigarettes: A Cultural History of American Advertising*. Belmont, CA: Wadsworth, 1997.

Sklar, Robert. *Movie-Made America: A Cultural History of American Movies*. New York: Vintage Books, 1975.

Stern, Jane, and Michael Stern. *Auto Ads*. New York: Random House, 1978.

———. *Encyclopedia of Pop Culture*. New York: HarperPerennial, 1992.

Stoddard, Bob. *Pepsi: 100 Years*. Los Angeles: General Publications Group, 1977.

Twitchell, James B. *AdCult USA: The Triumph of Advertising in American Culture*. New York: Columbia University Press, 1996.

Van Munching, Philip. *Beer Blast: The Inside Story of the Brewing Industry's Bizarre Battle for Your Money.* New York: Times Books, 1997.

Watkins, Julian Lewis. *The 100 Greatest Advertisements: Who Wrote Them and What They Did.* New York: Dover Publications, 1959.

Wernick, Andrew. *Promotional Culture: Advertising, Ideology, and Symbolic Expression.* London: Sage Publications, 1991.

Wyman, Caroline. *Spam: A Biography.* New York: Harvest Books, 1999.

WEB SITES

Many of the companies discussed in this book have their own corporate Web sites that include brief company histories. Other useful Web sites about advertising and its history include

<http://www.adage.com> (*Advertising Age* Web site)

<http://www.antiqueadvertising.com> (vintage advertisements)

<http://www.fitzroydearborn.com/chicago/advertassign.htm> (*Encyclopedia of Advertising*).

<http://www.scriptorium.lib.duke.edu/adaccess> (Duke University advertising collection)

Index

About the Contributors

MARY CROSS is a professor of English and former chairman of the English and Communication Department at Fairleigh Dickinson University. She is a former advertising copywriter and the editor of *Advertising and Culture*, also written with FDU faculty and published by Praeger. She has published articles and a book about Henry James and has taught at the University of Delaware and the City University of New York. She has a Ph.D. from Rutgers University.

WALTER CUMMINS is the editor of the *Literary Review*, an international journal of contemporary writing published at Fairleigh Dickinson University, where he is a professor of English. He has published several volumes of short stories and literary criticism. He received his Ph.D. from the University of Iowa.

MARTIN GREEN is an assistant to the provost and a professor of English at Fairleigh Dickinson University where he has also been acting dean and the chairman of the English and Communication Department. His publications include articles on advertising and the media. He received his Ph.D. from Indiana University.

JESSICA HAUSMANN is a Ph.D. candidate in English at Drew University in Madison, New Jersey, and an adjunct instructor at Fairleigh Dickinson University. She was a research assistant and writer for this book.

MARJORIE KEYISHIAN is an adjunct professor of English at Fairleigh Dickinson University and a published poet. She has written articles and reviews for the *New York Times* and other publications. She has an M.A. from Columbia University.

JENNIFER LEHR is an assistant professor of communication at Fairleigh Dickinson University where she teaches undergraduate and graduate courses in communication. She has published articles on corporate communication. She earned her Ph.D. at Rutgers University.

MARILYN RYE is assistant provost and former director of freshman writing at Fairleigh Dickinson University and an associate professor of English. She edited the book *Making Cultural Connections: Readings for Critical Analysis* and has published articles about composition, popular culture, and detective fiction. She has a Ph.D. from Rutgers University.

ELISE SALEM is an assistant dean and a professor of English at Fairleigh Dickinson University. She has published articles about literary criticism and Middle Eastern literature and holds a Ph.D. from the University of North Carolina at Chapel Hill.

SYLVIA SKAGGS-McTAGUE is Lecturer in English at Fairleigh Dickinson University. She received her Ph.D. in English from Drew University.

GEOFFREY WEINMAN is a professor of English and the chairman of the English and Communication Department at Fairleigh Dickinson University. He has published articles on literary criticism and corporate communication. His Ph.D. in English is from Johns Hopkins University.

WILLIAM ZANDER is a professor of English at Fairleigh Dickinson University and a published poet. A former reporter, he has published numerous news and feature stories. He earned his M.A. at the University of Missouri.